Success for All

A Comprehensive Educational Reform for Improving At-Risk Students in an Urban School in China

Success for All

A Comprehensive Educational Reform for Improving At-Risk Students in an Urban School in China

by

Yanyu Zhou
Confucius Institute at Maryland

≡IAP

INFORMATION AGE PUBLISHING, INC.
Charlotte, NC • www.infoagepub.com

Library of Congress Cataloging-in-Publication Data

Zhou, Yanyu.
  Success for all : a comprehensive educational reform for improving at-risk students in an urban school in China / by Yanyu Zhou.
       p. cm.
  Includes bibliographical references.
  ISBN 978-1-59311-939-3 (pbk.) – ISBN 978-1-59311-940-9 (hardcover)
 1. Urban schools–China–Shanghai–Case studies. 2. Students with social disabilities–Education (Middle school)–China–Shanghai–Case studies. 3. Educational change–China–Shanghai–Case studies. I. Title.
  LC5137.C62S539 2008
  371.009173'2–dc22
                                                                     2008021243

Copyright © 2008 Information Age Publishing Inc.

All rights reserved. No part of this publication may be reproduced, stored in a retrieval system, or transmitted, in any form or by any means, electronic, mechanical, photocopying, microfilming, recording or otherwise, without written permission from the publisher.

Printed in the United States of America

CONTENTS

Abstract vii

Acknowledgments ix

Introduction xi

1   Academic Success, At-Risk Students, and Educational Reform 1

2   Comprehensive School Reform in the United States and China 33

3   Educational Reforms and Its Social Context: The Radical Changes in China Politics, Economy, and Culture Since 1978 45

4   Social Inequalities in Urban China in the Era of Economic Reform and Its Impact on Education 61

5   The History of *Success Education* Reform 81

6   Multiple Levels of Leadership Support and the Crucial Roles of Principal Liu Jinghai 95

7   Professional Development in *Success Education* Model 115

8   The Quiet Revolution in the Classroom: Approaches to Help Students Learn and Succeed 131

9   The New Function of Moral Education in *Success Education*: A Network of Developing At-Risk Students Self-Confidence and Ability of Self-Education 161

10 The Role of the Class Director in Classroom Management 187

11 Parental and Community Involvement: Effective Resources and Active Support for At-Risk Students 211

12 Summaries, Reflections, and Conclusions 229

Appendices

- **A** Mission Statement 247
- **B** Class Schedule for Grade 7, No. 8 School, Shanghai, China (Fall, 2006) 248
- **C** Timetable of Teacher and Administrator Activities, No. 8 School, Shanghai, China 249
- **D** Middle School Students' Regulations in Shanghai, China (6–9 grades) 250
- **E** The Objectives of Cultivating Basic Qualities for Compulsory Education from Grade Six to Nine in Shanghai, China 251
- **F** Newspaper Report(translation from Chinese) (1): *Liu Jinghao Arrived in Hong Kong from Shanghai and Shared his Experience on How to Educate At-Risk Students: Carrying out Evaluation of Encouragement to Eliminate Students' Feelings of Frustration* 253
- **G** Newspaper Report(translation from Chinese) (2): *Success Education in Zhabei No. 8 School Has Achieved Remarkable Success: Helping At-Risk Students to Develop their Confidence in Learning* 255

Bibliography 257

ABSTRACT

Education for all and success for all are human rights as well as our common goals to achieve in the 21st century. However, schools in modern societies have failed largely to help build an equal society by offering equal educational opportunities for all children, fulfilling the "natural goals" of education as expected by functionalists (Feinberg & Soltis, 1998; Stromquist, 2002). Rather, as criticized by conflict and critical theories, it plays a major role perpetuating social and economic inequalities in society (Bowles & Gintis, 1976; McLaren 1994). Consequently, while most students from privileged families are guaranteed school success, a large number of students from low socioeconomic backgrounds have suffered from school failure. How can we help *all* students achieve success in school? This has been a key challenge for schools both in the West and the East. Success in school in our era of globalization is significant not only for individuals' personal development but also for a nation's economic growth and social development. School failure has caused many serious problems such as student dropout, juvenile delinquency, emotional and mental problems among students, unemployment, and so forth. To address these problems, over the past few decades many reform initiatives have been put forward, yet success stories are few.

This book provides a detailed account of an educational experiment in a middle school in Shanghai, China. The school, called Zhabei No. 8 Middle School (hereafter No. 8 School), is located in a run-down, lower working class district. Since the mid-1980s the school has experimented on an educational reform program called *success education*, aiming to help those at-risk students to be successful in school. This book illustrates how this educational experiment has been carried out and identified experiences that could be learned by the international educational community.

The book analyzes the critical role played by Principal Liu Jinghai, and particular attention is paid to the strategies adopted by the school to help enhance students' self-esteem through integrating love and care throughout the school's curriculum and activities. The pivotal roles played by teachers called "class directors" are meticulously studied, and efforts the school has made to collaborate with parents and the local community are examined. An ethnographic approach was used to gather data in this study. A combination of interviews, participant-observation, and document analysis was applied to arrive at a systematic and complex understanding of this educational endeavor in China.

ACKNOWLEDGMENTS

This book would have been impossible if it were not for the help and support of many people. As such, I would like to take this opportunity to express my sincere gratitude to all those people who have given me their selfless support for this research.

I am deeply grateful to Dr. Yan Xin, a world-wide known scientist in life science and biomedicine, and a renowned physician, for his miraculous treatment for my health problems. Without his help, it was impossible for me to maintain my health and finish my study. His profound philosophy emphasizing love and universal fraternity fundamentally transformed my view toward the world and taught me how to love and care for other people and all the existence in the universe. It is through Dr. Yan Xin's enlightenment that I decided to pour my energy into studying education for at-risk students, the topic of this book.

A most heartfelt thanks to you, Dr. Jing Lin, my advisor, my mentor, and my dear friend, for your wholehearted care, support, advice, and encouragement. It is hard to believe that without your help, I could have accomplished my research in such a smooth way. It is an unforgettable experience for me to know how you worked day and night, and went through line by line to help me with my scholarly writing and revise my book.

Special thanks is also extended to Dr. Steven Klees, Dr. Rebecca Oxford, Dr. Carol Anne Spreen, and Dr. Tom Weible for their valuable insights and support.

I must sincerely thank everyone who participated in the study—Principal Liu Jinghai for his strong support and precious time, Vice Principal Zhang Miaokun for his kind help during my investigation in Shanghai, Ms. Yan Yan for her assistance with my data collection, and all the other school leaders, teachers, staff, students, and parents I interviewed for their support and efforts.

I wish to express my great appreciation to Dr. Charles Mcelvaney, my respectful friend for his energy, time, and kind help in carefully editing the first draft of my book. Also, special thanks to Ms. Zhou Juan, my respected friend for her loving care and encouragement, Ms. Cai Chunyiing for her assistance in the diagram edition for this book, and all my friends for their direct and indirect support and their precious friendship.

Finally, to my family, especially to my parents, who gave me their unconditional love, who taught me the love of learning at a very early age. I want to especially acknowledge my beloved husband Pang Xiaojun, who is fully responsible for taking care of our child, and who is my soul mate to always understand me and totally support me in all circumstances. Without your love and care, I could not accomplish this book. A special thanks goes to my dear son Pang Yuzhou for your understanding and your hard work in learning. Sincere thanks to all my family members for their deep love and consistent support. Their reliable support have been extremely important for me to carry on and succeed in work and life.

INTRODUCTION

SCHOOL SUCCESS FOR ALL

School success and failure, educational equality and justice, accountability and school reconstruction, class, race and gender and the improvement of at-risk students, have become central issues in urban schools in North America since the 1960s (Bush, 2001; Spring, 2001). The trend of globalization that is sweeping across the world, characterized by rapid development of science and technology, has put education in a crucial and strategic role in almost every country in the world. Achieving education for all and enabling all students to succeed in life are becoming a prevailing trend in international educational reforms. How can urban students from disadvantaged socioeconomic family background be helped and assisted to become successful in school? What are the effective ways schools can adopt to help at-risk students? Governments, schools, and educators around the world have made great efforts to seek solutions to these questions. In North America, many experiments have been conducted in urban schools to help at-risk students succeed (Corbett, 2002; Datnow & Castellano, 2001; Slavin et al., 1996). However, little is known about the reform being attempted in China in this area.

Chinese education has undergone dramatic changes since China adopted the policy of economic reform and opening to the world in 1978. The reform and opening have transformed the country from a rigid, centralized economy to a more open and market-oriented economic and social system. Numerous research studies have examined the transformation of the Chi-

Success for All, pages xi–xvii
Copyright © 2008 by Information Age Publishing
All rights of reproduction in any form reserved.

nese educational system in terms of administration, finance, curriculum content, teaching methods, student's political activism, privatization, and so forth (Lin, 1993, 1999; Snowden, 2001). Few studies have focused on the issue of at-risk students in urban China, and the strategies that have been adopted by the Chinese government and schools to help enhance the learning and the chance of success of these students.

In the mid-1980s, an educational reform emerged in China, known as the "switching of tracks." The reform attempted to shift schools from an exam-oriented education (or yingshi jiaoyu) to *quality education* (or suzhi jiaoyu), which aims to educate the whole person by facilitating students' all-around growth including moral, intellectual, physical, aesthetic, and labor skill's development (Wang, 1997; Yan & Su, 1997). Since then, China has embarked on an era of many educational reforms.

Among the various kinds of educational reforms, *success education* conducted by No. 8 School in Shanghai since 1987, has attracted much attention domestically and internationally. Based on the principle, which holds that education should help every single student succeed in school and life, *success education* in No. 8 School has been considered to be highly effective, and the project has been recommended by the Ministry of Education in China as a role model within the nation (Liu, 1997). Yet, no study has been carried out that systematically examines these questions: What underlies the philosophy of *success education*? What has been done by the No. 8 School? What have been their achievements? What are the issues and challenges in conducting such a reform? What are the implications of this reform for improving low-achieving students overall? These questions have not been explored. This book aims to provide an in-depth understanding into the project, as this will add to and enrich our understanding of effective ways to improve education for urban disadvantaged children.

PURPOSE OF THE STUDY

This book is based on a research project which adopts a case study approach, and the purposes of the study are: (1) to study the development of Chinese education and its reforms in the era of China's economic reform and opening, and in the international context of globalization; (2) to examine a school reform through which to study how Chinese education is trying to transform from an exam-oriented model to an all-around developmental model in order to speed up its process of modernization; (3) to explore in depth how Chinese educators help at-risk students build up their self-esteem and improve their academic learning as well as develop and grow in other areas; (4) to reflect on school reform and ponder such critical issues as the nature and aim of education, the direction of education in the globalization era, the relationship of educational equality, quality and efficiency, and the holistic development of students; and (5) to attempt to generate theories and practical strategies from this Chinese case that may be applied to the international education community in terms of improving education for low-achieving and at-risk students.

RESEARCH DESIGN

Data for this book was mainly collected in 2004 but continuously through 2006. The focus of the data collection was the living experiences of the educators and the students in the experimental school, the rationales behind the phenomenon, the strategies used by the school, and the problems the school faces in a challenging social context. By a close examination of what has been undertaken in the school through observation and interviews with the principal, teachers, administrators, students, parents and government officials, the unique strategies Chinese educators have adopted in helping at-risk students were uncovered.

Research Questions

This book focuses on a set of central questions and their corresponding sub-questions:

I. What is the social context in which the experiment of *success education* occurs? Specifically,
   1. What is the international context in which China started its educational reforms? How does globalization influence Chinese education?
   2. What social changes have taken place since 1978 when China set out to undergo significant economic reform and open herself to the world? What impact did these changes have on the Chinese educational reforms?
   3. What is the exam-oriented educational system like? What are the disadvantages of this competitive system? What are the impacts of the exam-oriented educational system on students personal growth as well as on the national development?
   4. What is quality education? Why does Chinese education need to switch from exam-oriented education to quality education? What forces drove China to enter into an educational experiment stage since the mid-1980s?

II. How did the experiment of *success education* come into existence?
   1. What is success education? Who created this project? When and where did this program begin?
   2. What was the situation before the reform began in the experimental school? Why did the school conduct success education?
   3. What are the rationales behind success education? How does this mechanism work?
III. How has *success education* been implemented?
   1. What has been done to transform the school from a traditional education paradigm to the new model of success education?
   2. How did they train teachers to instill a belief in success education and develop specific knowledge and skills to carry out this reform? What has been done to help students build up a mentality of success and confidence in academic learning and life as a whole?
   3. What strategies the school has adopted to develop the literacy of success education for the parents? How were the parents involved in the school reform?
   4. What major issues and problems the experimental school has encountered when they implemented the experiment? How do they resolve these problems?
   5. What are the results of the experiment? How can we evaluate this educational reform? What are the reactions from the administrators, staff, and teachers? How do the students and their parents respond to this educational experiment?
   6. What are the roles of the Chinese government in this project? What special role did Principal Liu Jinghai play in the education reform?
   7. Are there any positive results of success education when applied to other schools? Does it present a trend of Chinese educational reform in the future?
IV. What do we learn from this Chinese educational reform case?
   1. What are the differences between the Chinese model and the experiences in other countries, in terms of improving at-risk students?
   2. What are the main contributions this Chinese educational reform made? What are the implications of success education for the international educational field?
   3. What theories, especially the theory of school success for all can we draw from this particular Chinese case? What are the experience and useful strategies we can learn from the reform?
   4. How can we learn from each other in order to achieve success for all in a global context? How can we build up a holistic, love-

based, caring, and meaningful environment that can facilitate our students to fully develop their potentials?

DATA COLLECTION

To collect data, I spent two months in No. 8 School, carrying out in- depth interviews with the principal and more than 100 students, teachers and parents during March–May, 2004. I observed classroom teaching and activities, attended teachers' meetings, and colleted many documents. The field work resulted in more than 100 interview tapes and three notebooks.

I also conducted classroom observations. With permission from the school, I observed classroom teaching, recorded teachers' teaching, took notes of teacher-student interaction patterns, observed and participated in all kinds of student activities, and attended the administrative meetings, the teachers' meetings, and parents' meetings, and visited students' families. By doing so, I explored how this holistic and comprehensive educational reform works and compared the differences that exist between this alternative approach and the traditional education.

In the interviews which were semi-structured, the principal was asked about his interest in helping at-risk students, the reasons he created and led *success education*, how he promoted this new educational concept and belief, and the difficulties he has encountered during the reform. Teachers were asked about their understanding of *success education*, how they changed from their traditional educational concepts to the new ones, how they integrated this alternative approach to their teaching, and what were the results of the reform. Students were asked about their feelings about this new educational reform, what are the differences between the traditional classroom and the alternative classroom, and how the new educational method helped them in terms of building up their self-esteem, improving their academic learning, and facilitating their social skills, and their personal growth. The parents were asked about their opinions on the experiment, how the reform affected their children, and for their comments and suggestions on this new educational perspective. I also did interviews on experts from outside the schools, governmental officers at district and city levels, and a principal from my hometown, who spent six months in No. 8 School to learn *success education as* a principal training program.

In addition, informal interviews were conducted during the study. Parents who happened to come to visit the school while I was there, and people I met on the campus were interviewed to obtain more details about the reform. In the meantime, during my class observations, I did a number of informal interviews with teachers and students to promptly identify any useful ideas and questions related to this research.

Besides observation and interviewing, I have collected many documents. These include 13 research books and 7 volumes of magazines on *success education* experiment, 6 books on math study material compiled by the school, 34 teachers' summarization papers and some brochures of the school. Collected were also school reform plans, government documents, the records of meetings and conferences for the reform from the governments and schools, the speeches of the principal and officers from all levels of government, annual report of the school, newspapers and other written reports of the event, school schedules, all kinds of evaluation forms, curriculum designs, students' achievement test reports, students' diaries, students' files, student agenda, and letters from parents and people outside school. I also received 77 VCR and DVD tapes containing Principal Liu's speeches, samples of excellent teachers' teaching, TV programs on the reform, TV series on the moving stories taking place in the school during the reform, and students' activities. In addition, I took hundreds of pictures of students, teachers, events and activities, the campus, students' families, and the community surrounding the school during my investigation. All these provide rich and vivid research sources. In all, the research findings from this wealth of information attempts to arrive at a systematic and complex understanding of the educational reform in China.

SIGNIFICANCE OF THIS RESEARCH

This case study provides a fresh perspective on how a school can work as a powerful organization that integrates respects and care for students throughout the whole schooling process. Examined is how success education in No. 8 School has helped or failed to help at-risk students. This attempt contributes to the global search for solutions to issues such as inequality in education, accountability, school reconstruction, and academic improvement of disadvantaged and at-risk students. The book also hopes to find out what principles advocated by the school and what experiences the school has accumulated that can be learned by the international educational community.

In practice, this study explores effective ways to help at-risk students from comprehensive and holistic approaches that integrate students' intellectual, emotional, and moral education as a whole to facilitate their academic learning and personal growth. The study examines how school leaders, teachers, parents, and the community work together to create a culture that centers on the caring of all students, making sure that *all* students experience education success. We examine the reasons behind students' low motivations to learn, and since most of the students come from low income families in this experimental school, we propose that the school's comprehensive approach, merging caring and love for students with flexible and innovative strategies in curriculum, teaching, learning, administration, and interaction with parents and the community, may be a fundamental way to deal with the problem of educational inequality and to achieve school success for all. In all, this study will contribute to our exploration of new approaches toward promoting school success for all children in the 21st century.

CHAPTER 1

ACADEMIC SUCCESS, AT-RISK STUDENTS, AND EDUCATIONAL REFORM

This chapter first examines the meaning of school success, the definition of at-risk students and schools, then identifies factors that lead to the disadvantaged students' difficulty and failure in school, discusses the negative results caused by at-risk students, finally studies the strategies done by governments and schools. Research in North America and in China will be reviewed. The focus is placed on middle school students as this book specifically concerns middle school students.

THE MEANING OF SCHOOL SUCCESS

What is the meaning of school success? Answers can vary a great deal based on people understanding of the aim of education in their specific social and cultural context. Different disciplinary and theoretical perspectives have pointed to different emphases. For example, in sociology of education, functional theory regards school as an agent of socialization. The function of school is to transmit the existing society's belief, culture, and value to the younger generation. Therefore, for functionalists school success means that students gain four key qualities, namely independence, achievement, specificity and universalism (Feinberg & Soltis, 1998, p. 18). Interpretive theorists, however, perceive school success to occur when students have a learning experience and take a positive role in the construction of knowledge. In another approach, critical theorists hold the view that "knowledge is power." They argue that school success should be measured by how knowledge empowers students from minority groups, those who suffer from gender/racial/social class discriminations, and those who are powerless to change the existing social injustices and inequalities (Greene, 1988; McLaren, 1994).

Philosophers of education have also held very diverse perspectives. For example, Plato, in his book *The Republic,* states that success is the full development of human nature in physical, moral, and mental excellence (Cornford, 1975). Rousseau (1911), as a naturist, perceives success as Emile's ability to be developed in a totally natural way, while success for Dewey is the development of each student to his fullest potential (Dewey, 1956), Freire (1970) sees success as a student's liberated mind, with the development of critical thinking and the cultivation of ability to take actions to transform society.

Thanks to a fast-growing information industry, we have been moving into a globalized world since the last decade of the twentieth century. As globalization is largely characterized by competition in science and technology, countries in the world view education as a powerful engine to develop its economy (Carnoy, 2000; Stromquist, 2002). Therefore, success in school is not only related to an individual's personal development but is also related to a nation's economic growth and social development. Success for all is becoming a common educational goal globally, as well as an inherent human right for the human race to achieve in the 21st century.

However, the task is daunting as in almost every society is that a substantial number of at-risk students are lagging behind in educational attainment. It has become one of the thorniest problems faced by educators, administers, policymakers, and parents regardless of where they reside.

THE DEFINITION OF "AT-RISK" STUDENTS

Research literature on at risk students is plentiful (Freiman, 2001; Mason et al., 2001; Swedner & Lubeck, 1995). What is the definition of "at-risk students?" The term "at risk," historically, has been used in medical and psychopathological context, focusing on patterns and rates of disease and disorder in populations (Masten & Garmezy, 1991). There are a variety of labels to identify students who are in academic or behavioral troubles such as "dropouts," "disadvantaged," "marginal," "impoverished," "alienated," "low achievers," etc. (Waxman et al., 1992). The category of "at-risk" has been introduced into educational field relatively recently (Winfield, 1991).

The definition of "at-risk" is very much a social construction. Some researchers regard at-risk students as those who could not complete high school while others argue they are students who have failed one or more grades (Slavin, 1989; Waxman et al., 1992). A common use of the term at-risk students is referred to as students who are more likely to experience problems such as poverty, drug abuse, gender, racial, and ethnic discriminations (Pellicano, 1987).

A helpful definition of "at-risk" students is provided by the Organization for Economic Co-operation and Development (OECD) as follows:

> The term "at-risk" refers to children and youth who are in danger of failing at school, or in making a successful transition to work. Educational, social and vocational failures are predicted by a range of factors, including: poverty, ethnic status, family circumstances, language, type of school, geography and community. (Day et al., 1997, p. 17)

Thus, the term "at-risk" refers in a general sense to children and youth from a disadvantaged background. That is to say, the at-risk students are those who are mainly minorities, the poor, and immigrants. They are regarded as the population who are culturally, socially, and educationally disadvantaged or deprived (Cox, 2000; Ensor, 2000).

However, researchers were cautious to use labels such as "culturally deprived" and "socially disadvantaged" to identify students who are put at-risk since the terms have easily caused many controversies (Natriello et al., 1990). Therefore, these labels have not been commonly used in the academic field (Stringfield & Land, 2002).

Literature on at-risk students in China is quite vast (Chen, 2003; Liu, 1997; Liu & Ge, 1991). Generally speaking, at-risk students are defined as those with normal cognitive ability but low motivation for study and low academic achievement (Chen, 2002; Xu, 2006).

Specifically, Chinese educators define at-risk students in a variety of ways. First, in terms of the learning process, at-risk students are regarded as those who need to take much longer time and spend a great deal more energy than other average students in learning, yet they still barely master the knowledge taught by the teachers in the classroom (Aimait, 2001). Second, in terms of school administration, at-risk students are usually classified as those who have problems in moral behavior and have low academic achievement. Third, in terms of psychological traits, *at-risk students* are characterized by such negative features as very low self-esteem, poor self-control, low concentration, short memory, and a narrow interest in subjects (Li, 2006; Tang, 2002). In all, in defining "at-risk" students, Western scholars tend to emphasize the connection of the problems to their political and economic contexts, while Chinese researchers tend to emphasize students' individual intellectual and psychological factors.

FACTORS ASSOCIATED WITH AT-RISK STUDENTS

The causes that lead to school failure are complex and diverse. Rossi (1994) points out that "no child is inherently at risk; rather, children are put at risk by external disadvantages" (p. xiii). Numerous studies have identified three aspects as the causes leading to students schooling failure, namely family background, community conditions, and school environment (Cox, 2000; Stringfield & Land, 2002; Waxman et al., 1992).

Family Background

Research shows that children's school performance is largely influenced by their environment such as family and local community (Bronfenbrenner, 1986; Maccoby & Martin, 1983). Family is the first place where socialization takes place for children to learn about their social roles in the future through interacting with their parents (Santrock, 1996). Parents' beliefs, values and behaviors have a great impact on the adolescents' academic achievement (Patrikakou, 1997; Wong & Wang, 2002).

Also, from the teacher's point of view, research finds factors leading to educational failure usually lay not in the classroom but outside school walls, in short, in the home and students' family background. For example, Schorr (1988) observed that most at-risk students who experienced academic failure were:

- Growing up in persistent or concentrated poverty and in a family of low social class;
- Being born unwanted or into a family with too many children born too close together;
- Growing up with a parent who is unemployed, a teenager, a school dropout, an illiterate, a parent who is impaired (as result of alcoholism, drug addiction, or mental illness), and/or who is without social supports;
- Growing up in a family or neighborhood with such high levels of social disorganization at to leave a young child unprotected from abuse and violence, and with little exposure to healthy role models;
- Growing up outside one family, especially in multiple foster care or institutional placements; and

- Growing up with the sense that one has bleak prospects for good employment or a stable family life and little power to affect one own destiny and that one is not valued by the outside world (Schorr, 1988, p. xxiii).

From another angle, Levin (1989) describes at-risk students as those who have been exposed to insufficient education resulting from a lack of family and community resources.

More specifically, Natriello, McDill, and Pallas (1990) discuss five key individual/family-level indicators associated with the educationally disadvantaged: Poverty, race/ethnicity, limited language skill, poorly educated mothers, and single-parent families. Among these five factors, I would like to specifically examine poverty, race/ethnicity, parents' educational level, and single-parent family. These are factors that will be related to the case I am studying in China.

Poverty

Research reveals that among the factors related to students' low achievement test scores, dropout and violent crimes, poverty is regarded as the greatest risk indicator. Schorr (1988) argues that poverty causes many negative outcomes among poor children, such as "bad health in infancy and childhood, being abused or neglected, not having a decent place to live, and lacking access to services that protect against the effects of these conditions" (Schorr, 1988, p. xxiii).

There is strong evidence that the issue of poverty is a persistent and worldwide problem in both developed and developing countries. A figure from the United Nations Development (UNDP, 1998) indicates that in OECD countries more than 100 million people have less than 50% of the median disposable income while 37 million are unemployed. Another study shows that in 1999, around 12.1 million children in the United State less than 18 years of age lived below the poverty line. In particular, a wide disparity of income existed between the Blacks and Whites, the Hispanics and the Whites. For example, approximately 33.1% of Black and 30.3% of Hispanic children lived below the poverty line in 1999, as compared to 9.4% of White children (Bennett et al., 1999).

Students' low social class background and their conditions of poverty have been consistently linked with their poor academic achievement and school failure. "The Nation Report Card," released by the National Assessment of Educational Progress (NAEP), states that in 1998, 58% of 4th graders, 44% of 8th graders, and 43% of 12th graders who were eligible for free or reduced-price lunch, a federally assisted meal program for supporting students from low income families, scored below basic levels in reading achievement, as compared to 27% of 4th graders, 19% of 8th graders, and

20% of 12th graders who were ineligible (Donahue et al., 1999). The gaps in mathematics were even worse than in reading. For example, in 1996, 58% of 4th graders, 61% of 8th graders, and 60% of 12th graders who were eligible for the National School Lunch Program, scored below basic levels in mathematics achievement, as compared to 26% of 4th graders, 29% of 8th graders, and 26% of 12th graders who were ineligible (Reese et al., 1997).

Dropout rates are also inversely related to family income. In 1999, the estimated national average dropout rate—the proportion of 15- to 24-year-old students leaving high school between October 1998 and October 1999 without successful completion—for students from the bottom 20% of the family income distributions was 11.0%, compared to 5.0% for students from the middle 60%, and 2.1% for students from the top 20% of the family income range (Kaufman et al., 2000).

Race/Ethnicity

Evidence that race/ethnicity is also indicators of poor academic achievement and school failure has also been well documented. In the United States, the achievement gap between Black and White and between Hispanic and White has been a major challenge facing American educators, researchers, and policymakers. As early as in the 1970s, Greer (1972) noticed that more than 40% of school children were permitted to fail in school. Most of them were minority students.

After more than two decades of Greer's research, what is the situation of public schools in America in recent years? Research shows that large gaps remain among races in reading, math, and science achievement. Generally speaking, the test scores of *at-risk students* are two years behind other students by grade 6 and four years behind at the end of grade 12. In 1999, data from National Assessment of Educational Progress (NAEP) reveal that the average seventeen-year-old black student only gained the 13th percentile of the distribution of white students on the math exam and the 22nd percentile on the reading exam (Chubb & Loveless, 2002). About half of minority students cannot complete high school, which is a minimum requirement for getting into the U.S. labor force (Huston, 1991).

In addition, there exists a big disparity in terms of dropout rate for different racial groups. For example, in 1999, the dropout rate was 12.6% for Black high school students, 28.6% for Hispanic students, and 7.3% for White students (Stringfield & Land, 2002).

Parents' Educational Level

Parents' level of education, especially the mother's educational attainment, plays a very important role in children's school performance in today's technological society (Natrillo et al., 1990). Parents' educational level affects children's academic outcomes in that better educated parents tend to be more involved in activities such as attending school-sponsored activities, contacting with teachers, helping their children with homework, providing their children with study materials and diverse learning experiences, supervising their children's academic choice, and monitoring their children's school progress. In contrast, less well-educated parents, particularly those parents who have not graduated from high school, tend to be less involved in their children's schooling (Campbell et al., 2000; Waxman et al., 1992).

Stringfield and Land (2002), in their book, *Educating At-risk Students,* cite research data obtained through both qualitative and quantitative approaches to examine the relationship between parents' level of education and children's achievement test scores and dropout rates. These research data show that the higher level of education the parents have obtained, the higher scores students got in academic tests, and the lower dropout rate for them. Stringfield and Land summarize the research findings in the following:

> In 1998, 48% of 8th-graders and 43% of 12th-graders whose parents' highest education level was less than high school completion scored below basic levels on reading achievement, compared to 34% of 8th-graders and 32% of 12th-graders whose parents highest education level was high school graduation (Donahue et al., 1999). In 1996, 63% of 4th-graders, 56% of 8th-graders, and 58% of 12th raders whose parents highest education level was less than high school completion scored below basic levels on mathematics achievement, compared to 41% of 4th-graders, 48% of 8th-graders, and 42% of 12th raders whose parents highest education level was high school graduation (Reese et al., 1997). According to dropout data for the 1990 cohort of the National Education Longitudinal Study of 1988 (NELS: 88), students whose parents had not completed high school dropped out at a rate three times greater than students whose parents had exceeded high school completion. (Kaufman et al., 1996, p. 9)

Single-Parent Families

In the past few decades after World War II, the divorce rate has steadily increased in the Unites States. As a result, an increasing number of children are living in single-parent families, especially, living in mother-only families. For example, the percentage of children under the age of 18 living with a single parent for 1968, 1978, 1988, and 1998 was 11.8%, 18.5%, 24.3%, and 27.7% respectively. These ratios show the number of children living in disrupted families has increased dramatically (Lugaila, 1998; U.S. Bureau of the Census, 1999a). Research also presents a tendency that families headed

8 *Success for All*

by single mothers have increased very rapidly. In 1960, only 7% of children in the United States were living in fatherless families; by 1985, the rate had reached 21% (U.S. Bureau of the Census, 1960, 1961, 1989). In 1998, of the children under the age of 18 years who lived with a single parent, 84.1% lived with their mothers (Lugaila, 1998).

Studies on the correlation between family structure and children's educational achievement found that offspring from one-parent families have lower grade point averages, more delinquency problems, and higher dropout rates than offspring from two-parent families (Matsueda & Heimer, 1987; McLanahan & Sandefur, 1994; Rossi, 1994). Based on NAEP's reading and mathematics achievement scores in 1986, researchers point out that a large number of third-grade students from single-parent families were at least a year behind their peer from intact families (Natriello et al., 1990). Also, on average, children from disrupted families are less likely to finish their high school than children from two-parent families. Kaufman et al. (1996) state that the dropout rate for students from one-parent families in 1990 was about double the proportion for students from two-parent families.

The main reason for single-parent family to become a risk indicator of children's poor school achievement is that these families usually have less income. For example, in 1983, approximately 50% of all female-headed families were poor, compared to only 12% of married-couple families (Garfinkel & McLanahan, 1986; Huston, 1991). Because of income insecurity, single parents have less money and invest less of it in their children. In the meantime, a family of low socioeconomic status usually limits children's participation in extracurricular activities, in travel experiences, and in summer camps, all of which are associated positively with school performance (Heyns, 1985).

Moreover, it has been reported that more married mothers (56%) than single mothers (49%) and single fathers (46%) spend a significant amount of time with their children and are more involved in their children's school (Nord et al., 1997). In all, children of single parents may not perform as well academically than children of married parents because single parents tend to have fewer financial and educational resources and less time available to assist and supervise children (McLanahan & Sandefur, 1994).

Community Conditions

"Community" is defined as a formal or informal group of people who share common values and common goals and who help each other to meet their needs. By providing common attitudes, local networks, and peer-group activities, a community exerts a strong influence on individuals' life. Loss of community may cause individuals to have mental problems or abnormal behaviors (Huston, 1991; Waxman, et al., 1992).

Studies found that families living in a run-down inner city neighborhood with high levels of poverty and disorganization not only are more isolated from mainstream society but also are likely to have weakened parental control. In the absence of adult leadership, children are easily influenced by antisocial youth cultures and associated with gangs and the drug trade as a result (Wilson, 1986). Some neighborhoods in inner cities are so crime-ridden and unsafe that children are in danger playing outside and walking to school (Halpern 1991).

We are discovering that children living in poor communities have fewer opportunities and less incentive to devote themselves to develop their own educational potentials. One of the important reasons for this is that students who are marginal lack a learning environment from the community which is supposed to highly value academic success and encourage adherence to proper attitudes and tradition. Many marginal children received conflictive views toward study, that is, while schools and mainstream society expect students to do well in learning, families and communities in poverty may not. To gain membership in a community, marginal students often adopt behaviors learned at home and expected in the neighborhood. Lacking supportive resources from the community, marginal learners eventually experience poor academic achievement and school failure (Waxman et al., 1992). On the other hand, a caring, integrated community in which education is highly valued and expected is likely to be most beneficial for children in high poverty schools (Boyd & Shouse, 1997; Shouse, 1996).

School Environment

Educators found that school itself could also be a factor linked to the poor academic outcomes for students. A school environment may promote or not promote students' learning by creating a positive or a negative climate (Sinclair & Ghory, 1987). Rather than facilitating students' academic achievement, some schools may put students at increased risk by having a poor learning environment (Kagan, 1990; Montgomery & Rossi, 1994). What is an at-risk school? Waxman (1992) suggests that if a school is characterized by the following features in its environment, it is an at-risk school:

- The school alienates students and teachers;
- it provides a low quality education;
- it has differential expectations for students;
- it has high noncompletion rates for students;
- it is unresponsive to students;
- it has high truancy and disciplinary problems; or
- the school is not adequately preparing students for the future (pp. 5–6).

Land and Legters (2002) group a variety of school risk factors into three categories: Sociodemographic characteristics, school climate and culture, and school policies.

In terms of Sociodemographic characteristics, the authors examine the correlation between students' poor academic outcomes and school environment from four aspects: School-level poverty, class size, school size, and urbanicity. Several research studies show that there is a negative impact that a high poverty school exerts on students' academic achievement. For instance, according to a statistical figure from NAEP in 1996, the scores in reading achievement and in mathematics for 9-year-old children in high poverty schools (75% students received free or reduced lunch) were respectively 37 and 21 points lower than their peer in low poverty schools (25% students having free or reduced lunch) (Bandeira, de Mello, and Young, 2000). Also, high poverty schools tend to have a lower graduation rate, fewer financial and human resources, less qualified teachers, and lower teacher salaries than low poverty schools (Jencks & Mayer, 1990).

A study on Tennessee's Project STAR (Student/Teacher Achievement Ratio) reveals that through providing more contacts with teachers and more opportunities in learning activities, students in small classes (13–17 students) have better academic performance than in regular classes (22–26 students) (Nye et al., 1999).

Also, although the results of studies on school size are controversial, most research finds that having less contact with teachers or other adults, large schools with poor and minority enrollments are more likely to have a poor school climate that may alienate students. As a consequence, students in large schools tend to experience more academic failure and a higher dropout rate than small schools do (Cotton, 1996; Pittman & Haughwout, 1987).

In addition, schools located in inner cities appear to have greater risk of poor academic performance than suburban and rural schools. Largely serving low socioeconomic minority communities, students living in high poverty urban schools are more likely to have lower academic scores, with students less likely to graduate on time from high schools (reaching 50%), and more likely to be unemployed later in life as compared with students in suburban and rural schools (Edwards, 1998; Lippman et al., 1996).

School climate and culture have also been considered as a school risk factor that influences student performance. A school should provide a positive environment with warmth, love, care, and support for all students. However, unfortunately, school climate and culture are often discouraging to those students with poor academic performance and behavioral problem (Montgomery & Rossi 1994). For example, since there are not enough psychological services in many schools, students with emotional problems or students of color may not have access to school counseling (Gibbs & Huang, 1990).

Land and Legters (2002) state that expectation and school violence are very important components of school climate and culture. Research shows that a teacher's expectation has a strong influence on students' performance. Low teacher expectations bring about low students' performance, regardless of what students' real abilities are (Rosenthal & Jacobson, 1968). Higher expectations and higher supportiveness have been reported to be associated with not only higher academic achievement but also with better behavioral outcomes for poor and minority students (Boyd & Shouse, 1997).

In the meantime, school violence may have a negative impact on students academically, emotionally and physically and lead them to avoid school (Kingery et al., 1998). Although the rate of school violence has gone down in recent years, large urban schools with high poverty level are still at greater risk of serious violence (*Education Week*, 2001).

School policies play a very important role in school administration. As part of school environments, school policies influence students' performance to a great extent. For example, Land and Legters (2002) show that tracking, which has been practiced in schools to manage students' academic diversity, may negatively affect students' achievements. Through grouping students by ability, scholars criticize that, the tracking practice segregates low achievers—usually the poor, Black, and Hispanic children (Ress et al., 1996), and offers these disadvantaged students a substandard education. Labeling minority students and those from working class background as low track students, tracking and ability grouping may harm students' self-esteem which will contribute to poor academic outcomes.

Special Education, Retention, and Suspensions and Expulsions

These are also factors associated with at risk students. Originally, special education was designed for children with disabilities to meet their special needs in education. Although research found that separate special education programs facilitate some students' academic achievements, special education students are generally more at risk of dropping out and do not do as well in national standard tests as nondisabled students. Furthermore, special education services have been reportedly provided to a disproportionate number of minority students, especially to African American children. For example, Black students are 2.9 times more likely to be identified as having a mental problem than their White peers, 1.9 times more likely to experience emotional disturbance, and 1.3 times more likely to be identified as having a special learning disability (Toppo, 2001). As a result, special education has been charged by some scholars to have discriminated against Black and other minority students.

The purpose of *retention* policy used by many schools is to help low performing students to catch up with their same-grade peers through repeating the year's work. Although in the early grades retention may assist children in keeping them with their same-age cohort, an increasing body of research presents that retention contributes to a greater rate of school dropouts (Jimerson, 1999; Roderick, 1994). Since 1980s, federal and state governments have been promoting greater accountability, which requires schools to implement high-stakes standard tests; as a result, there was a rise in retention rates. For example, in 1998 approximately 28.7% of students who were 14 years old did not reach the appropriate grade for their age (U.S. Bureau of the Census, 1999b). Poor, Black, and Hispanic students have been put at greater risk of retention. Reflecting on students' educational failure, retention is regarded as a potentially harmful solution to improving students' academic outcomes and solving their behavioral problems.

As school policies, s*uspensions* and *expulsions* are used to punish unruly and troublemaking students. Research indicates that since 1980s because of an increased rate of school violence, the number of suspensions and expulsions have been rising dramatically. For instance, in the country, about 6.8% of students were suspended from schools in 1997, as compared to 3.7% in 1974. Alienating students from school, suspensions and expulsions more likely than not increase the rate for student detainment, lead students to permanently drop out, or be involved in criminal behavior (Gordon et al., 2000). Poor and minority students, particularly African American male students, have been found to be disproportionately suspended and expelled (Skiba & Peterson, 1999). Racial discrimination and cultural differences raise equity concerns which place students at greater risk of school failure.

CHINESE SCHOLARS ON RISK FACTORS FOR STUDENTS

The literature on factors associated with at-risk students in China is also rich and varied. Chinese scholars explore the causes that link to students poor academic outcomes mainly by examining what they call internal, external and integrated factors (Liu & Ge, 1991). Internal factors are related to students' personal drawbacks such as physical and mental problems, delinquent behaviors, poor study skills and a passive, even negative attitude toward learning. On the other hand, external factors include family background, school environment, and social context. Most research, however, regards at-risk students to be connected to a set of integrated factors that include both internal and external factors (Jin & Guo, 1991; Li, 2002; Tang, 2002). The following section will review these factors in greater detail.

Focusing on Students' Personal, Internal Factors

Compared to researchers in the West, who place more stress on external disadvantages, researchers in China pay much attention to at-risk students' personal characteristics, namely internal factors. Many studies examine the causes that may bring about school failure by examining students' physical, psychological, and personal relationship problems (Liu & Ge, 1991; Zhang, 2006). For example, Gu (1991) found that more than 80% of at-risk students have psychological problems. Other research also indicates that low academic achievers usually have experienced some emotional, behavioral, mental, and social skill problems (He, 1991a). Lacking the motivation to learn, at-risk students do not have a big goal; they get sick of study and do not want to work hard; they are easily distracted, and they are careless, nervous, depressed, and sensitive; they also are very lonely, isolated, and cannot get along with other people. Particularly, fearing failure, they are easily discouraged, have low self-esteem, are timid, and have no confidence in study. All these personal features may put students at risk, leading to an academic failure or eventual dropout. Some physical disadvantages such as diseases, low intelligence, and hyperactivity have also been cited as risk factors (He, 1991c).

The National College Entrance Exam as an External Factor

Drawbacks of the school system have also been examined by Chinese educators as a risk factor for students to experience academic failure. The most severe criticism centers on the country's exam-oriented education system. Closed down for 10 years during China's chaotic years of the Great Cultural Revolution (1966–1976), the system was restored in 1977. To select students to receive higher education and train highly skill labors to speed up its economic development, China has set up a three-day National Unified College Entrance Examination (National Entrance Exam hereafter) that took place every year in July (now in June). Every year, millions of secondary school students take part in this exam. With only 3–4% of the students admitted to university in the 1980s and the early 1990s, this exam-oriented educational system basically labeled only a small number of students as academic success while the vast majority of students were treated as "educational failures." As a result, instead of developing students' full potentials, the aim of education in Chinese schools is to pursue a high rate of students passing the national exam. "Examination wars" have broken out and "examination hells" have placed tremendous pressure on students and damaged students' intellectual, psychological, and physical development (Li, 1997; Lin & Chen, 1995; Ren, 1998). Thus, this highly competitive system has created numerous problems that produce many at-risk students.

In school administration, all school policies made by all levels of governments and schools have given high priority to the needs of this exam-oriented system. The number of students passing the national exam has long been the essential criterion to evaluate the quality of a school. More specifically, to achieve "school success" on the National Entrance Exam, education in China places more emphasis on high schools than on middle schools; pays much more attention to a small number of outstanding students while a large number of ordinary students are neglected; schools focus more on students exam-taking skills than on students' all-around development.

Focusing on students' performance in all kinds of tests, which are given to students frequently to prepare them for the final battle, curricula are very narrow and rigid, with all teachers following a unified teaching outline. Also, to select only the best students through the National Entrance Exam, generally speaking, the contents of the textbooks compiled by the Ministry of Education go beyond students' real ability to learn. According to a statistical figure in 1990, 80% of high school science students found it difficult to learn their textbook contents. As a consequence, many students lose interest and motivation in learning and become low-achieving or at-risk students (Cheng, 1991).

Teachers' Poor Qualities

Chinese scholars have highlighted teachers' poor qualities and the relationship between teachers and students as factors related to academic failure for students. Lacking professional training and following a teacher-centered teaching approach, some teachers' classes are very boring. A study conducted in Beijing in 1990 shows that among 10 investigated middle schools 25% of the teachers were not qualified to teach (Study group on at-risk students in Chaoyang district in Beijing, 1990). With an emphasis on test-taking, teachers usually give their preference to those top students and ignore or even look down upon the low academic achievers. Lacking respect and care, these students feel alienated from their teachers and from the school. The negative schooling experiences render students to lose their enthusiasm for study and eventually drop out of school.

Parents' Social Class and Educational Level

Students' family background and social context have been examined by Chinese scholars to analyze factors that place students at risk. In terms of family background, similar to researchers in the West, Chinese scholars have also found a close correlation between parents' social status and students' poor academic achievement. Li (1989) discussed five individual/family-level indicators that are among the most frequently cited and studied in explaining how students become at-risk students: the parent's education level, income, expectation, strategies of educating children at home, and family structure. In the following, I will summarize findings from national studies that associate each of these indicators with academic failure.

Ji (1989) investigated 402 students from four middle schools in Shanghai and revealed that parents' educational level had a great influence on students' academic achievement. The more education parents have, the higher academic achievement students demonstrate. Li (1989) conducted a survey with 1056 students from five primary schools and five secondary schools in Beijing in 1988. The research shows that the father's educational level plays an important role in students' academic success. That is, well-educated fathers can help their children with school work in many more ways such as doing drills with their children, holding a positive value toward education, building up a supportive study environment at home, and assisting with their children's homework. The mother's educational level is also very significantly related to children's academic achievement, especially to children at elementary school level.

In terms of family income, a special phenomenon that is unique in China is that students from poor and rich families can both become low academic achievers. It is not a surprise that students from low socioeconomic background families experience academic failure because of a lack of financial resources and family support. However, many children from wealthy families also demonstrate a low motivation to study since they think they can rely on their parents to have all the money they want and thus it is not necessary for them to work hard and improve their life by obtaining better socioeconomic status through higher education (Su, 1991; Gan, 2008).

16 *Success for All*

Parental Expectations

A growing number of research studies show that parents' expectation of their children's education exerts a huge impact on students academic achievement. Generally speaking, Chinese scholars assume a direct relationship between parents' educational expectation and students' school success. In other words, they believe if parents have high educational expectation for their child, the student will do a better job in school. Conversely, low expectation from parents will result in a poor academic outcome for their children. That is because parents who value education more will pay more attention to their children's schooling. Also, they will provide more support to their children in school and create a better learning environment at home. On the other hand, parents who have low expectation for their children may not care about the children's study and give less support to their children. Yan (1991) examined 45 at-risk students and found that most of those students' parents had lower expectation on education for them, as compared to the parents of the high achieving students in the same school.

Studies indicate that although there is a positive relation between parents educational desire and their children's success in school, the educational aspiration from parents has to correspond with their children's ability. If too high, students will get too much pressure from their parents, which may discourage students' learning interests. Wu (1991) investigated 1898 middle students' families in two districts (Xu Hui and Nan Hui) in Shanghai. The research showed that only 26.5% students achieved high academic scores, meeting the goals set by their parents. Seventy-three and a half percent of students' achievements were not as good as their parents expected. Therefore, Chen (1991) suggests that parents should set two levels of goals for their children: one is a short term goal and the other is a long term goal. The short term goal should be very specific while the long term goal provides a direction toward future achievement for their children.

Strategies parents adopt in educating their children at home have been regarded as an important factor linked to at-risk students by Chinese scholars. China has a very long history of valuing children's education. There is saying in China that "a child cannot grow up to be useful without parents' [beating them] with sticks." As a result, many parents, especially those who are less-educated, curse or beat their children whenever they receive reports showing their child's poor academic outcomes in school. Living in fear, children may lose their interest in study and become at-risk students (Gao, 1991).

In contrast to abusing children, some parents go to the opposite and spoil their children. In today's China, most urban families have only one child because of the imposition of the government's one-child-per-family policy over the past two decades and a half in order to control the growth of population. Treating their child as a little emperor or empress, many parents coddle their child and do not require them to work hard on their studies. As a consequence, these children do not like to study and eventually become at-risk students.

Changes in Family Structure

Similar to Western scholars, Chinese scholars also found that family structure influences students' academic achievement significantly. In terms of the stability of a family, China used to be viewed as the country with the lowest divorce rate in the world. However, since 1978 when China opened its door to the world and introduced a competitive market economic system with relaxation in social control to replace the rigidly managed, tightly controlled social economic system, family structure in China has undergone a rapid change. For example, in 1980 there were 270,000 divorce cases in the court nationally. In 1990 the figure had gone up to 790,000. In Shanghai, the rate of divorce was 1.95% in 1980, 4.61% in 1986, and 13.4% in 1989. According to a report, among the children who live in single-parent families in China, 37.35% live with their father, 50.36% with their mother, 10.83 with their grandparents.

Research shows that, generally speaking, the academic score of children from one-parent families is lower than that of children from two-parent families. A comparative research with 929 students from single parent families and 804 from two-parent families examines grade point averages for Chinese language and mathematics and found that students from divorced families scored 3.44 on average for the Chinese language subject, while students from two-parent families scored on average 4.25. The same disparity existed in mathematics achievement scores: on average, students from disrupted families scored 3.33, and students from intact families scored 4.22 (Fu & Shi, 2001).

Studies indicate that parental divorce often hurts children's feelings and damages their psychological development which may affect their study negatively. Without both parents' constant caring, support, and help, children from divorced families are found to have greater difficulties to achieve in school (He, 1991a).

Influence from Commercialism

In terms of social context, scholars in China note three aspects which may relate to at-risk factors for students. First, influenced by the culture of a new market economy, many students as well as many parents view that studying is of no use in today's commercial society. In particular, at the beginning of China economic reform in the 1980s, there existed a big salary gap between businessmen and intellectuals. Taking advantages of the chaos which were created by the government getting into uncharted water, daring businessmen with only an elementary education could earn much more money than a teacher or a professor who has received higher education. Therefore, some students deemed it unnecessary to study hard and lost their drive to learn (Gao, 1991). As mentioned above, students from wealthy families did not work hard either since their parents have already made a lot of money for him/her. Also, due to competition in the job market, the reality that many college/university graduates cannot find a job discouraged students from achieving a higher goal in education.

A seldom-studied, but a big challenge facing educators in both the West and the East today is the rapid development of computer games and many other games. To earn profits, many game companies have set up their businesses around schools, which have tremendously distracted students' attention from study. Games featured by these businesses are highly addictive. Once students become addicted to them, they do not like to study any more. Scholars also found that pornographic books and DVD programs can become a risk indicator for students. If students indulge in those kinds of books or VCD or DVD programs, they will lose their interests in study.

Neighborhood Influence

Unstable community and run-down neighborhoods also produce at-risk students. Wu (1990) conducted a research on the impact of different cultural areas on students' academic outcomes. He divided culture into four different kinds based on locations: advanced cultural area, a drawback cultural area, regular cultural area, and railway cultural area. The advanced cultural area is referred to as administrative area, IT area, and key school area. A drawback cultural area consists of self-employers, small retailers, individual producer, and at-risk or low performing schools. Regular cultural area is the area with manufacturing and ordinary schools. Finally, the railway system areas in China are usually those huge state-own companies with their own schools. The percentage of at-risk students in these areas is different. They are respectively 2.33% for intensive area, 1.40% for railway system area, 9.29% for regular cultural area, and 10.73% for a drawback cultural area.

THE NEGATIVE RESULTS OF AT-RISK STUDENTS

Although it is difficult to estimate the ratio of the disadvantaged population in both the West and the East because of differences in the criteria to determine "at-risk students," nevertheless, school failure is a major concern for educators and scholars around the world.

Liu (1997) points out that the average ratio of low achieving students in the schools around the world is around 6%–10%. A 1976 U.S. government study revealed that there were 13% of all 17-year-olds identified as functionally illiterate and half of illiterates were from educationally disadvantaged population (National Assessment of Educational Progress, 1976). Natriello et al. (1990) found that at least 40% of children in the United States were at risk of school failure in the late 1980s. These students are mainly from poor and single-parent families, minority groups, and non-English-speaking populations, representing about one-third of all students in primary and secondary schools in the United States. The proportion is rising rapidly since immigration has brought in many people from impoverished and rural areas of Asia and Latin America. Those students' academic achievement falls far behind the majority children. Specifically, they are two years behind other students by grade 6 and four years behind at the end of grade 12. Approximately half the students do not finish their high school education, which is a minimum requirement for getting into the U.S. labor market (Huston, 1991). Although the percentage of students completing high school has increased steadily for several decades, the dropout rates remain high in some areas, particularly in some major cities, and among certain races such as Hispanics and African Americans. According to recent dropout statistics, about 11% of American students are not able to complete high school (Kaufman et al., 2000). Roughly a third of the children are doing poorly in reading and math (Bourque & Byrd, 2000).

The problem of at-risk in the East is also very serious. For example, in Japan, the ratio of at-risk students is measured at 20%. In China, Liu (1997) found that about ten million primary and secondary students failed their studies every year. At-risk student population has been growing. According to Yang (2001), in China, in 2001 fifty million or 30% primary and secondary students have been placed at-risk.

The negative impacts of at-risk students on the society have been well documented. At-risk students directly result in many social problems: prejudice against studying, increase in dropout rates, repetition of the year's work, antisocial behaviors, school violence, students with low self-esteem, students suffering emotional and mental disorder, and unemployment (Finn, 1987; Lin, 1993; McLaren, 1994).

Moreover, the expansion of the disadvantaged student population leads to dire economic consequences such as an unskilled labor force and the high cost of public services (Levin, 1991). An increasing number of educationally disadvantaged students will lower the criteria of admission to higher education. Public institutions of higher education will have to invest more time on providing students with remedial academic work. As a result, it will produce a disadvantaged population which may not be able to contribute the development of the economy and the democratic society.

Further, a large number of disadvantaged students will lead to a serious problem in the future labor force. Today's technological society demands more educated and skilled work forces. Even entrance-level jobs such as clerical, cashier, and sales work today need some training in computer, oral and written communication, and reasoning, etc. However, lacking family and community support, large numbers of disadvantaged students are unable to take full advantage of the educational opportunities available to them. Therefore, they will be unprepared for the highly competitive job market. From a society's point of view, without successfully resolving the plight of the at-risk students, economy in a country will lose its power to compete in the global community in which we now live.

The direct negative results of these economic losses will lead to a rising cost of public services. Without adequate educational attainments, these disadvantaged future citizens will depend on public assistance for survival which will raise costs substantially for society. James S. Catterall (1985) even calculates that "each year's class of dropouts will cost more than $200 billion in both lost earnings and unrealized tax revenues during their lifetimes. Additionally, billions of dollars will be spent for welfare, medical aid programs, and expenses in the criminal justice system" (Waxman, 1992, p. 11).

In all, because of many problems caused by a growing disadvantaged student population, a worldwide educational crisis looms before us in dealing with the education of at-risk students. Educators, scholars, policy makers, and parents are looking for an alternative approach toward educational reform on improving at-risk students.

STRATEGIES FOR IMPROVING AT-RISK STUDENTS

One of the most pressing issues facing policymakers, educators, and parents in both East and West is how to effectively help students who are placed at risk. As we have mentioned, in the globalization era, the issue of at-risk students is not only related to personal development but associated with a nation economic development. Governments, having realized this, have waged waves of school improvement efforts beginning in the middle to late 1980s. Numerous alternative programs for at-risk students have been designed and implemented (Goldenberg, 2003). Generally speaking, those programs adopted two approaches: preventive and remedial, namely substance abuse prevention and treatment, and a general area which focuses on the at-risk students' needs (Rogus & Wildenhaus, 1991).

Research shows that the majority of strategies for at-risk students focus on the high school setting or on early intervention at the primary level. Middle-level education has been regarded as "the forgotten segment of public education." Especially, dropout prevention programs for middle schools have lagged behind (Barr & Parrett, 2001; Weir, 1996). Because this research focuses mainly on middle school education, the following literature review will highlight those studies that touch on changes in middle school education. According to Barr and Parrett (2001), the guideline for transforming middle school education should include the following:

- Smaller components where cohorts of students and teachers work together for most of the school day.
- High academic standards that align the curriculum to content standards.
- A curriculum which focuses on the developmental needs of young adolescents and includes interdisciplinary course subjects that foster communication, critical thinking, social development, and healthy lifestyles.
- Flexible scheduling to provide blocks of time for interdisciplinary study with teams of students in shorter periods of time for career exploration and specialized studies.
- Programs that provide cooperative learning, mentoring, computer and technical education, and so on, should be employed for the middle-level student.
- Teachers that serve as classroom counselors and advisors.
- Out-of-school programs in the community. These may be more crucial at the middle level than in either the elementary or high-school years, for it is during early adolescence that students are placed most at-risk during their time away from school (pp. 162–163).

These guidelines can also be seen as a tendency toward educational reforms for at-risk students in North America for the past two decades.

Although a variety of programs have been initiated for students who have learning and behavior problems, Finn (1989) summarized three main categories of successful programs for at-risk students: organizational, instructional, and interpersonal. In this section, I will borrow Finn's three categories to sort out the literature on alternative programs for at-risk students.

Organizational Components

Organizational components are related to school-wide efforts to improve middle schools supported by administrative and building policies. Characterized by comprehensive whole-school reforms, they have demonstrated significant promise toward enhancing the academic achievement of youth at risk. In accordance with Finn, the organizational components that are associated with successful programs mainly include these:

- Creating small learning communities;
- Setting alternative environments dissimilar to traditional schools;
- Linking to agencies outside the school institution;
- Having a fair discipline, encouraging students to participate in the decision-making process of the school;
- Designing different types of dropout prevention programs.

In other words, these organizational components emphasize the entire school's reform, encompassing its staff, students, and the community.

Among numerous whole-school reforms in middle schools, developing small schools is regarded as one most effective way for alternative education. Growing numbers of studies show that successful model programs in small schools have proven to have provided academic, social, and financial benefits for all students, especially those who are at risk (Barr & Parrett, 2001; Carnegie Council on Adolescent Development, 1989). The idea of downsizing schools is to enable every teacher to know every student better so that the school can employ more effective ways for at-risk urban students to learn and grow than participation in traditional schools.

Of small school models, one that is getting increasing favor is "schools within schools." "Schools within schools" is defined as "large public schools that have been divided into smaller autonomous subunits" (McAndrews, & Anderson, 2002). The purpose of designing schools within schools is to develop small learning communities while sharing the resources of the larger existing facilities. The benefits of small schools have been reported to have created happier, safer, higher achieving students (Oxley, 2001); to have enhanced students' self-perceptions (McPartland et al., 2001); and to have increased higher rates of attendance than large schools have (Gewertz, 2001).

There has also been research on multiple methods, or multiple team structures, to improve students learning (Datnow & Stringfield, 2002). For example, Trimble and Peterson (2000) investigate the relationship between a multiple team structure and student achievement in a school with a high enrollment of minority students and students from low SES family background. The research examined the composition and interactions of the executive team, leadership team, grade level teams, cross-content teams, interdisciplinary and study teams, and their influence on student learning outcomes. The findings from the observation show that the multiple team structures resulted in changed classroom practices and increased student performance.

To provide more detail about school-wide efforts, in their book, *Hope Fulfilled for At-Risk Youth: K–12 Programs that Work*, Barr and Parrett (2001) describe some successful reform models such as Multiple-Intelligences Middle Schools, Accelerated Middle Schools, Community for Learning, School Development Program, and Coalition of Essential Schools.

Instructional Components

Curriculums and teaching are always very important parts of school reform efforts. Merely changing the grouping of students without innovation in the curriculum and teaching methods is not likely to achieve success with at-risk students. Instructional components of at-risk programs include adopting alternative approaches with regard to curriculum, teaching methods, assessment, and academic demands according to at-risk students' needs. According to Weir (1996), the following instructional components have demonstrated effectiveness in improving at-risk students' learning: cooperative learning and peer tutoring, vocational education, computer-assisted instruction, a climate supportive of and tailored to each student's need and abilities, a diversity of instructional techniques, an integrated curriculum that allows students success in many ways, and a wide variety of curriculum materials that are different from traditional textbooks.

At middle education level, programs on reading, writing and language arts, mathematics, cooperative learning, and summer schools have been documented as positively effecting at-risk student achievement. Barr and Parrett (2001) list a number of effective at-risk student achievement programs as following:

- Cooperative Learning: Cooperative Integrated Reading and Composition (grade 2–8).
- Reading, writing and language arts: Exemplary Center for reading Instruction (grades 1–10); Reciprocal Teaching (grade 1–8); Profile Approach to Writing (grades 3–12); and Multicultural Reading and Thinking (grade 3–8).
- Mathematics: Project SEED (grades 3–8); Skills Reinforcement Project (grades 3–8); Maneuvers with Mathematics (grades 5–8) (p. 1444).

Holliday (2002) states that cooperative learning is conducive to creating a positive learning environment for at-risk students to achieve academic success. He conducted a study on using cooperative learning to improve the academic achievement of inner city students in a middle school located in Northwest Indiana where most of the students are minority students and are from low socioeconomic backgrounds. The research found that cooperative learning strategies work well with inner city students who are labeled at-risk.

Summer school programs can also be viewed as an effective way of offering at-risk students an opportunity to receive credit for class failure or non-attendance (Borman & Hewes, 2001). With a flexible schedule, summer schools usually focus on remediation. In other words, students who have failed in some areas in regular classroom setting can make up through summer schools. It has been instrumental in helping students to catch up with their class as well as keeping students from dropping out of school (Cale, 1992).

Interpersonal Components

Interpersonal components of programs for at-risk students aim at helping at-risk students who have mental, physical, and/or emotional problems to develop their confidence and self-esteem. The strategies include creating a supportive climate that is tailored to students' individual needs and abilities, raising students' self-esteem and fostering students' positive attitudes about school, increasing students' opportunity for informal interactions with adults, encouraging parents' and the community's participation in alternative programs, developing cooperative learning, counseling, and mentoring.

Research found that building student's self-esteem is crucial for developing a successful at-risk student program. There is a direct correlation between healthy self-esteem and the following behaviors: higher educational aspirations, academic excellence, lack of involvement in drugs and alcohol, and lack of antisocial behaviors. Therefore, developing students' self-esteem must be a goal for administrators, educators and parents (Friedland, 1992).

Bateman and Karr-Kidwell (1995) review two programs focusing on raising students' self-esteem and achievement and reveal that increasing student's self-esteem had a positive impact on students' behaviors and achievement. One program, called "Building Self-Esteem," was implemented in the Parlier Unified School District, and throughout the United States. It showed that discipline problems in the middle school dropped approximately 75% in the first year of the program and by 85% in the second year.

Students in this program had fewer discipline problems and were more cooperative and more highly motivated. Another study conduced in Dahlonega, North Carolina also indicates that compared to the control group, the tutorial group and the tutorial-counseling group made significant progress in achievement, behavior and self-esteem.

One of the most promising programs to help middle-school students grow socially and emotionally employs service learning which includes peer teaching, cross-age tutoring, and a host of public service activities (Barr & Parrett, 2001). Through those activities, students develop the value of giving, positively participate in learning and make contributions to their community. Studies show that few school programs have as many effective results in enhancing students' self-esteem as service learning is able to produce (Nathan, 1989). In particular, researchers recommend cross-age tutoring as a very effective approach toward building students self-esteem and reducing dropout rate (Massachusetts Advocacy Center, 1988).

Building up a trustful relationship with adults and having an adult model are crucial for children entering adolescence. Therefore, at the middle-school level, three aspects of programs for at-risk students are seen as extremely important: parental involvement, counseling, and mentoring (Barr & Parrett, 2001). Research shows that parents may exert a powerful influence on their children education through caring about their children's schooling (Orgen & Geminario, 1994). Effective middle schools should implement a policy to encourage parental involvement. However, unfortunately, parents are found to be not actively encouraged to involve in schooling in many middle schools.

Counseling programs serve at-risk students who need advice on academic problem, sexual and physical abuse, dysfunctional families, gender-related issues, and drug and alcohol problems. Waterman and Walker (2001) studied a counseling program called SPARK, initiated at UCLA with Los Angeles areas schools over a period of six years. Aimed at helping youth at risk for academic, behavioral, and emotional difficulties to cope with the stresses they face, the research found that the SPARK group counseling curriculum appears to be effective in a variety of areas, including academic achievement, psychological adjustment, self-esteem, attachment to peers, and gang involvement.

Defined as a sustained relationship between a caring adult and a student, mentoring has become an essential part of programs for at-risk students in an effective middle school (Barr & Parrett, 2001). Educators, policymakers, researchers, parents agree that adolescents need adults to supervise and support their development (Reglin, 1990). Mentoring is regarded as a powerful way to provide adult connections to youth who are isolated from adults in their schools, homes, communities, and work places (Flaxman, 1992). Since more and more children are living in poverty or in single families, our students need mentors to help them more than ever. Literature on mentoring shows consistent effects mentoring has on improving students' academic attainment, helping them to be successful in life, and reducing the possibility of student dropouts (Reglin, 1998).

In recent years, there has been rapid growth in after-school programs to deal with the increasing risky behaviors of youth. Studies have discovered that a high proportion of youth risk behaviors such as sexual activities, drug and alcohol abuse, gang-activity, crime etc. occurred between the hours of 3:00 p.m. and 6:00 p.m. in the afternoon, a time when the students finished school and their parents are not at home from work (Barr & Ross, 1989; Hollister, 2003). After-school programs were initiated as a strategy to address students' low academic achievement and to reduce the occurrence of at-risk behaviors. Integrating academic remediation, counseling services, and community and parent involvement, after-school programs have been found to increase levels of achievement and motivation for at-risk students and facilitate the connection between school and community (Collins & Onwuegbuzie, 2001; Edmondson & White, 1998; Posner & Vandell, 1994). However, critics argued that there is limited empirical evidence to evaluate the results of those programs (Fashola, 1998).

Strategies to Improve At-Risk Students in China

Through an extensive review of literature on strategies to improve at-risk students in China, I found that instead of focusing on socioeconomic analysis and national policymaking, Chinese educators deal with the issues of at-risk students by focusing on what kind of individual and collective efforts teachers can make in their teaching in the classroom to help the students. They have chiefly put their efforts on helping at-risk students by creating a loving and caring learning environment, by adopting a flexible curriculum to meet at-risk students' needs and by building up a close connection with families and communities (Shen, 2000; Zhang, 2006).

Chinese educators and scholars believe that teachers should love, respect, and work in enthusiasm with at-risk students. Research shows that although different teachers may use different methods for assisting at-risk students in their teaching, there is a fundamental belief or philosophy which all Chinese educators strongly hold: love is the panacea for at-risk students. In every research paper I read, it was mentioned that only strategies that integrate loving and caring students can students be transformed from the at-risk situation to be successful in school (Duan, 1989; Song, 2001; Tang, 2004). Because of repeated failures in school, at-risk students usually have been blamed a great deal by teachers and parents, and also looked down upon by their classmates. As a result, they have become sensitive, passive, and even hostile toward other people and the society. Only teachers who fully respect, trust, love, and pay a lot of attention to those children can bring miracle changes to these students (Deng, 2006; Gong, 1991; Huang, 2004; Li, 2001).

To create a caring and accepting learning environment, the teacher should not only build up a close personal relationship with students who are considered to be at-risk but also facilitate all the students in the classroom to have a harmonious atmosphere in which students can learn from each other, take care of each other, and help each other. Under such a friendly and positive circumstance, children with learning and behavioral problems will feel warmth, feel respected and loved, which may consequently motivate them to develop a normal life and make progress in their academic achievement (Cao, 1991; Chen, 1991; Wu, 1991).

Sharing the same view with educators in North America, Chinese scholars also advocate that building up of students' self-esteem as the essential way of helping students who underachieve in school and have behavioral problems. Studies revealed that the at-risk group was less able, more anxious, and less confident than the not-at-risk group. Due to repeated failure in school, these students had a negative self-concept and very low self-esteem. Therefore, a main concern for educators is to help these students build a positive self-concept and foster high self-esteem. A growing body of research documents indicates that letting at-risk students experience success in their studies and life is a highly effective approach for building up disadvantaged students' self-esteem (Lou, 1991; Xie et al., 2006; Zhu, 2003).

Identifying at-risk students' talents and giving them positive reinforcement is recommended by many experienced Chinese classroom teachers as very efficient strategies to help at-risk students be successful (Li, 2005). Chinese scholars argue that everyone has his or her special talents that make his or her different from others. Some students may not be good in academic achievement due to factors related to their socioeconomic status, family background, or their community setting. However, they may have talents in social skills, arts, sports, or technology, etc. An excellent teacher should know each at-risk student well, be aware of their talents, and provide as many opportunities as possible for students to explore, present, and develop their talents. Li (2004) suggests using a multiple intelligence theory for transforming Chinese at-risk students. Using a multiple evaluation standard, prizes and awards will be based on a variety of accomplishments, thus letting at-risk students experience success and receive recognition for their success. In such a supportive and encouraging school climate, students' self-esteem may be enhanced. With high self-esteem, students will have a positive attitude toward school and feel confident in their studies which may eventually bring about academic success.

On another front, developing and offering a flexible curriculum to meet the needs of at-risk students is another significant strategy proposed by Chinese educators. There is a well-established literature in Chinese education on transforming at-risk students by "teaching students in accordance with their aptitude" (*Yin Cai Shi Jiao*), a famous Chinese saying originated from Confucius. Therefore, finding ways to effectively identify the specific needs of each student who displays at-risk behaviors within the school setting becomes one of the most major challenges faced by school teachers. To do so, school teachers are urged to set up a file for each "problem student" to record their studies and behavior, to visit students' families from time to time, to have one-on-one conversations with the students after class, and to observe these students closely through teaching, learning or extracurricular activities (Chen, 1991; Huang & Xu, 1991; Wang, 2006).

Studies have found that common characteristics exist among at-risk students: for example, they lack basic learning skills and good study habits, have limited knowledge, short attention spins and are easily distracted (Chen, 1991; Fan & Li, 1991). The regular curriculum which is designed to transmit a huge body of information to students to do well in examinations causes at-risk students to experience failure. To solve the problems of at-risk students in academic learning, some educators made efforts on adjusting the core curriculum to be at a lower level, and made it more engaging and relevant. In order to stimulate students' interest, they tried to reform the traditional forms of instruction by shifting away from a teacher-centered mode of instruction to a more student-centered mode. Other teachers explored ways that not only impart to students knowledge but also teach them how to learn. Strategies such as increasing students' personal resources (e.g., remediation for students' skill deficiencies), giving extra lessons to at-risk students after school and during the weekend, and helping students with their homework have been adopted by many teachers in China to improve student achievement (He, 1991b; Wei, 2006). Although the evidence of success from those alternative approaches has been reported, Chinese schools still pay much less attention to at-risk students than to those outstanding students since Chinese education is still largely exam-oriented. Strategies of helping students who are placed at-risk are more often personal efforts and experiences than stipulated as policies and actions initiated by schools and governments.

In our literature review, it is found one of the most obvious features of Chinese education to deal with the issue of at-risk and violent youth is that they put a lot of efforts on building up a strong connection between family, school, and community. China has a long tradition of viewing education as a comprehensive endeavor which need parents, school, and community to work together to achieve a common goal. Research shows that, in efforts to be effective with at-risk children and youth, the primary focus for

Chinese educators has been on establishing and maintaining good communications with students' families, helping students' families to provide a home environment that can fully support students, and educating parents on how to assist their children studies (Wang, 2005). Specifically, teachers in Chinese schools are required to visit students' families as much as they can. Also, parents can phone school teachers at any time and ask for help with their children. Research on improving schools has documented positive results of what Chinese schools have done to help parents become caring, loving, and supportive parents and set up good examples for their children through the parent school, seminars, and regular parent meetings (Chen, 2004).

In their book, *Studies on At-Risk Students*, based on literature review Liu and Ge (1991) summarized 27 strategies to improve at-risk groups. These strategies include: Helping the student enhance his/her academic achievement through remediation one by one; inspiring students' study interests by setting up a new goal; choosing a peer role model for at-risk students to imitate; teaching students how to control their emotions, manage their time, and train their willpower; assigning problem students as teachers' assistants to help other students study; providing more learning opportunities for at-risk students in the classroom; awarding at-risk students through multiple evaluation systems; encouraging students consistently; and conducing cooperative learning. Although Chinese scholars have provided a diversity of alternative approaches toward educating disadvantaged youth, lack of evidence is also obvious in this book.

In summary, governments, schools, families, and communities in both Western and Eastern societies have put in tremendous effort to facilitate school improvement. Many reforms and programs aiming at improving educational equality and productivity have been initiated. These programs can be found at different school levels and have been studied over the past two decades through both quantitative and qualitative research methodologies. However, the effectiveness of these strategies in serving at-risk children is controversial and complex.

Research conducted by CRESPAR Systemic and Policy researchers over an 11-year period clearly indicated that some schools have improved, while others have fallen back. Research even found that although using the same alternative approach, some schools have improved dramatically, others have not (Datnow & Stringfield, 2001). Borman and Hewes (2001) argue that few American policies for school improvement have revealed convincing evidence of long-term benefits to students and society. A number of early intervention programs might show some positive results. However, these impacts generally diminished after several years. As a consequence, many program participants showed no difference in academic achievements than those of non participants. Moreover, Borman et al. (2004) state that although the latter half of the 20th century is characterized by continuous and intensive educational reforms in the United States, these efforts on school improvement have been moving from one to another with little evidence of national progress. Some data on urban school academic achievement also demonstrate that educational reforms in the last two decades in the United States, including the effective schools movement, school choice, and school restructuring, have been largely ineffective (Sanders, 2000).

In China, the situation of education for at-risk students is even worse. With only a 3%–4% rate of students who could be admitted to universities, this exam-driven educational system failed 95% students for a long time.[1] Serving the single goal of helping students to pass the National College and University Entrance Examination, Chinese schools pay little attention to at-risk students. Strategies for helping students who are placed at-risk are rather more personal efforts and experiences than consistent institutional efforts supported by policies and actions initiated by the government. Although the Chinese government started a national educational reform called *quality education* (suzhi jiaoyu) in 1985 to facilitate the success of more students, the consensus on this reform is that the effort has made little change in today's Chinese education because the exam-oriented educational system still functions intact. The educational experiments initiated by schools to inspire students learning since the mid-1980s have also faded away as time passed, and experimental schools reported academic outcomes not different from those of non participants (Yang, 2001).

SUMMARY

In conclusion, study on at-risk education in both North America and China indicates the problem of at-risk students is a worldwide phenomenon. In today's highly competitive world, the disadvantaged children are losing behind faster than ever, which will place them in the bottom of the society with little chance of social mobility. The factors associated with at-risk students are complicated. Literature both in the United States and China shows that, poverty, single-parent families, parents' low educational level, minority background, poverty in the community, and high-poverty school contributed to conditions that place students to be at-risk. Although the strategies for helping at-risk children might be different, great efforts have been initiated by governments around the world. However, stories of success are few. Thus, policymakers, educators, and school administrators are still looking for alternative approaches to help improve the learning of the disadvantaged students effectively.

NOTE

1. Since 1998, China has been undergoing higher education expansion, increasing student enrollment to about 20% of the student cohort in 2006. However, the pressure on school is still huge, as in an increasingly competitive job market, people's expectation have gone up as well, with parents and schools pushing harder than ever to have their children enter well-known universities.

CHAPTER 2

COMPREHENSIVE SCHOOL REFORM IN THE UNITED STATES AND CHINA

This chapter reviews a school reform model, which has been developing rapidly since the 1990s—the Comprehensive School Reform (CSR). Since CSR is a school-wide reform, which is very similar to the success education, I have drawn from these models and identified components and issues to be examined and analyzed in the study of success education reform in Shanghai, China.

DEFINITION, THEORY AND PRACTICE OF COMPREHENSIVE SCHOOL REFORM

What is CSR? The definition of CSR can be viewed as the following:

> Comprehensive school reform focuses on reorganizing and revitalizing the entire school rather than on isolated, piecemeal reforms. It provides teachers with the training, materials, and support they need to help students reach challenging academic standards. In comprehensive school reform, a "design" becomes the basis for all operations and activities within the school, and provides a vision that helps the school focus its efforts, engage teachers in

their work, and build strong parent and community support (New American Schools 1998, p. 7).

More specifically, CSR "is a federal program incorporated under the reauthorization of the Elementary and Secondary Education Act, and No Child Left Behind Act of 2002" (Pearson, 2002, p. 9). Described as a new direction for the American educational reform, CSR is deeply rooted in two important ideas the belief in applying research-based practices as a key to school reform, and the federal government's evolving strategies for utilizing the Title I program to help disadvantaged students in America's high-poverty schools (Cross, 2004).

For decades, American public schools have been criticized for failing many students, especially those in high-poverty settings (Berends et al., 2002). Thus, policymakers and educators have been trying to improve instruction and student achievement. The Title I program initiated in 1965 was intended to provide funding to schools to serve a high percentage of economically disadvantaged students. Through pullout models the additional funds directly targeted those eligible students, hoping that this measure would serve as a lever to make changes in America's high-poverty schools. However, after several decades, research has demonstrated that the planned educational change efforts on enhancing at-risk students' academic outcomes through the Title I program had produced little change in the nation's test scores (Desimone, 2000; Protheroe, 1998). Therefore, the 1983 report, *A Nation at Risk* (National Commission on Excellence in Education, 1983) warned that the American Educational system was in a crisis. Deep concern for the quality of public schools has led to calls for an educational innovation.

New American Schools (NAS), which was founded in 1991 as a nonprofit, nonpartisan organization by business leaders, emerged in response to the educational needs of poor children (New American Schools 1998). NAS founders believed that to help the disadvantaged students in the highest-poverty schools to achieve high levels, school-wide change, instead of a fragmented approach which featured programs in the past, must take place. They also believed that when an entire school is changed, the lowest-achieving students can achieve success along with other students. Thus, this comprehensive school-wide reform focuses on school-wide programs to help not only the disadvantaged students but *all* students to succeed.

Aimed at working on all elements that effect teaching and learning in a coherent manner, the CSR programs suggest the following components for school reforms:

1. Employ proven strategies based on scientifically based research and effective practices;

2. Integrate a comprehensive design for effective school functioning, including instruction, assessment, classroom management, professional development, parental involvement, and school management, that aligns the school's curriculum, technology, and professional development into a comprehensive school reform plan, and state content and student academic achievement standards;
3. Provide high quality teacher and staff professional development;
4. Include measurable goals for academic achievement and benchmarks for meeting the goals;
5. Seek support from the school staff;
6. Provide support for staff;
7. Provide for meaningful involvement of parents and the local community in planning, implementing, and evaluating school improvement activities;
8. Use high quality external technical support and assistance;
9. Plan for an annual evaluation of implementation;
10. Identify other resources to sustain reform efforts (Pearson, 2002, p. 9).

These components are also considered as the criteria to evaluate if a program is CSR or not.

With strong support by the government at all levels, the school-wide reform movement has been developing rapidly, especially in those low-performing, high-poverty schools. In 1994, the Improving America's Schools Act rewarded schools with student poverty rates of at least 50% to use Title I funds to make school-wide improvement (Protheroe, 1998). In 1998, Congress appropriated $145 million per year for low-performing schools to develop and implement comprehensive reform programs (Hertling, 2000). Through a competitive process, a school can be granted to have a minimum of $50,000 per year for three years to run a CSR program (Cross, 2004). Some recent data show that so far 5,160 schools have received funding from CSR programs and more than 800 NAS models have been implemented (Rowan et al., 2004).

Although research on the effects of school-wide reforms is still limited, the movement is seen as one of the most promising approaches toward reforming American schools in the improvement of student achievement (Murphy & Datnow, 2003). It might be too early to determine the effects of CSR models on student performance. However, NAS believes that if all of their designs are fully implemented, it will have positive results in schools' attendance rates, parental involvement, and student outcomes (Church, 2000).

Effective school reform literature provides evidence on effectiveness of CSR models. For instance, by examining CSR programs for at-risk elementary and middle school students, Fashola and Slavin (1997) identify some essential elements which work well in implementing CSR programs. These elements include research-based curricula, integrative instruction, dynamic classroom management, clear criteria of assessment, and skills for building understanding with students.

Moreover, cited by Ross (2000), several detailed research studies on the 34 Memphis schools that have adopted CSR designs shows that most schools have made year-to-year progress. Also, student outcomes have improved compared to the achievement in schools that have not implemented CSR models. In these schools, teaching strategies have become more dynamic by using cooperation learning, discussion, projects, teacher coaching, and technology. Another research study, conducted by RAND researchers, found that after implementing CSR for three years, while students in Memphis and Kentucky schools have achieved major success in their mathematics achievement, Cincinnati and the state of Washington schools have improved a great deal in reading. That is, among 163 schools, 81 or 50% of the schools outperformed their control groups in mathematics, and 76 or 47% of the schools did better than those non-CSR schools in reading (Ames, 2004).

Even though only three CSR programs present "strong evidence of positive effects on student achievement," research conducted by the American Institutes for Research (AIR) provides 24 comprehensive school reform models in detail as a guide to educators who are interested in those approaches. Among these programs, a number of famous models such as "Success for All," "Roots and Wings," "High Schools That Work," and "Talent Development High School with Career Academicism" etc. have enjoyed increasing popularity across the country because of their positive effects (AIR, 1999).

With more than a decade of practice, and despite uneven successes, research demonstrates that some lessons have been learned from the implementation of CSR. By reviewing five major comprehensive school reform models, Borman et al. (2002) summarize the following factors that affect the success or failure of a CSR program:

1. Schools that implement their selected models with the greatest fidelity are more likely to see positive effects;
2. Models that are more clearly defined tend to be implemented with greater fidelity and, in turn, have stronger effects on teaching and learning;
3. Well-implemented reforms usually have strong professional development components, including follow-up support that addresses specific classroom-level problems in implementing change; and

4. Teachers and administrators must support or even co-construct the selected reform design (Holdzkom, 2002).

In particular, research emphasizes the significant role of leadership in implementation of CSR. The importance of leadership in school reforms has been focused on by researchers for decades (Brookover et al., 1979; Purkey & Smith, 1983). As a school-wide reform, the role of leaders is even more crucial than ever before.

Specifically, leadership in establishing effective CSR efforts can be examined at different levels. At the state level, legislators and other policymakers set the tone for CSR reform. They provide a strong voice for change, apportion funding, initiate policies that allow districts and schools to make decisions to implement school-wide reform, and build coalitions to support reform efforts (Education Commission on the State, 1999). At district level, leadership provides the active support for schools implementing CSR models. Those supports include promoting CSR programs to local schools, facilitating local schools to adopt a reform design that best fits their features and matches their needs, coordinating the program, and evaluating the effects of CSR (New American Schools). Without such sustained support, even a promising CSR effort can be abandoned (Hess, 1999).

All of the NAS studies, with no exception, stress that the school principal capacity is critical in the success of urban school improvement (Berends et al., 2002). In the book entitled *Leadership Lessons from Comprehensive School Reforms,* Murphy and Datnow (2003) draw attention to the correlation between principal leadership and success of CSR programs. The principal's leadership is described as "the single most important predictor," the "catalysts for change," and "the gatekeepers for their schools' change efforts." Being "often at the heart of successful deployment activity," the principal can provide "the capacity, coherence, and ownership needed to sustain deeper reform." Another study done by Berends et al. (2001) also mention that schools with strong principal leadership had higher levels of implementation than those schools without strong principles.

Other components such as faculty buy-in, professional development, and parent and community involvement have also been regarded as essential factors for making a CSR model successful. According to a number of researchers, without intensive support of a large segment of teachers and other school staff, school-wide reform is doomed to failure (Ames, 2004; Stringfield & Land, 2002). Since this research-based and standards-based reform changes classroom instruction dramatically, it requires teachers to be involved in the program from the very beginning. In other words, the alternative program needs teachers to fully understand the significance of the reform, help set the goal, make their decisions to select the model, and actively participate in the reform. Otherwise, without a clear picture of the design requirements as well as lack of ownership, teachers will not put in their full effort by ignoring comprehensive reform efforts. This passive role teachers adopt may cause the program to perform poorly (Balfanz & Mac Iver, 2000).

In the meantime, CSR fundamentally shifts away from the traditional way of teaching and learning. Both research and practice found that professional development is the key to reach the goal of CSR (Bodilly et al., 1996; Mid-Continent Research for Education and Learning, 1999). New American Schools (1998) reinforce this point and explain by stating that "Professional development is at the heart of design-based school reform, because raising student achievement depends on the skills, knowledge, and effectiveness of teachers" (p. 6). Therefore, CSR demands for high quality professional development which should cover the following elements:

- Focus on teachers as central to student learning, yet include all other members of the school community;
- Focus on individual, collegial, and organizational improvement;
- Nurture the intellectual and leadership capacity of teachers, principals, and others;
- Use the best available research and practice;
- Enable teachers to develop further expertise in subject content, teaching strategies, uses of technologies, and other essential elements in teaching to high standards.
- Promote continuous inquiry and improvement embedded in the daily life of schools;
- Is planned collaboratively by those who will participate in and facilitate that development;
- Invest substantial time and other resources;
- Is driven by a coherent, long-term plan;
- Is evaluated ultimately on the basis of its impact on teacher effectiveness, and student learning (U.S. Department of Education, 1995).

It is true that professional development needs to involve the entire teaching faculty in a focused and collaborative effort to improve teaching and learning in a school (Maciver et al., 2000; Nelson & Hammerman, 1996).

We have also learned that few significant reforms are successful in at-risk and high-poverty schools unless the reform obtains multiple layers of implementation support including parents and community involvement and support. Much of the existing literature shows that parental involvement and community engagement present positive results for student outcomes, attendance, and classroom behavior (Epstein, 2001; Jordan et al., 2000). Thus, many CSR models emphasize a central role for families and communities in the schooling and implementation process of reforms. These important roles of family and community in children's education can range from offering home support to sharing decision making to providing resources. Research found positive outcomes occurred when adults participated in classrooms. For example, in Memphis, the 25 schools implementing CSR models have shown greater gains in student achievement than non-CSR schools due to the efforts of teachers, students, parents, and communities (Office of Elementary and Secondary Education, 2000). However, some research states contrarily that a majority of the measured outcomes did not show a significant improvement in students achievements resulting from parent involvement (Cross, 2004).

In summary, research and history tell us that schools will improve when teachers and students, with the support of parents, administrators, policymakers, civic and business leaders, and other community members, become engaged in the teaching and learning process, and have access to the research and resources they need to excel (New American Schools, 1998, p. 9). High academic achievement is most likely when schools, homes, and communities contribute to students' ability, willingness, and opportunities to invest in education. Academic failure is most likely when a student has few or no sources of encouragement, practical support, and educational opportunities.

COMPREHENSIVE SCHOOL REFORMS IN CHINA

China has also been undergoing "comprehensive education reforms" or "comprehensive educational experiment" movement, starting from the end of 1970s and the early 1980s (Wang, 1995; Wu, 1995). In 1978 China carried out its economic reform and opening-to-the world policy which have brought about tremendous social changes. Viewed as the engine for China's economic development, education has become the first priority for Chinese government to reach its goal of modernization. In 1980, the Editorial Department of Educational Research, a core journal in the education field in China, held a conference on educational experiments in Beijing. Based on the experience of a number of educational experiments conducted by educators in the former Soviet Union as well as in some schools in China before the Cultural Revolution, Chinese educators in this conference reached a consensus that "the life of education science lies in educational experiment." The implementation of various educational experiments became a new tendency after the proceedings of the conference was published by the journal (Liu, 1998; Zhang, 1995). Since then, Chinese education entered into its experimental stage.

Lei (1995a) divides Chinese comprehensive educational experiment movement into three phases. The following is a brief history of comprehensive educational reforms in China.

The *first phase*: Restoration and development period (1979–1982). With the ending of the Cultural Revolution in 1976, Chinese education began to enter a rapid developmental age. In 1977, China restored the annual National Entrance Examination which was halted for ten years by the Cultural Revolution (1966–1976). In 1981, "The National Working Conference on Educational Experiment Reforms in Primary and Secondary Schools" was held in Beijing. Educators, policy makers, and school administrators from 28 provinces and cities attended this conference. After the conference, some schools decided to resume various educational experiments interrupted by the Cultural Revolution while other schools conducted new experimental reforms.

The *second phase*: The upsurge of reforms (1983–1988). In 1983, Deng Xiaoping made his famous speech that "education should orient toward modernization, toward the world, and toward future," in Beijing Jingshan Middle School, a well-known experimental school in China. Inspired by Deng's speech, Chinese education made great progress during the mid-1980s. One indication is that many educational experiments were conducted across the nation at that time. These experiments have been given various names such as "harmonious education," "pleasure education," "success education," "affective education," "hope education," "motivation education," "self-ownership education," "love education," "creative education," "art education," "frustration education," "comprehensively optimized education," and "community education" etc., just to name a few (Liu, 1997).

These educational experiments are described as comprehensive, schoolwide, or whole-school, quite similar to CSR in the United States. Reviewing the research, three reasons can be identified to explain why school-wide reforms become an increasingly popular school improvement strategy in China.

First, Chinese educators realized that to transform piecemeal, fragmental, and isolated approaches characterizing efforts in the past into integrated and comprehensive school reforms, changes are needed in all aspects of a school—school management, government, curriculum, instruction, professional development, assessment, and parent and community involvement (Lei, 1995b; Liu, 1993; Wang, 1993). Research shows that after the Chinese Communist Party took over in 1949, China had carried out reforms of one after another. However, these programs did not effect much change in improving the quality and performance of schools. To speed up national economic development, education needs to be changed in an alternative way.

Second, Chinese educators responded positively to the systems theory that was created in the 1940s in the West. In the 1980s, when China opened the door to the world, many theories from the West have influenced this oldest country of the world tremendously. In 1984, Liu's long article on the implication of system theory, information theory, and control theory for education was published respectively in *Educational Research* (Liu, 1998). After that, attention increasingly focused on using a systematic approach to improve schools. In fact, the typical Chinese thought model is holistic and comprehensive, deeply rooted in Chinese philosophy and Chinese culture. Therefore, the conception of "the whole is more than the sum of its parts "from system theory was readily accepted by Chinese policy makers and educators.

Third, whole school reform was perceived to be needed to resolve the problems caused by Chinese exam-oriented educational system. As mentioned before, the national entrance exam had been reinstated in 1977. On one hand, this practice inspires a huge enthusiasm for youth to study science and technology that eventually make great contributions to modernizing the country. However, on the other hand, the fierce competition for higher education has resulted in exam-driven education in Chinese primary and secondary schools. The most serious problem caused by this exam-oriented educational system was that only a small number of people at the top of the educational echelon succeed while most students experience "educational failure." Research shows that "examination wars" and "examination hell" have placed great pressure on students and damaged students intellectual, psychological, and physical development. To deal with these problems, in 1985 the State Educational Committee held a conference and pointed out that, instead of serving the single objective of helping students to pass the National College and University Examination, a cardinal purpose of educational reform should be to improve the overall quality of the Chinese citizens' education. All of these aforementioned factors resulted in a booming of comprehensive educational experiments.

The *third phase*: The deepening of development period (after 1989). An obvious feature for this stage is that a national debate took place regarding the defects of an exam-oriented education (yingshi jiaoyu) and the need for *quality education* (suzhi jiaoyu) since the mid-1980s. Through this nationwide debate, Chinese educators and policy makers realized that the ultimate purpose of education was not the preparation of students for the National Entrance Exam but to develop all students' potentials to the fullest. In 1993, the Chinese government promulgated *The Outline of Development and Reform of Education in China* and officially directed that the basic and secondary education in China should switch from exam-oriented education (or yingshi jiaoyu) to *quality education* (or suzhi jiaoyu) (Commentator of China Education Daily, 1997; Jia, 1997).

Efforts on improving school quality through *quality education* which aims at helping all students at all aspects have been made by Chinese government for two decades. The biggest challenge faced by Chinese educators is that the exam-oriented educational system still exists largely intact today. Passing the national exam to pursue higher education is still a big pressure for every single student, and parents, teachers, and school administrators' work and life still evolves around helping students to achieve this purpose. Although numerous educational experiments have emerged, most of them disappeared a few years later because of a deep conflict with and a big burden from the exam-driven system. To promote *quality education* and deal with this up-and-down in school reform, Chinese government, on one hand, encourages every school to design their own model that best fits their needs. On the other hand, it strongly recommends those effective comprehensive educational experiments as a role model to be implemented across the country. *Success education* is the one that can be considered as a highly effective project promoted by the Ministry of Education in China (Gong & Xu, 1995; Liu, 1997; Wang & He, 1995).

Starting in 1987, the *success education* experiment is regarded as a schoolwide program that has involved every aspect of teaching and learning in the school. Therefore, in this research, the investigator will use CSR models as a conceptual framework to analyze this Chinese case. This comprehensive approach allows one to see what are the similarities and differences of school-wide reform between the West and the East, and to synthesize helpful strategies, methods and principles for improving at-risk students.

In all, we intend to anchor this research in China's social context by using a CRS model to guide the research's theoretical framework. This project, as a case study, will try to provide a complex but a clear picture of *success education* as a new educational reform in China.

SUMMARY

This chapter consists of two parts. The first part examines theories and practice related to an American educational reform model—the Comprehensive School Reform, which has provided concepts and practical ideas to build the theoretical framework for this research. The second part discusses the movement of comprehensive educational reforms in China starting in the late 1970s and early 1980s. It provides background information for the happening of the success education reform, which we study in this thesis.

The literature sources point to a convergence that educational reforms are moving toward a comprehensive approach which is the new direction for education systems both in the West and the East.

CHAPTER 3

EDUCATIONAL REFORMS AND ITS SOCIAL CONTEXT

The Radical Changes in China Politics, Economy, and Culture Since 1978

This chapter examines the social and education context of success education and provides a comprehensive picture of the national environment within which the reform was carried out. Changes in politics, economy, and culture in China since 1978 will be discussed. Particularly, educational reforms that have been implemented since 1978 will be reviewed. The Chinese public educational system will be examined to situate the success education reform in context.

CHANGES IN CHINA'S ECONOMIC SYSTEM SINCE 1978

Success education appeared in Shanghai, China in the context of radical changes since 1978. With the end in 1976 of the Great Cultural Revolution which brought a devastating disruption to the country's economic development, China found itself lagging far behind the Western countries in terms of economy, science and technology. The old inefficient model of Mao

Success for All, pages 45–60
Copyright © 2008 by Information Age Publishing
All rights of reproduction in any form reserved.

which emphasized political movements and ideological control in isolation from the world led the country's economy to a near total collapse. The per capita grain output in 1977 was in the same level as in 1957 (Xue, 1981). With only 134 yuan ($16.8) per annum for rural per capita income and 315 yuan ($39.4) for urbanites in 1978, the population of the country lived in extreme poverty (Wong & Mok, 1995). To catch up with advanced Western countries, under Deng Xiaoping's leadership, the People's Republic started to carry out dramatic economic reform measures and adopted the open-door policy in 1978. The overall goal of the reform was China would achieve modernizations in industry, agriculture, national defense, and science and technology. This more-than-two-decade reform has overhauled major policies under Mao and resulted in tremendous changes in economy, politics, and culture.

In economics, China has been undergoing a fundamental transformation from a highly concentrated state-planned economy to a market economy. The reform began from the rural areas in 1978 by introducing the household responsibility system as a way of resolving the problem of chronic low productivity in Chinese agriculture. The remarkable success in rural reform was expanded into the industrial sector starting in the mid-1980s. Many policies had been initiated to make the urban economy more dynamic and to improve efficiency and accountability. The urban reform could be measured by a rapid development of private enterprises, the establishment of special economic zones which offered low tax or no tax advantages to foreign companies, the opening of the stock market, significant restructuring of state enterprises, and encouragement of foreign investment (Bhalla, 1995; Lu, 2004; Yao & Liu, 2003). All these measures have established a new economy in the country, tremendously increasing national productivity.

For example, in the 1980s and the large part of the 1990s, China's economy registered a double digit GDP increase, and in some years, the increase reached 20%. Although since late 1990s the government has tried to reign in the overheated economy, GDP increase has remained at around 9–10% per year. In 2005, GDP reached Rmb18.23 trillion yuan or US$2.3 trillion. China was ranked as the world's sixth largest economy by the World Bank in 2005. In other words, from 1978 to 2005 China's GDP increased by 11 times in dollar terms, from $215.3 billion to $2.3 trillions, or from $225 to $1,707 in per capita income (Yang & Campbell, 2006).

Reforms and rapid economic growth have made China one of the world's top traders and favorite destinations for foreign direct investment. For example, in 1980, China's foreign trade volume was $38 billion, ranked as the 28th world foreign trader. However, by 1997, China's merchandise trade volume, not including Hong Kong, had reached $325 billion, rendering the country to become the world's tenth largest trader (Yang & Su, 2000). For the past decade, China has been the world's second largest recipient of foreign direct investment after the United States, attracting 50 billion dollars a year on average.

Globalization has played a catalytic role in China's rapid development. With a record 15 years of continuous effort, China finally succeeded in joining the World Trade Organization (WTO) on November 11, 2001, becoming the 143rd member of this international organization. Able to open its domestic market to all other WTO countries, China's trade performance has reached unprecedented scale since 2001. These numbers are significant: Foreign trade grew by 22.4% in 2002, 34.6% in 2003 and 35.4% in 2004 (Tong, 2006). By 2005, China had attracted US$603 billion in direct investments. Exceeding Japan, China's foreign currency reserves stood at one trillion in October 2006. More than 80% of the Fortune-500 companies and the world's top 100 information technology forms have set up their businesses with China (Yang & Campbell, 2006). In addition, China has joined more than 100 international organizations including International Monetary Fund (IMF), Asian Development Bank, Asia-pacific Economic Forum (APEC), and the World Trade Organization (WTO) (Wen, 2006). There is no doubt all of these have integrated China more deeply into the global economy.

CHANGES IN THE POLITICAL SYSTEM SINCE 1978

In politics, although scholars criticize that the rapidly growing economy has not significantly contributed to the country's political reform (Mackerras et al., 1993; Zhang & Li, 1998), wide-ranging changes in political structures and processes have taken place in China. One most crucial political change since 1978 was a dramatic shift of the Chinese Communist Party (CCP)'s core work from waging class struggles which was the main task before and during the years of the Cultural Revolution (1949–1976), to focusing on economic development and modernizing the country. The Third Plenum of the Eleventh Party Central Committee held in December 1978, was the milestone to usher in such a transformation. It was in this meeting that the new leadership under Deng Xiaoping declared that the "main concentration of Party work and the full attention of the people of China would shift toward socialist modernization and construction" (Lin, 1994). From then on, the focus of the three generations of Chinese leaders after Mao is to devote their energy to push for the building of "socialism with Chinese characteristics" and to eventually lead the Chinese people into Xiaoking Shehui, namely to bring China into the rank of middle level developed country. Politics has been reviewed as a tool to facilitate and promote economic reforms. The purpose of many government restructuring efforts is to enhance efficiency and ensure social stability (Smith, 2000). In the National

48 *Success for All*

People's Congress held in early March, 2006, both Premier Wen Jiabao's government report and the eleventh five-year economic-development plan (2006–2010) reiterated the CCP's firm will that the first priority of government policies is to continue to push for economic reform and deepen market changes. As Premier Wen said, "We must consistently and unwaveringly press ahead on the road of reform... to retrogress or backpedal offers no way out" (Chen & Oster, 2006).

Another obvious political change in the Chinese society after 1978 is that with the government relaxing its tight ideological control on the people, ordinary citizens began to demand democracy. The massive student movement of 1989 involved hundreds of thousands of students and millions of ordinary citizens (Hunter & Sexton, 1999).

In addition, because of the impact of economic development and globalization, a large number of private business enterprises have been established. Millions of individuals now own their own private businesses. As a result, the Chinese society has become more fluid, flexible, and dynamic. The trend of privatization has reached a rather deep level. Wong and Mok (1995) describe this situation as follows:

> Decollectivization and diversification of ownership forms, decentralization of state control over direct management of social and public policies becomes a central feature.... For example, the state encourages local communities and individuals to take more responsibility in the provision of welfare services. Besides, autonomy is given to enterprises, schools, universities, other social organizations and even the private sector to cater for social needs (p. 9)

Within this sociopolitical context, China has become the ground for the rapid development of civil society (Dorn, 1998).

CULTURAL CHANGES

In the culture arena, China has also been experiencing a revolutionary transformation since 1978. These unprecedented changes in culture can be described with four key words: depoliticization, diversification, commercialization, and globalization.

Depoliticization

Before the reform era and under Mao's leadership, a centralized political culture dominated every aspect of people's life through direct or indirect influence imposed by CCP. In such a "political conquest of society"

(Vogel, 1969), any free discussion and liberal thinking were not allowed and individual interests were neglected and respect for personal dignity were downplayed (Wong & MacPherson, 1995). The continuous economic reform after 1978 has not only promoted economic growth, but has also greatly changed people's thinking, lifestyle, and behavior. For example, leisure time and personal life space have significantly expanded after 1978. People in their leisure time can seek all kinds of entertainment such as watching TV, playing sports, shopping, reading, and traveling. With an enhanced living standard, ordinary people's life has become diverse and colorful. Instead of seeing the whole nation wearing only blue uniforms with short, straight hair as was the typical dress and hair style during the Cultural Revolution, people in China today can choose whatever clothes they like and decide to have whatever hair style they want. Although people in government offices and universities still have to attend the weekly political studies which have been used to pass down government policies or for forming a collective consciousness, the political nature of these meetings have been greatly watered down, with people talking about making money or complaining about their leaders much of the time.

Diversification

According to Qi and Tang (2004), "cultural diversity is an expression of various beliefs, values, and attitudes to life" (p. 471). Cultural diversity in China in the reform era means a huge non-governmental media and entertainment enterprise have arisen, and different cultures such as popular culture, marginal cultures, and elite cultures coexist. Since 1978 the state has gradually lost its monopoly over the mass media due to the development of market economy. All forms of media communication have been undergoing an enormous expansion (Liu, 1991). After the mid-1980s, television, radio, newspapers, and magazines were available for nearly every family in the urban areas and many families in rural areas as well. In spite of careful surveillance conducted by CCP, different voices can be heard through a much more diverse and open network of communications such as Internet, satellite transmissions, and broadcasts from Taiwan, Hong Kong, and countries of the world. For instance, Gospel radios, Voice of America and BBC are three famous foreign radio broadcasts in China. CNN and other several media companies like Star and MTV are popular throughout the country. Chinese people are no longer limited to government information sources (Stockman, 2000).

Also, a sharp cultural transition can be witnessed with the striking rise of multimedia popular culture after the 1990s. These cultural productions

50 Success for All

made by both domestic and multinational corporations include pop music, DVD films, soap operas, radio talk shows, books, tabloid newspapers, sitcoms, game-shows, and comedies. In this multicultural context, the society is becoming much more open and dynamic than before the reform era. However, on the other hand, traditional culture and the arts are declining in value for the younger generation (Liu, 2004; Zha, 1995).

Commercialization

One of the most significant changes in culture during the reform era is that market oriented values have gained prevalence in the Chinese society because of the development of a market economy since 1978 (Wong & Mok, 1995). The growth of a consumer culture is manifested in the rapid growth of advertising, for example. With the opening of the country to the outside world, all kinds of advertisements seemed to appear all of a sudden out of nowhere in the late 1970s: on billboards, on TV and radio, in newspapers and magazines, a stark contrast from no advertisement at all anywhere in the country (Stross 1990). Starting from 1992, the government controlled media enterprises entered into the market and advertisements have become their major source of income (Berger & Huntington, 2002).

Another noticeable phenomenon of cultural transformation is that popular culture played an important role in the process of cultural commercialization. At the beginning of reform, consumerism focused on household appliances such as washing machines, TV sets, and refrigerators. After their basic consumption needs have been met, more and more Chinese people become interested in a variety of popular cultural productions such as sports, MTV, pop music, body building, karaoke bars, and so on. With a growth of hedonistic values, people have been encouraged to consume more and more.

Globalization

In the Chinese cultural landscape, research evidence shows that China today is moving into a true stage of globalization (Wang, 2004). With an "open-door policy" and a rapid development of communication technology, Chinese culture has been influenced by Western culture significantly. To quote James L. Watson:

> Looming over Beijing's choking, bumper-to-bumper traffic, every tenth building seems to sport a giant neon sign advertising American wares: Xerox, Mobil, Kinko's, Northwest Airlines, IBM, Jeep, Gerber, even the Jolly Green

Giant. American food chains and beverages are everywhere in central Beijing: Coca-Cola, Starbucks, Kentucky Fried Chicken, Haagen-Dazs, Dunkin' Donuts, Baskin-Robbins, Pepsi, TCBY, Pizza Hut, and of course McDonald's. As of June 1999, McDonald had opened 235 restaurants in China (in Sjursen, 2000, p. 52).

Popular culture has not only contributed to a diverse society as mentioned above, but also become a test to measure China's entry into a globalizing cause. In today's China, it is not surprising that Chinese ordinary citizens can access all kinds of popular cultural productions: films from Hollywood, cartoons from Japan, TV sitcoms from South Korea, the NBA finals from the United States, pop songs from Hong Kong, and romance fiction from Taiwan.

As a new form of culture, Internet is a very important indication of globalization. China started to develop the Internet in 1994. Since then, hundreds of thousands of Chinese-language Internet websites have been built up in China and the number of Internet users has increased dramatically. For example, in June 2003 the number of Chinese Internet users was 68 million, and in early 2006 this has been increased to more than 100 million (Xinhua News Report, 2006). The Internet provides a useful platform for people to understand, communicate, and interact with each other in today's information age.

REVIEW OF CHINESE BASIC EDUCATIONAL REFORMS SINCE 1978

The dramatic social changes in China have brought about significant transformation in Chinese education. China has a long tradition of using education as the vehicle to build a centralized society, and individuals have used it to move up the social ladder. From as early as the Sui Dynasty (581–618) to 1905, China had used an imperial examination system as the channel to select bureaucrats for governing the country. Therefore, after China opened her doors to the outside world, the Chinese government realized that in order to catch up with developed countries, education was an engine to push this old country forward (Chang, 1996; Miao, 2002; Sui, 1996). As a first step to divert from the ultra political orientation during Mao's era and realign education to meet the needs of national economic development, the annual National Entrance Exam was restored in 1977 (after ten years of cancellation), to select talented students to study in universities and help modernize the country.

In 1977, when Deng Xiaoping regained power, he set up a clear and strong tone for the country that: "The key to achieving modernization is through the development of science and technology" (Deng, 1984, p. 53).

Since then, China's education entered a new historical phase and has been experiencing rapid development at all levels. In the following section, I will focus on great changes in China's basic education since 1978.

Considered as the cornerstone of education, the Chinese government recognizes that basic education plays a fundamental role in improving the quality of the national labor force in the information era. Therefore, the Chinese government has placed top priority on the development of basic education (Tao, 1999). In 1985, the Chinese Communist Part (CCP) Central Committee initiated "The Reform of China's Educational Structure" (known as *tishi gaige* in Chinese). As a guideline, the regulation impacted Chinese education in many ways. This was the first time since 1949 when the Chinese government called for a major change in the system that affected administration, financing and structure of education (Tsang, 1991). Specifically, under this framework, the obvious innovations in basic education can be seen in the following aspects: the decentralization of administration, popularization of nine years of compulsory education, implementation of measures to replace examination-oriented education with quality-oriented education, and structural changes in secondary education.

Decentralization of Administration and Finance

The mid-1980s was a very important stage of the Chinese basic educational development. As mentioned before, in 1985 the CCP Central Committee announced its decision to reform education. One of the net results of the reform on basic education is turning over basic education administrative power to local governments. Since then, China entered its decentralization era.

Decentralization in Chinese educational system was a result of economic reform, which emphasized giving more decision-making power to the local government and autonomy to peasants and workers to stimulate their productive abilities and their sense of responsibilities for work and life. Decentralization in Chinese education is most apparent in administration and finance. Specifically, in terms of administration, since 1985, a series of policies have been issued for decentralizing the organizational system, empowering local schools and communities to have more opportunities to participate in school administration, and separating the power of the party from school administration. Through doing so, schools would be more efficient, effective, and productive (Lin, 1993; Ngok, 2007).

The change first came from the state level. In 1985, the Ministry of Education was renamed as the State Education Commission, giving it a status right below the State Council yet above all other ministries to show the importance of education. Under the direct control of the State Council, the commission was responsible for formulating general educational policies and guidelines, mapping out overall reform plans, and coordinating the educational programs of various departments and ministries (Snowden, 2001). The second change could be seen at the local level. In this new form, local officials who used to have little independent power, have gained greater decision making power in administration, especially in authorizing the use of school funds, personnel affairs, and the like. At the elementary and secondary school levels, the reform was embodied in the "principal responsibility system." Under such a system, "principals increased their responsibility for personnel, finance, teaching, and instruction, while the schools' Party committee became more narrowly defined, overseeing ideological work and supervising and inspecting compliance with Party policies" (Delany & Paine, 1991, p. 31).

In terms of financing, local schools under the new educational system have been given more power to make decisions regarding school financing. Before the reform started, the state provided major funding and the local government could be considered as the second important resource of funding to schools. However, since the mid-1980s, the Chinese government decentralized financing responsibility to lower units of government offices and to end users of education services including students, parents, and employers. Therefore, local governments and local communities had to subsidize basic education (Cheng, 1995; Mok, 2004). Through this decentralization measure, the share from the central state in public education finance decreased from 13.8% in 1990 to 11.7% in 1995; on the other hand, the average share of non-government expenditure increased from 39.2% in 1993 to 45.2% in 1995 (Law, 2000).

Popularization of Nine Years of Compulsory Education

In the history of Chinese basic educational reforms, the major achievement gained by the Chinese government was the popularization of nine years of compulsory education since the mid-1980s. After ten years of disruption in educational development during the Cultural Revolution (1966–1976), the first challenge facing Chinese education reform was its huge poorly educated labor force. In 1980, 93% of school-age children entered primary school, and by 1985, only 68.4% of elementary school students graduated (Delany & Paine, 1991). A 1984 national survey of those who were employed also showed that less than 1% of them had received higher education, 10.53% had received secondary educations, and 60.34% had received primary or junior high educations. The illiteracy and semi-illiteracy rate was 28.26% in the urban area. In the rural area, the illiteracy and semi-illiteracy rate even reached 36.55% (Lin, 1993).

Therefore, the Chinese government realized that basic education is the foundation for the country to reach the goal of modernization. Consequently, in the 1980s, the Chinese government set up two targets for basic education to achieve: universalizing compulsory education and wiping out illiteracy (the "two basics"). On April 12, 1986, China promulgated its first Compulsory Education Law approved by the Fourth Session of the Sixth National People Congress. The Law required that by 2000 all children who had reached the age of six, regardless of gender, ethnicity or race, must enter school to receive compulsory education for nine years. Specifically, the Commission set up different goals in line with local conditions. According to the Law, the most developed areas of the country including cities and coastal provinces were scheduled to complete the goals of universal compulsory education by about 1990. Towns and regions with mid-level development were required to offer the nine years basic education by 1995, while economically backward areas were told to try their best to universalize education at various levels (Rosen, 2000).

To implement the Compulsory Education Law, the Chinese government has devoted major effort to make compulsory education universal. For example, the Chinese central government required that government at all levels must guarantee to increase their educational funding for basic education year after year. As a result, the amount of the government appropriation for education had been increased by about 15% annually during the period from 1995 to 1999. Educational expenditures as a percentage of Gross National Product (GNP) have grown from 2.46% in 1995 to 2.79% in 1999 (Wang, 2004). In particular, since 1993, the funds for basic education were separated from any other educational expenditures. From 1993 to 1995 the special fund for basic education from the central government increased from RMB33.3 billion to RMB54.6 billion, or an increase of 28% annually (National Basic Education Bureau, 1997).

After making persistent efforts for a decade, China has made remarkable progress in basic education. For instance, by 2000 85% of the areas of the country had achieved nine years compulsory education for all children. The illiteracy rate among people aged above 15 was reduced to 4.8%. The gross enrollment rate of primary school students reached 99.1% in 2000 while the enrollment in junior middle schools was 88.6% (Zeng, 2001).

Implementation of Measures to Replace Examination-Oriented Education with Quality-oriented Education

The issues of equality and quality are also very important aspects of Chinese basic education reforms. The educational system in China is featured by a test-based or exam-oriented education. The competition for the National Entrance Exam every year was so fierce that only 4% of the students were admitted into universities in 1980s (Lin, 1999). Thus, having made only a small number of people at the top succeed, the exam-oriented education system resulted in most students' failure. This creates unequal opportunity for students to obtain a good quality education. Also, focusing only on preparing students for the National Entrance Exam, the current educational system has been criticized for having a narrow curriculum and ignoring students' full potentials (Liu, 1998).

To deal with this problem, in 1985 the State Educational Commission held a conference and pointed out that the cardinal purpose of educational reform was to improve the overall quality of Chinese citizens' education and life. In the ensuing years, a national debate took place regarding the defects of an exam-oriented education (yingshi jiaoyu) and the need for *quality education* (suzhi jiaoyu). Despite different opinions in terms of the definition and the contents of *quality education*, and the strategies and approaches to achieve *quality education*, the debating parties generally agreed that the ultimate purpose of education was not the preparation of students for the National Entrance Exam but to develop all students' potentials to the fullest. In 1993, the Chinese government promulgated *The Outline of Development and Reform of Education in China* and officially directed that basic education and secondary education in China should switch from exam-oriented education (or yingshi jiaoyu) to *quality education* (or suzhi jiaoyu) (Feng, 2004).

In the era of globalization, Chinese educational reform is not an isolated phenomenon. Rather, it is a response to various initiatives in international education reform. From the late 1970s to the end of the 1990s, the three themes—"learning to live," "learning to learn," and "learning to care," promoted by the United Nations Educational, Scientific and Cultural Organization (UNESCO) in the International Education Conferences, have influenced Chinese education tremendously. Especially, "the International Educational Conference of Facing the 21st Century" held in Beijing in 1989, and "the 1990 World Conference on Education for All" in Jomtien, Thailand, acted as catalysts to push forward Chinese education transformation from exam-oriented to *quality education*. Much research has been done to reflect upon this transformation (Bao & Huang, 1995; Tan, 2000).

In action, to implement *quality education* and to act in response to international education reform as well as to implement the Compulsory Education Law, many educational experiments have been conducted in China since the mid-1980s. With China entering into its educational reform stage, overnight, numerous experiments appeared throughout the country. These experiments use various names such as what we have previously mentioned. Of these experiments, *success education* conduced by the No. 8 Middle School of Zhabei in Shanghai in 1987, has been regarded as a very successful one. However, in the real world these experiments did not affect the main body of Chinese education. The magic baton of the National Entrance Exam still determines the direction of education in China today.

Overall, the quality education reform is still a controversial issue. The biggest challenge faced by Chinese educators is as long as the National Entrance Exam exists, the core work for basic education will always evolve around the preparation of students for the exam and quality education will never come true. Also, what is quality education? So far there are no uniform definition and criteria. Schools are undertaking educational reforms in their own way according to their understanding of the meaning of quality education. Recently, I met a scholar from Beijing Normal University, the top teacher training university in the country. She told me that quality education in fact has not worked well. The real situation in basic education in China is that: The competition for higher education is even fiercer than before because of the existence of the one-child-per-family policy. Parents expect their only child to enter key universities, not just ordinary ones. Also, learning from Western countries under the name of implementing quality education, schools add extra activities to students after schools such as engaging them in selling products, social investigations, and outdoor research activities while by all means academic tasks remain paramount. Therefore, children are facing even more pressure from parents and schools. The scholar described that her daughter, who is a high school student in a key, secondary school in China, usually gets up around six o'clock in the morning and goes to bed at midnight. Therefore, a heavy burden for students is still a big issue in China.

Structural Changes in Secondary Education

Besides the decentralization and implementation of nine-year compulsory education, structural change in secondary education and the development of vocational/technical (VT) education are also seen as major changes in Chinese education since 1978. VT education was the weakest part of the whole Chinese educational system when China's educational reform began in mid 1980s. Before the economic reform started in 1978, China only had general education at its secondary level. The monolithic education structure brought about a big problem when large-scale industrialization emerged in the late 1970s. China was facing an acute shortage of technicians and skilled laborers. For example, the labor force aged 15 to 59 in 1990 was 730 million and was expected to increase at a rate of about 27 million a year in the 1990s. In the mid-1990s, nearly 40% of the labor force did not receive any training in vocational and technical skills (Law, 2000). In the meantime, since narrow access to higher education allowed only a small number of students to enter colleges and universities, the majority of students have to choose vocational education as their alternative before they join the work force. Therefore, the Chinese government has attached great importance to developing vocational education. As a result, student enrollment in the vocational track increased from 18.9% in 1980 to 56.8% in 1996 (State Education Commission, 1997). For the first time in China's history, the student population in VT schools has exceeded that in general academic schools at the secondary level.

According to Tsang (1991), there are three types of VT schools at the senior-secondary level: Senior-secondary vocational schools; skilled-workers schools; and secondary specialized schools. With them, junior secondary school graduates can have choices to either go into the above three kinds of VT schools or general senior secondary schools which prepare students for university education after passing the National Entrance Exam. Providing more opportunities for both students and parents, the rapid development of VT education fundamentally changed the structure of Chinese basic educational system. However, low quality, inadequate funding and resource support, and the inability to secure employment for their graduates are the main problems faced by VT education in China. Therefore, the success of vocational education has been limited.

All in all, Chinese basic education has achieved a remarkable degree of progress over the last two decades. China has made great stride in offering at least nine-years compulsory education in most parts of the country, and illiteracy rate is declining. For example, the rate of enrollment for children of school age was only 20% in 1949, but it had reached 95.9% in 1985, and 98% in 2000. Compared with 80% of illiteracy in 1949, the figure had been reduced to 26.8% in 1988 and 6% in 1997 (National Development and Reform Commission, 2005; Liu, 1997; Wu, 1992). Also, it is evident to see a dramatic expansion at higher levels of education and a fundamental structural change in the secondary education in China. The rapid changes in education are the results of economic reform and financial decentralization. Therefore, one significant impact on Chinese basic education caused by the reform is that it has brought the ideology of the market to the school.

Within such a context, new resources are garnered while differentiation of educational opportunities becomes much more serious. Education in China today in its policymaking process is much more sensitive to local community needs and students' career prospects than before.

A recent new development is very significant. During the 4th Session of the 10th National People's Congress that opened in Beijing March 3, 2006, the central government declared that to speed up the pace of educational reform, one major imitative being to make compulsory education totally free, especially in the minority areas, the poorest parts of China. This policy will be spread to the entire country in 2007. In "The Eleven-Five-Year Plan of Chinese Economic and Social Development" passed by the Congress in March of this year, the Chinese government has set up a higher goal for educational development to 2010: the educational expenditure will account for 4% of GDP annually; the state will be in charge of nine-year basic education financially; the graduate rate of junior secondary students will reach 95%, and VT students will be increased to eight million every year. All these strategies may bare far-reaching implication for enhancing citizens' quality in China. However, serious problems remain. The biggest challenges faced by Chinese basic education are financial problems, poor school conditions, low quality of teachers, and poor treatment of teachers. There is still a long, long way to go for China.

THE CHINESE PUBLIC EDUCATIONAL SYSTEM

With a total enrollment of 320 million students at all levels, China possesses the largest educational system in the world. In 1999, the number of primary schools numbered at 582,300 and the number of senior secondary schools stood at 78,500 (Wang, 2003).

The goal in China is to develop a well-rounded educational system. The mission of schools should be to train students to be strong in five areas: moral aptitude, intelligence, physical fitness, a sense of aesthetics, and an aptitude for labor. Through schooling, students are expected to become dedicated citizens with "lofty ideals, knowledge, and discipline" and eventually make contribution to the country.

The educational system in China is generally designed along a 6–3–3–4 pattern (a 5–4–3–4 system remains in some areas as well): six years of primary school, three years of junior secondary school, three years of senior secondary school and four years of university. "Basic education" in China refers to non-vocational public education which consists of regular primary and secondary school with a total of 12 years. Children in China go to school at a very young age. Many attend nurseries in their first year; kindergartens care for children from 3 to 6; children begin primary school at about 6 and get into secondary school at about 12. About 65% of the children finish their elementary education in six years while the others complete it in five. Even though 2% of the children take four years to complete junior secondary school, most of the children follow the three-year pattern to finish the same level of education. Senior secondary education (high school) covers another three years, but is not compulsory (Wang, 2003). According to Bush et al. (1998), only 44% of junior secondary students progress to the senior secondary system while the rest of students go into VT education or move directly into employment.

The public educational system is very hierarchical. The schools are divided into key and ordinary tracks. Governments at all levels usually invest more money in key, primary and secondary schools. Therefore, key schools can provide high quality education through hiring excellent teachers and possessing the best teaching equipment and facilities. Although students entering the key primary schools do not need to take entrance exams, students must score very high to pass the provincial unified entrance examination in order to enter the key junior and senior secondary schools. Parents have a high expectation for their children to enter key schools because these schools earn a good reputation in helping a very high ratio of their students to pass the national unified entrance examinations and enter very prestigious universities and colleges.

The Chinese public educational system is an exam-driven system, as we have reiterated. For most people, including students, parents, and school teachers, the current Chinese education system is viewed as a tool to help children get into higher education. Therefore, it seems that the ultimate goal for K–12 education in China is to facilitate students to pass the National Entrance Exam. As a consequence, tests and examinations play a crucial role in the whole education system in China. Students must take not only unit tests, midterm and final exams but also graduation exams and higher school entrance exams. Only about 1% to 4% outstanding students can be recommended by schools authorities to a higher level school without examinations.

Because of the national entrance examination system, the curriculum of basic education in China is very academically oriented and heavily loaded. Since each [mainly urban] family only has one child (while rural families still have two or more children), parents want their children to prepare for higher education beginning from primary and secondary schools. Schools also work very hard to meet the final goal to help their students to go to universities. Thus, the courses in basic education in China are designed to be very complex. For example, in junior secondary schools students are required to study more than ten subjects, including Chinese, mathematics, physics, chemistry, biology, English, politics, history (both Chinese and world), geography, fine arts, music, information technology, physical hygiene, physical education, work skill, and moral character. Some junior secondary courses in China are only available in high schools in the United States such as physics, chemistry, and biology. The schools usually run for a whole day from 8:00 a.m. to 6:30 p.m. with a noon break from 12:00 to 2:30 p.m. If it is a boarding school, the class will not end until 10:30 p.m.

All these factors demonstrate that Chinese basic education is a highly competitive system. Students shoulder a heavy study load. To reduce a student's workload, as mentioned before, the Chinese government has promulgated several regulations since the mid-1980s and called for an educational reform of shifting test-based education to the quality education. However, the effect is weak since the national entrance exam still predominates.

CHAPTER 4

SOCIAL INEQUALITIES IN URBAN CHINA IN THE ERA OF ECONOMIC REFORM AND ITS IMPACT ON EDUCATION

As discussed in chapter 3, the economic reform launched in China in 1978 has fundamentally changed the Chinese society. China has enjoyed an unprecedented growth in economy over two decades. Chinese culture, value, and education have been experiencing much change as well. However, like other countries in the world, China is also facing many dilemmas during its process of modernization. One of the biggest dilemmas confronted by the Chinese government is that China's rapid development was accompanied by a sharp increase in inequality. Evidence shows that inequality can be seen at all levels in China. In this chapter, I will examine the issues and problems of inequality and poverty in urban China. Since the reform case occurred in Shanghai, the study will also look at the rapid social development and educational reforms in Shanghai since 1978. The negative impact of economic reform on education in Shanghai will be studied as well.

ECONOMIC REFORM AND INEQUALITY IN URBAN CHINA

Since 1978, the Chinese government has implemented Deng Xiaoping's policy that diverted away from strict egalitarianism and that allowed a proportion of people to get rich first through taking advantage of the mechanism of a market economy. The idea is the wealth created through this process will trickle down to all levels of the society and inspire all people to improve their economic conditions. The policy has shown dramatic effect from the very beginning, improving peasants' living condition quickly, and bringing urbanites along into the rush for establishing businesses. Intellectuals also joined the trend, and by early 1990s, it seems the whole nation was involved in setting up companies, opening factories, running restaurants, and selling all kinds of goods. After economic boom for two decades, the Chinese economy has developed tremendously and people's living conditions have been enhanced greatly. However, on the other hand, social classes in China have experienced a fundamental transformation. The income gap between the rich and the poor began to widen. The issue of inequality has reached such a sensitive degree that it could seriously affect the stability of Chinese society (Geng, 2005; Wu, 2002; Xong, & Liu, 2004).

During the Mao era, following the principle of equalitarianism—that is, everybody "eats from the same big pot," people's incomes under the planned economic system did not have too much difference. However, in the market-oriented economy, new social groups have emerged and social structure has become much more complex than that in the Mao era (Lin, 1999). First, there appears to be a new upper class in China. This wealthy group is mainly comprising private entrepreneurs, government administrators, corporate administrators, and processional groups and specialized personnel such as lawyers, professors, agents, entertainment program hosts, well-known singers, actors/actresses, dancers, etc.

In his book, *China in the Post-Utopian Age*, Smith (2000) provides a vivid picture of how this group has enjoyed their luxuries:

> Evidence of new wealth is ubiquitous, especially along the so-called golden coastline, with the emergence of five-star hotels, new golf courses, luxury apartment buildings, and a conspicuous fetish for expensive consumer items like French brandy, jewel-encrusted gold watches, and luxury foreign cars (especially from BMW, Mercedes, and Lexus). (p. 209)

Another net result of economic reform was the emergence of a broad-based middle class. They are government officials, managers of companies, artists, intellectuals, white-collar employees, and small business owners, accounting for 25%–35% of the total population of China (Ye & Zhu, 2004).

Although they do not earn as much as the upper-class does, they have their personal property such as houses, cars, and a decent salary. Some of them have their own businesses or work in joint Chinese-foreign ventures or foreign ventures. They can afford to travel from place to place, buy some luxury consumer items, and join expensively aristocratic clubs. Research shows that their wealth accounts for 50% of the total wealth in the country (Wang, 2005).

The third class is the urban working class. Ranked together with rural peasants at the bottom of the social structure, they are regarded as the socioeconomically disadvantaged population (Wu, 2002). Urban workers used to be the leading class during the Maoist period from the 1950s to the 1970s. Holding an "iron rice bowl," they had a permanent job and enjoyed enviable social welfare. However, by introducing a mechanism of competition into businesses, most state enterprises have lost money and have been undergoing restructuring since the 1980s. Not only have urban workers seen steep reduction in their actual income, they also lost their health and other benefits, and millions of them (especially women) were laid off starting in mid-1990s. For example, between 1995 and 2003 the number of state-owned enterprises shrank from 118,000 to around 34,000. Seventeen percent of urban workers lost their jobs in 2003. Research also found that the rate of unemployment among urban permanent residents increased from 6.1% in 1995 to 11.1% in 2002 (Garnaut et al., 2005). In 2004, the number of unemployed urban workers in cities and towns reached 30 million or 5% of the total labor population in the country (Hu & Yang, 2004). Many urban workers were forced into retirement at age 40. Lacking an adequate unemployment insurance system, those unemployed workers live in poverty with only 100–300 yuan monthly living allowance from the government.

Meanwhile, during the 1980s, labor migration in China increased dramatically, as a result of the massive program of agricultural reform in 1978. Hundreds of millions of surplus labor force migrate from the countryside to cities in search of job opportunities. By 2003 there had been 90 million peasants who poured into cities for job hunting (Li, 2004). Working on construction sites, in restaurants, as housemaids, or as cleaners, their pay usually was very low. As a result, one can see in China today:

> In the cities the poor are panhandling on the streets, the homeless camping outside bus and rail stations;... The massive migration of peasants out of the countryside and the appearance of a huge floating population in the cities provides visible evidence that gaps and discrepancies have developed in Chinese society. (Smith, 2000, p. 210)

Overall, the problem of income inequality in China rose in the late1980s and at a faster rate in the 1990s. Using the Gini coefficient to measure inequality in China, the statistical figures have presented a sharp increasing tendency: 0.15 before 1978, 0.382 in 1988; 0.397 in 1998; 0.414 in 2000; 0.465 in 2004; and 0.47 in 2005. Some research even shows 0.53 or 0.54 in 2004 (Wang, 2005; Xu, 2004).

Although inequality between urban and rural areas has been the dominant pattern of inequality in China, urban inequality has become very serious during the reform era. Comparing the average income of urban households between the top 20% of the income bracket and the bottom 20% of the income bracket, the income gap increased from 4.2 times in 1990, to 9.6 times in 1998 (Yang, 2005). Recent research reveals that currently among the deposit accounts in the country, 80% belongs to the 20% of the rich families, only 1% for the 10% poorest households. In China today, more than 30 million urban residents are still living in poverty, earning 130–150 yuan (less than $20.00) a month (Wang, 2005).

As mentioned above, increasing unemployment, wider wage differentials, and insufficient social welfare and benefits are considered the main contributing factors to the rising poverty and serious condition of inequality in urban China. Also, government corruption that links to their possession of economic and political power is another factor leading to the worsening state of inequality in China. Government officials can wield their political power to be involved in the economic sphere to rake in huge profits, many becoming a millionaire overnight. This issue has become a major problem faced by the Chinese government.

The growing social inequality in China during the reform era has impacted education greatly. According to functionalist theory, school is a tool to achieve social equality through providing equal educational opportunity for every child regardless of his/her family, race, sex, or religion (Feinberg & Soltis, 1998). However, evidence suggests that equality in education for all children remains far from a reality in China's case because of an increasing income disparity after the end of the 1980s. The economic reform has not narrowed the gap between the poor and the rich in terms of equal access to educational opportunity. Rather, it has increased the inequality. Public education in China, in return, has legitimized and reinforced social inequality.

Research based on significant field work finds that in the Chinese highly competitive educational system, students from disadvantaged family background are consistently disadvantaged (Lin, 2004; Ross & Lin, 2004; Lin & Ross, 1998). In terms of equality of access, although China promulgated the Compulsory Education Law in 1986, the nine-year compulsory education is not free for nearly 20 years because of the introduction of the market mechanism to education. Further, the decentralization reforms that started in 1986 has been implemented often with local and central government shedding their responsibilities for funding education (Lin, 2000).

Within this context, school administrators must take responsibility for "creating income." To make a profit, elementary and secondary schools charged student fees in all kinds of excuses such as school maintenance, supplementary classes, use of classroom equipment, and so forth. Therefore, not only poor people in rural areas but also poor families in the cities and towns are finding themselves unable to afford to send their children to attend public education anymore. For example, urban public schools require nonresidential students (mainly migrants) to pay a "school support fee" of about 20,000–30,000 Chinese yuan to get into the school, on top of an annual tuition of more than 10,000 yuan. That has given parents, especially those migrant parents, a huge burden. While the small portion of wealthy families can send their children to "elite private schools," many children from low income working class families may lose their opportunities to access education because of lack of money.

Research also found that a daunting problem in primary and secondary education in China is the high number of dropouts. Studies showed that, during the 1980s, an average of four million middle and primary school students dropped out of school every year. In other words, in the late 1980s the dropout rate was 5 to 8% per year, leading to a total dropout rate of about 20% over the three years of junior secondary education (Cheng, 1995). Although the enrollment rate of primary school had been above 98% between 1995 and 2001 after having implemented the Compulsory Education Law for more than ten years, the gross enrolment ratio at junior secondary level was only 88.95% in 2001.

The reason for students leaving school, as research consistently has found, is mainly related to social inequality that was caused by the economic reform. While wealthy people with financial freedom to have school choices for their children, schooling seems to be out of reach for many disadvantaged families due to the increased cost of education. A study which investigated 200 parents with children attending primary and middle schools in Chongqing, one of China's largest cities, found that at the start of the fall term of 1994, the average cost of miscellaneous fees for primary students was 95.93 yuan, for junior high students, 155.5 yuan, and for senior high students, 257.3 yuan—in the mid-1990s, the monthly income of an urban worker was about 150 yuan a month. In addition, other sharply increasing expenses such as textbooks and school supplies, the high cost rendered the parents who made barely 100–200 yuan a month and lived in poverty unable to keep their child in school (Rosen, 2000).

The tracking system in urban education which divides schools into key and ordinary schools have perpetuated educational inequality. Established in the early 1950s and restored in 1978, key schools serve to select elite youth and accelerate the development of those talented students for the universities. Following the same idea as allowing a group of people to be rich first, the rationale for setting up key schools is to employ the limited resources of the country in a concentrated manner to develop high quality personnel, which eventually would speed up the economic development. Since key schools register a high admission rate for their students to enter colleges and universities (more than 90%), they have many privileges over the ordinary schools as mentioned before. Receiving more benefits in human, financial, and material resources from the governments than ordinary schools, key schools are a reflection of the inequality in the possession of power in China's political system. Increasingly researchers found that the students who attend key schools mostly come from the family of government officials and high-level intellectuals. On the other hand, lacking resources from the families, most children from a working-class background can only choose ordinary schools in which students have much fewer opportunities for getting into colleges and universities. Also, the key schools have been criticized for being open only to those promising ones and not all students (Hayhoe, 1984; Lin, 1999; 1993; Zhou et al., 1998).

ECONOMIC REFORM, SOCIAL DEVELOPMENT, AND EDUCATIONAL REFORM IN SHANGHAI SINCE 1978

Economic Reform and Social Changes in Shanghai

As one of the pioneering Chinese educational reforms, s*uccess education* was not conducted by accident, rather it is a reflection of the transformation in politics, economy, and culture in Shanghai during the era of reform. Located at the mouth of the Yangtze River in China Eastern Coastal Region, Shanghai comprises fourteen urban districts and six suburban counties. Beginning as a fishing village, Shanghai has experienced dramatic changes in modern time. With a total area of 6,341 square kilometers and a population of more than 20 million, today it is the largest Chinese metropolis and the fourth largest in the world. As one of three municipalities in China directly under the central government, Shanghai is also an economic, commercial and transportation center.

Because of a solid industrial base with more than 40,000 enterprises (He, 1992a) and a Pacific coastal line, Shanghai plays a pivotal role in the country's economic development, leading in production, science and technology, management, and transportation. It became the center of China's modernization drive since the central government decided to develop Pudong into the largest special economic zone in April 1990. Acting as a "dragon head" for the cities along the Yangtze Delta, Pudong has injected "old Shanghai" with new blood. By the end of 1993, Pudong's GDP grew to

12 billion yuan, a figure that had doubled just during the period of twelve months (Smith, 2000).

The important position of Shanghai in the national economy can be indicated by the following figures: With incredible inflow of capital and talents, Shanghai kept an extraordinary annual economic growth rate of 14.3% during the period 1978–1998. In 1999, the gross output value of industry in Shanghai reached more than 630 billion yuan, accounting for one twelfth of the national output or one sixth of the national profits (Shanghai Municipal Commission for Education, 2000a).

Another study on Shanghai economic growth over the period from 1952 to 1998 shows that in 1998 Shanghai's GDP represents a rise of 53 times more than 1952 in constant prices. Per capita GDP increased at a rate of 8% per year during the same period, and reached $3400 at the end of 1998; its fiscal revenue accounted for one ninth of the national total. As one of the largest international trade centers and financial centers in Asia, Shanghai has attracted increasing foreign direct investment (FDI) since the1980s. From 1991–1998 the FDI inflows reached US $23.2 billion, accounting for 94% of the total amount over the entire period from 1981 to 1998 (Zhang, 2003). The above statistics confirms that "Shanghai has gained back its status as the most important economic center, a symbol of rapid economic growth and deep institutional reforms and a prospective major financial center not only for the East Asia but also for the entire world" (Zhang, 2003, p. 87).

Serving as a cash machine or "cash cow," Shanghai has its special political role in the country's development, namely to provide the revenues to the central government (Sun, 2000). To achieve this goal, in 1979 Shanghai government began to explore some urban reform policies. As did other cities, the main political achievement of the Shanghai government was to successfully transform from the central planning economy to the market economy. By giving wide decision-making powers to enterprises, a diversified economy has been established in Shanghai (He, 1992b). The process of privatization in Shanghai started in the mid-1980s—up to then the city lagged behind other coastal provinces such as Guangdong, Fujian, and Zhejiang. But in the 1990s private enterprises had developed rapidly. Their number increased by 260% from 1991–1993, and the number of workers in these companies rose by 212% to more than 100,000 in only these two years (White III & Li, 1998). In 2002 the number of private enterprises had reached 210,000, hiring 2.3 million people, or one in every three Shanghai workers (Zhu et al., 2005). This change, on the one hand, has contributed to a remarkable economic growth. However, on the other hand, it also correlated with class differentiation and inequality between the rich and the poor. I will discuss this issue later in this chapter.

In terms of culture, Shanghai plays a very important role in cultural transformation in the country during the reform era. Shanghai culture is usually called as "the sea style of culture" due to its location near the sea and Yangtze River, meaning "the sea can contain all the rivers." Therefore, openness, changes, and creations are regarded as the characteristics of Shanghai culture, compared to Beijing's culture which is considered as more orthodox, traditional, and hierarchical. As a result, for the last hundred years, Shanghai has presented itself at heart of the radical cultural changes. In today's era of reform, rather than uniformity, culture in Shanghai tends to have diverse and multiple dimensions (Rimmington, 1998). Mainly influenced by Western culture (American culture) after China opened its door to the world, life style, behavior, and philosophy among the younger generation in Shanghai are more dynamic and Western-oriented than that in the older generation. For example, Liu (2004) cites a story from a Reuters news report on December 14,1996 that describes how people in Shanghai celebrated Christmas holiday as a popular culture:

> Holiday commercial promotions in Shanghai department stores started earlier than ever this year, expecting a major kick-off with Christmas shopping season. The stores, especially joint-venture ones are working hard to promote the idea of Christmas as a gift-sharing holiday among young people in their 20s. Christmas decoration, trees, and cards can be seen everywhere in the stores. Some stores give out a 10% gift certificate for every 500 yuan spent in the store, to encourage spending. One young salesman told the reporter that he planned to spend 500 yuan on Christmas gifts and cards for friends. According to him, "we young people in Shanghai like to copy Western habits." The traditional holiday shopping season in China is during January and February before the Chinese New Year, which is still the case to most older people in Shanghai. (pp. 78–79)

In summary, the opening of the Pudong New District in 1990 indicated a significant shift of Shanghai's economy. After more than a decade, with a pace of extraordinarily economic growth, Shanghai's multiple functions and key national role as an economic hub have been established. All these provide a solid foundation for its educational reform.

Basic Educational Reform in Shanghai in the Era of Reform

Dramatic and significant transformation has been taking place in the educational sectors in Shanghai in response to a fast-growing economy since 1978. Shanghai currently has 640 primary schools and 807 secondary schools with a total enrollment of more than 1.3 million students at basic education level. Children in Shanghai begin their primary school at six years old. The educational system in Shanghai follows a 6–3–3 pattern: 6 years of primary school, 3 junior secondary school, and 3 years of senior secondary school (Shanghai Municipal Commission for Education, 2006).

Looking back today, the Shanghai government has always put its priority in educational development and linked the key role of education to Shanghai economic development and social progress. As a municipality under the direct leadership of the Chinese central government as well as being China's dragon head in economic reform, Shanghai has to play an important role in implementing the educational policies promulgated by the central government. On the other hand, as a city with the country's largest special economic zone—Pudong, and a model of opening policy, Shanghai has enjoyed relatively high autonomy in education policymaking. Moreover, in order to serve local economic development, Shanghai has been encouraged to act as a leader in terms of taking educational policy initiatives and making innovation. Indeed, Shanghai is a good example of a combination of centralization and decentralization in education reform (Lun & Chan, 2003).

In 1985, the Shanghai government initiated "The Regulation on Universalizing Compulsory Education in Shanghai," one year before the Compulsory Education Law was issued by the central government in 1986. As a result, by 1986, Shanghai had achieved the universalization of nine years compulsory education, becoming the earliest area for reaching this national goal (Hook, 1998). With the support of rapid educational development, Shanghai created more than 200,000 job opportunities in industry in the 1980s. Educational development not only brought about a tremendous increase in production but also provided solid manpower resources for its stable, continual, and fast economic growth in the 1990s. From this experience, Shanghai government authorities noticed that today's education is tomorrow's economy (Cai, 1995). Therefore, they continue to support and encourage educational reforms.

To implement the 1985 "Decision on Reform of the Educational Structure" as set down by the central government, Shanghai has reformed its education by emphasizing the adoption of research-based strategies ever since June 1986. During the period of the city "Seventh Five-Year Plan" (1986–1990), educational development was viewed as a major research program in the research plan for the domain of "philosophy and social sciences." Lun and Chan (2003) describe this situation in detail:

> (At that time) more than 200 experts, scholars and practitioners, who came from over 80 units in the various departments of education, economy, science, culture, organization and personnel, were involved in that research which lasted for three years. The research topics were concerned with various educational issues including: educational development strategy, educational

investment, basic education, higher education, vocational and technical education, adult education, pre-primary education, social education, cadre education, and the education personnel system. It proposed a general strategy for educational development to meet Shanghai increasing basic demands, its main strategic targets, as well as key measures to promote Shanghai's educational development. (p. 85)

In such a context, many new educational reforms had emerged during that time. The success education program launched in 1987, which I am studying, is one of these educational innovations in Shanghai.

In the 1990s, facing the challenges of a globalization era, the Shanghai government formulated an ambitious goal: To develop itself as a "first-class city with first-class education" (Su & Chen, 1994, p. 6). In response to the "Program for Education Reform and Development in China" issued by the central government in 1993, Shanghai outlined its educational blueprint in the twenty-first century as "a first-class lifelong educational system in Asia with reasonable structure and a focus on people's all-rounded development" (Leading Group of the Project on Shanghai into the 21st Century, 1995, p. 447). In all, Shanghai attempts to build up a great modernized education system that can connect all levels of education including preschool, primary, secondary and tertiary schooling, and link up general education, vocational education and adult education.

To achieve this goal, in the mid-1980s, the Shanghai government made an important decision on reforming low performing and at-risk schools at primary and secondary education levels. They altered and reconstructed 230 low performing schools in only three years (Shanghai Institute of Human Resource Development, 2005). The No. 8 School which I am investigating is one of these at-risk schools.

In 2001, the Shanghai government further confirmed that its education goal was to construct an advanced, modernized, and well-organized lifelong educational system that are world-oriented and well matched with the world-class status of Shanghai and that eventually will build Shanghai into a Learning City (Shanghai Municipal Commission for Education 2000b).

In the intersection of rhetoric and actions, Shanghai educational reforms have experienced a process of "re-centralization" and decentralization (Hawkins, 2000). In 1995, the Shanghai Municipal Commission for Education was established as a unified educational administrative unit, ending a history of being administrated by three fragmented government departments: the Municipal Bureau of Education (for general education), the Municipal Bureau of Higher Education, and the Office of Education and Health under the municipal government (for the coordination of education and health affairs). This reconstruction of management made Shanghai a more efficient and effective educational administrative system.

The course of decentralization in Shanghai can be seen in four aspects (Lun & Chan, 2003). First, it is called territorial decentralization, meaning "a transfer of power from higher to lower levels" (Chan et al., 2004, p. 98). The obvious feature of this education reform in Shanghai is that the municipal government has given more autonomy to schools in decision-making. They encouraged schools to have their own developmental goals, to create their own styles, and to form their own school culture. Under such a context, Shanghai has become a pioneer in many kinds of educational experiments in the nation since 1980s.

Secondary, in order to increase educational investment, Shanghai has adopted an open and flexible policy to attract nongovernmental social forces and individuals to run schools. As in other provinces in China, schools in Shanghai, for a long time, used to be directly controlled by the central government in terms of financing, curriculum, and management. By the 1990s, "non-state bodies" started to be involved in the formal education sector in Shanghai. Currently, using multiple channels to run schools, the provisions of educational services in Shanghai are very diverse. They have public schools and *minban* schools (people-run private schools). In particular, Shanghai has spearheaded an alternative strategy to transform the management system of the public primary and secondary schools (*zhuanzhi xuexiao*) since 1993. Under this policy, the ownership of the public schools still belongs to the government, however, they are managed by the enterprises, business organizations, social organizations, or individuals through making a contract with the government. Those kinds of schools are usually called "public schools run by social forces." By the end of the year 2000, there were a total of 125 *minban* primary and secondary schools and 67 public schools run by social forces (*guoyou minban*) in Shanghai.

With a diversity of investment from the state, society, and individuals, a new education finding system has been formed in Shanghai. For example, research found that of current educational expenditure in Shanghai, approximately 50% comes from government while 30% is from society and communities, and 20% from individuals (Kang, 2001).

Third, in terms of curricula, textbooks, and examinations, Shanghai initiated a number of important reforms to implement quality education, reduce students' burden, and make school more diverse and more creative. Since the 1950s up to the late 1970s, education was regarded as a political tool to serve the country. Thus, a centralization policy was adopted in the education sector, characterized by a unified system of an administration, curricula, syllabus and textbooks, etc. However, this policy has been changed during the age of economic reform. It was Shanghai that began to publish and use its own textbooks suitable for local economic development and social progress right after the central government relaxed its tight control on textbooks in an attempt to increase a diversity of textbook production options in 1986. Later on other economically advanced areas followed Shanghai's example.

So far, Shanghai has been carrying out two rounds of reform in the school curriculum and textbooks. The first round started in 1988 by a Special Task Force to innovate teaching materials. After almost ten years of great efforts, a whole set of school curriculum and teaching materials from K–12, which are to meet Shanghai's own needs of economic, political, and cultural development, were created and accepted by authorities in the Fall of 1997. To better implement quality education and to construct first-class education, Shanghai has been continuing its second round of reform in the school curriculum and teaching materials after September 1997.

China started to reform its examination system in 1995 through abolishing the uniform middle school entrance examination. Shanghai implemented this policy in 1997. Also, Shanghai was among the first to reform the university entrance examination. Beginning to conduct its own university entrance examination in 1996, Shanghai has adopted a "three-plus-one" model of examination. Under this model, instead of students taking examination in six subjects as was the case before the reform, the students are only required to take examinations in three basic subjects: Chinese, mathematics, one foreign language (mainly English), and an optional subject. In such an alternative examination system, students feel much relieved from the heavy pressure of examination. Furthermore, rather than only taking the summer university entrance examination, students in Shanghai can have an option to take the examination either in spring or in autumn.

Fourth, the appearance of community education is seen as a form of decentralization in education in Shanghai. Early in the 1980s Shanghai started to develop community education activities in order to develop a good relationship between schools and communities and fully use community resources to facilitate education. According to Lun and Chan (2003), from 1985 onward, "community education committees," which consist of schools, local government offices, business enterprises, public institutions and the local military units, have been set up in a number of districts in Shanghai. In 1995, there were 14 districts and 125 streets having established a Community Education Committee. In this way, school, family, and society are well connected and play an integrated role in education development.

After more than two decades of reform, as one of the most advanced cities in China, Shanghai boasts a high concentration of educated human resources. In the 1980s, an average Shanghainese had 7.4 years of education, much higher than the national average which was only 4.5 years in the same period. In 1999, the average year of education of the labor force reached 11 years in Shanghai (Shanghai Municipal Commission for Education, 2000b). In the same year, the rate of enrollment among school age children was 99.98 % while both the proportions of students entering and completing junior secondary schools also reached more than 99%. The admission rate to senior secondary education increased significantly from 62% in 1986 to 97% in 1999. All these figures indicate that Shanghai is the number one in educational access and attainment in China (Shanghai Municipal Commission for Education, 2000a). With 187 people having received higher education per 10,000 population, the ratio was impressively high (Hook, 1998). These factors indicate that Shanghai has made great progress in education since 1978.

Social Inequality and School Problems in Shanghai

Although Shanghai has achieved spectacular development in economy, culture, and education, like other industrial cities in China, Shanghai is also facing many major challenges and serious problems such as unemployment, huge number of migrants, poverty, and inequality in education. In this section, I will examine issues and problems the Shanghai government is confronting in the reform era and their impact on education, aiming at providing a context that can explain why *success education* reform happened in Shanghai.

The first challenge faced by the Shanghai government is an increasing unemployment rate since 1990s, a problem that did not exist during Mao's era. As one of the negative results caused by the economic reform and opening policy, the large number of the unemployed in Shanghai is the product of the restructuring of state-owed enterprises (SOEs) initiated by the central government in 1984 (Garnaut et al., 2005). The purpose of this reform is to shift a large number of low productivity SOEs into profitable ones by reforming their ownership. As a center of industry in China, Shanghai has been undergoing a significant transformation in SOEs structure since mid-1980s (Ngan et al., 2004).

It has been reported that in the booming market economies which stress competitiveness, in 1997 37% of SOEs and collective enterprises in Shanghai struggled with financial difficulties, and 8.5% had already bankrupted or were on the verge of bankruptcy (Shanghai Statistical Bureau, 1999). However, on the other hand, private enterprises have developed very rapidly. For example, in the first half of 2002, 30,000 new private enterprises were registered in Shanghai. In 2004, there had been 210,000 private enterprises in Shanghai, employing 2.3 million people (Lee & Warner, 2005).

Another noticeable transition that occurred in Shanghai in the 1990s was that the city industry has been experiencing a dramatic shift from the primary production sector to the secondary and tertiary sectors. Shanghai used to be the main base of manufacturing industry in China. However, from the 1990s Shanghai became an international center of economic, finance, and trade. For example, in 2000 3,720,800 persons were engaged in establishments in the service sectors, 3,670,400 in the secondary production, and only 892,300 in the primary production (Lee et al., 2004).

Due to this restructuring, massive unemployment and labor force redundancy became inevitable in Shanghai. The figures in the following two tables reflect the situation of unemployment in Shanghai since 1990.

Table 4.1 shows that urban unemployment rate in Shanghai had increased sharply from 1.5% or 77,000 persons in 1990, to 4.5% or 274,300 persons in 2004. This number only refers to the urban registered unemployed persons, not including "hidden unemployment" or redundant workers who are laid off (*xiagang zhigong*). According to the fifth census in Shanghai in November 2000, the unemployment rate had reached 9.66% or 548,300 persons, 2.76 times more than the registered number (3.5%). A study shows that in the end of 2001, there were already 1.5 million redundant workers, accounting for one third of all the employees in SOEs in Shanghai.

TABLE 4.1 The Number of Unemployed People and the Unemployment Rate in Shanghai (1990–2004)

Year	Unemployed People (Unit: 10,000)	Unemployment rate (%)
1990	7.70	1.5
1991	7.61	1.4
1992	9.42	1.7
1993	12.97	2.4
1994	14.85	2.8
1995	14.36	2.7
1996	14.54	2.7
1997	14.90	2.8
1998	15.96	2.9
1999	17.47	3.1
2000	20.08	3.5
2001	25.72	4.3
2002	28.78	4.8
2003	30.11	4.9
2004	27.43	4.5

Source: Shanghai Municipal Statistic Bureau, http://www.stats-sh.gov.cn/2003shtj/tjnj/nj05.htm?d1=2005tjnj/C0322.htm

Table 4.2 reveals that the disadvantaged groups who were first laid off in the SOEs reform were workers around their 40s–50s with low education level as well as women. That is the generation who experienced the Cultural Revolution and lost their educational opportunities because of the political disturbance. Since 2000 a new phenomenon appeared, that is, younger people less than 35 years old became the main body of unemployed persons. For example, in 2001 the number of unemployed persons with age 16–25 had reached 105,000, accounting for 39.3% of total unemployed persons (Zhou & Xiao, 2006).

Losing their jobs, the unemployed workers possess little political, economic and intellectual power to make a new career and usually live in poverty. Shanghai is the first urban city in the nation to have established the

TABLE 4.2   Profile of Employees Laid Off in Shanghai as of 30 June 1999

Demographic	Percentage (%)
Job type	
Worker	70.5
Service staff	9.1
Administrative staff	5.0
Technician	2.7
Others	12.8
Total	100.0
Education level	
Junior secondary	72.2
Others	27.8
Total	100.0
Sex	
Male	46.6
Female	53.4
Total	100.0
Age	
35 and below	20.9
36–40	31.9
41–45	29.3
45 and above	17.9
Total	100.0

Source: Shanghai Tongji Nianjian 1999 (Shanghai Tongji Chubanshe 1999). Cited from Lee et al, 2004) p. 140.

"minimum-living-standard guarantee scheme" (*zuidi shenghua baozhang*), starting in 1993. However, the support money from the government is very limited (185 yuan per month in 1996, 195 yuan per month in 1997, 280 yuan per month in 1998, and at 300 yuan per month from August 2005 onward) and these people can basically only survive (Ngan et al., 2004; Yang, 2006). With cost of living rising year by year, many working class families have to pinch every penny to survive.

The second problem for Shanghai to deal with is the inflow of migrants since 1978. As the national economic center, Shanghai has been seen as one of those cities full of opportunities for outsiders to find work and to live in. Since the late1970s hundreds of thousands of people from all over the country have moved to Shanghai seeking jobs and for a better life. Becoming the biggest city of migrants or a "floating" population in China, Shanghai held 3.87 million migrants in 2000, about one-sixth of the total population in the city. Among them, 3.2 million were peasants, accounting for 85% of outsiders (Li, 2004). The urban-rural income disparity and better living conditions in the city are main factors for the inflow of migrant workers. As rural peasants make very little, migrants working in the city could double the income they would earn in the rural areas (Yep et al., 2004).

Having only received junior high or primary level education, most of the migrants work in construction sites. The rest work in various service sectors such as restaurants, hotels, stores, etc. To survive in the city, they are willing to accept any less-than-favorable and even demeaning jobs. They work harder and longer but get less pay. Research shows that migrant workers, on average, work around 55 hours per week, but only earn about 50% of the income the local workers make. For example, even though migrants made 869 yuan a month in 1999, much higher than 665 yuan in1997 and 555 yuan in 1995, their incomes were still low, as compared with urban workers who average 1,167 yuan per month plus bonuses and all kinds of welfare and benefits (Zuo, 2003). Lacking living protections and any welfare and benefits, the migrants become one of the most vulnerable groups in the city, living in poverty and experiencing all kinds of discriminations.

Owing to the above reasons, the income gap between the rich and the poor in Shanghai is significantly widened in the era of reform. A newspaper in Shanghai in April 2000 investigated family incomes in the city and provided a profile of Shanghai's families' income: the top 1% wealthy families earned more than 120,000 yuan per year, the next 5% middle class earned 50,000 to 120,000 yuan per yean, and the majority 71% ordinary families made around 50,000 yuan a year (Chen, 2005). According to the Shanghai government, families with incomes between 300 yuan and 16,683 yuan per year belong to middle-and-low income families (Shanghai Management Bureau of Housing & Land Resources, 2005). In December 1998, the average monthly income of a poor family was 243 yuan, accounting for only 31% of a local person's average income per month (731 yuan) (Tang, 2004). Moreover, research shows that low-income groups have been growing so dramatically that in a short four-year period from 1999 to 2003, the number of people who received the minimum-living-standard guarantee increased six times, namely from 70,000 or 0.72% of the population in 1999, to 445,600 or 4.5% in 2003 (Huang, 2005).

Figure 4.1 presents the amount of living subsidy spending by the Shanghai government each year from 1996 to 2003. Through the table, one can see a rapid increase of money invested by the government as basic subsistence living allowance to support the poor people from nearly 400 million yuan in 1996 to around 1 billion yuan in 2003 (Huang, 2005).

Social inequality has been a continuing problem in the education field in Shanghai. One of the profound impacts from the economic reforms and globalization on education is that education is not a public good anymore. To a great extent, it is more and more becoming a commodity. As in other places in China, compulsory education in Shanghai is not free. Extra charges under many names are a big problem for Shanghai parents to worry about. For example, although tuition is free for nine years' compulsory education in Shanghai, students have to pay a fee of 210 yuan (for primary students) and 280 yuan (for junior high students) each semester, called "one time charge fee," which includes miscellaneous expenses, textbooks and notebook fees. Other expenses are charged for students under the names such as school costume, lunch, interest group, accommodation, extra or make-up courses after class or weekend, just to name a few. The fee for private primary and secondary schools is much higher: in 2003, it cost around 5,500 per semester for private schools and 5,000 yuan for "public schools run by social forces" (Su, 2003). If parents want to choose

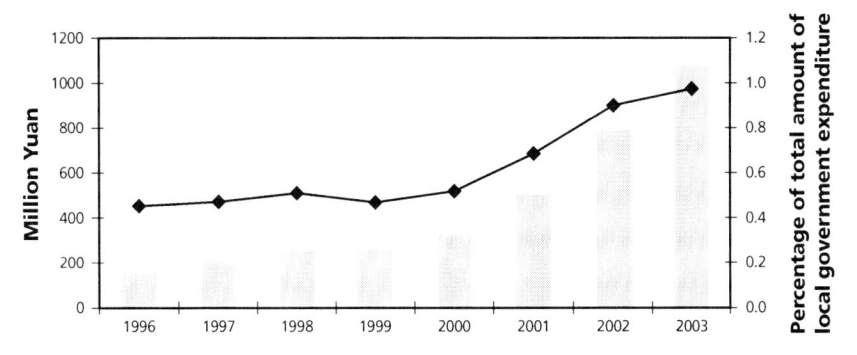

Figure 4.1 The expenditure of Shanghai government for support of people below the poverty line 1996–2003.

a better school for their child, they have to pay a school option fee and a lump-sum school support fee that range from 10,000 to 30,000 yuan, even to 50,000 yuan.

Because of these various kinds of charges, the cost of education has increased very rapidly since the mid-1990s. Recent research on 3,000 families in Shanghai shows that the average education expense for Shanghai residents is 937 yuan per person in 2003, an increase of 23.2% from 761 yuan in 1995. Specifically, the average cost for a student in Shanghai from primary to high school for each semester is as follows: 1,603 yuan for primary students, 2,402 for junior high, and 4,447 yuan for high school students (Shanghai Statistical Bureau, 2005). Another investigation conducted by the Shanghai Women's Committee and Shanghai Social Science Academy also shows that Shanghai parents today generally invest one-quarter or 23.6 % of their total family incomes on their child's education, much higher than 10% of education expenses in the United States and Canada families (Gong, 2005). All those expensive education fees are a huge burden to the working class families.

Thus, inequality in education is obvious in Shanghai. For instance, there is a big gap in the amount of investment in children's education between rich and poor families. According to the figures from the Shanghai Statistical Bureau (2005), at high school level, in 2003 wealthy families in Shanghai spend 2.8 times more than that of poor families in supporting their students' learning within school, spend 2.1 times than that of low-income families in after school activities, and spend 5.7 times more than that of disadvantaged families in home tutoring. At the primary education level, the expenses for children's education among low-income families, ordinary working class families, middle class families, and rich families were 905 yuan, 1,538 yuan, 1,964 yuan and 3,390 yuan respectively. In terms of school choice, while 8.4% of high-income families in Shanghai in 2003 were able to select a better school or key school for their children by paying an expensive fee, only 0.8% of low-income families did the same thing. The above information provides evidence that a direct negative impact of Shanghai's social change is that parents who live in poverty cannot afford quality education for their children.

Moreover, education for migrant children has become a complex and knotty problem in Shanghai (Zhu, 2001). According to the sixth survey to a sample of the floating population in Shanghai, there were 190,000 immigrant children under age 15 in 1997. However, only 60.75% of them were enrolled in local schools. The major reason for the other 39.25% of migrant children who failed to have access to education was their parents could not afford the high amount of school support fees as mentioned above (Zhou & Yang 2001). Working as construction workers, cleaning ladies, and housemaids, etc., their parents' incomes usually were around 1,000 yuan monthly. With such a low income, it was impossible for them to pay an annual tuition fee of 10,000 yuan and a lump sum, the so-called school support fee ranging from 30,000 to 50,000 yuan for their children (Li, 2004). As a consequence, living in a low standard and unstable life, many migrant children cannot obtain a good education.

In summary, as the pioneer of radical reform in China, Shanghai has achieved a lot in economic and educational development. However, it is also facing many challenges in education. Hoping to play a key role in leading China into the 21st century, Shanghai has never stopped seeking any alternative ways to reform its education. This provides the context in which *success education* was born and has been growing since 1985.

CHAPTER 5

THE HISTORY OF *SUCCESS EDUCATION* REFORM

This chapter and the next six chapters will detail the process of the reform, strategies adopted by the school, and the results of the reform. This chapter will provide background information of the Zhabei District, the situation of the community and the school before the reform. Finally, the chapter will give a brief review of the history of success education experiment.

INTRODUCTION

Why did success education experiment occur in the Zhabei District in Shanghai? What are the reasons for No. 8 School to conduct success education? What was the situation before the reform? How was the experiment designed? What are the results of the program? The purpose of this chapter is to answer these questions and try to provide a profile of the reform. Specifically, the chapter will first give information about the Zhabei District in general. Then, it will examine what the investigated school looks like and why the reform is necessary. Finally, the study reviews the process and stages of the success education program. Before doing all these, I would like to provide some background of the school since situations have changed during the 20 years' since implementation of the program.

Success for All, pages 81–94
Copyright © 2008 by Information Age Publishing
All rights of reproduction in any form reserved.

Originally, *success education* was initiated in No. 8 School of Zhabei in Shanghai in 1987. After having implemented the experiment for nearly two decades, Principal Liu Jinghai, the initiator of the reform, has been running two schools using the same idea of *success education* in the Zhabei District. As a "public school run by social forces," Tian Jia Bing Middle School was established in 1997, donated by a wealthy businessman, Tian Jia Bing from Hong Kong. Built in 2001, the new campus of No 8 School was the replacement of the old one in 2006. With a rapid growing economy, the Shanghai government is planning to remove all old and shabby houses of the city in order to improve people's living standard. The houses surrounding No. 8 School, the slum area in Shanghai, have been targeted by the government to be rebuilt in the next five years. That reason led to the establishment of the branch in 2001. The old campus was closed down in 2006 and will become a school for special education in 2007.

Based on my research questions, I selected the old and new campuses of No 8 School as my samples. Because Tian Jia Bing Middle School mainly serves students from the middle and wealthy families, I did not select it for study. Furthermore, with the changes in China's social and economic contexts, a majority of students in the new campus of No. 8 School are not from the poor working class any more, but from Shanghai peasants with rather decent income. My research focus was mainly on the old campus, where the reform originated, expanded, and many innovative measures were tested and proven effective there. Meanwhile, I will also explore the development of *success education* in the new campus and examine the new situation and new challenges facing the school.

THE ZHABEI DISTRICT OF SHANGHAI

To better understand the success education program, it is necessary to look first at the school's environment—the Zhabei District in Shanghai. With a total area of 29.2 square kilometers and a population of 810,211 in 2003, the Zhabei District is located in the North of Shanghai and consists of eight streets and one town. Called "the area of slum-dwellers," it was one of the poorest areas in Shanghai with a large number of migrants and most people who lived in this district were low income workers.

There is a historical reason that caused Zhabei to become a poor area. Developing in the late Qing Dynasty, Zhabei used to be one of the most prosperous areas in the city during the 1920s–1930s. At that time, Zhabei was a center of social service, finance, industry, and culture in Shanghai. Called "The Northern Door into Shanghai," the Shanghai Railway Station and the North Suburb Train Station of Shanghai (freight transport) were also situated in Zhabei. However, all of these were destroyed by Japanese bombing during the World War II. The disasters happened on January 28, 1932 and on August 13, 1937 when the Japanese army invaded Shanghai. The bombing and invasion killed thousands of people and razed 95% of the buildings including stores, factories, schools, hospitals, resident houses to the ground. Zhabei was left with nothing but catastrophe and poverty (Feng et al., 2002).

After the War of Resistance against Japan, a large number of refugees from the countryside of Jiangsu, Anhui, and Zhejiang provinces arrived in the Zhabei District close to the Shanghai Train Station. They settled down in the areas of the train station and built their houses with old and waste bricks and tiles, pieces of cement, worn asphalt felts, and broken glasses. Those small, low, dilapidated houses were crowded together, looking like fish scales. Within the neighborhood, the zigzagging streets are very narrow and small. New comers find it difficult to find their way around. Also, because of the crowded condition, usually three generations live in a very small room. When the children are grown up, they often add a loft on the top of their houses. Then, one can see all kinds of small rooms on the roofs that look like boxes. That is Shanghai's special houses called "garrets." An area full of "garrets" is called "the area of shack-dwellers."

The economy and people living standards in Zhabei have been enhanced greatly after 1949 when the CCP took over. In particular, since China adopted the economic reform and opening policy, Zhabei's economy has been growing very fast. For example, from 2001 to 2004 Zhabei's cumulative GDP reached 18.73 billion yuan, an increase of about 13% per year. Especially, in 2004 GDP in Zhabei increased so rapidly that it had reached 5.62 billion yuan that year, or 17.8% increase from previous years (Chen & Yang, 2005).

In spite of a sharp growth in economy, the Zhabei District is still one of the poorest and the most undeveloped areas in Shanghai due to the historical conditions mentioned above. It was reported that in 2005 16,906 householders in Zhabei had registered for the minimum-living-standard guarantee money (300 yuan monthly) offered by the government. Among those poor families, 43% of them had a per capita income less than 300 yuan per month, 13% a little bit higher than that of minimum-living-standard guarantee, and 53% less than 435 yuan per month (Feng, 2005). Zhabei today is still a concentrated area of migrants to Shanghai. In 2003, 100,000 migrants poured into Zhabei. Therefore, the Zhabei government faces a lot of problems such as social security, employment, education, housing, and so on. Particularly, the crisis of housing is so serious that in 2005 Zhabei had an existence of 130,000 square meters of "the area of shack-dwellers," and 60,000 families were living in "garrets" (Zhang, 2005). It indicates that social inequality and poverty are big issues and challenges for the Zhabei government to deal with.

84 *Success for All*

Photo 5.1 The slum area surrounding No. 8 School, Zhabei Distract, Shanghai, 2004.

Photo 5.2 The "garrets"—the street surrounding No. 8 School, Zhabei Distract, Shanghai, 2004.

THE SITUATION OF NO. 8 SCHOOL BEFORE THE REFORM

Founded in 1963, No. 8 School served the poorest community near Shanghai Railway Station in the Zhabei District, which assumed "ghetto-like status" with the majority of the residents living in poverty. With an area of 4,000 square meters and the construction area of 6,735 square meters, it is a junior secondary school. In March 1996, the former Zhongxing Middle School was merged with No. 8 School adding an area of 3,062 square meters and a construction area of 2,865 square meters. After joining two schools together, the total area of No. 8 School is 7,235 square meters and the construction area of 11,500 square meters. In 2000 before the new campus was built up, there were 45 classes with an enrollment of 2,197 students, 100 teachers, and 50 staff in the merged school. In 2004 when I visited the school, the old campus had been reduced to 15 classes with 607 students, 47 teachers, and 21 staff.

Despite many attempts, it is difficult for the author to get very detailed original information about what the school looked like before the *success education* program started and how the reform began since the school did not keep those kinds of records on purpose. However, all the collected documents and all the interviewees who have experienced the reform de-

Photo 5.3   The old campus of No. 8 School, 2004.

86 *Success for All*

Photo 5.4 The living room of a student in No. 8 School, 2004.

Photo 5.5 The bedroom of a student in No. 8 School, 2004.

scribed a very severe situation at the school in the mid-1980s. The evidence indicates that for a long period of time, No. 8 School had been categorized as an at-risk school with the lowest student achievement level in the District, the highest rate of crime, and very poor academic discipline. Most students in the school were those who had failed a primary grade. They were discouraged and uninterested in school. Local people even called this school a "garbage school" or "the concentration camp of at-risk students." There was a popular saying in the Zhabei District at that time: "No. 8 School, No. 8 School, the door is toward the East, hooligans are in crowds, and fighting is the order of the day."

Some figures show that in 1986, only 22% of the students in the school could pass the standard graduation final exam. With nine students committing an offence, the students' crime rate was the highest in the District (Zhao, 2005). In 1987 among 35 junior secondary schools in the District, the total average entering scores of Chinese, mathematics, and English (three major subjects) of the school were ranked in the bottom last two schools. Thirty percent of the students in their primary school education had played truant while 37% students had repeated a year's work. Some of them even stayed behind two or three years.

Because of its very poor reputation, most parents did not want their children to go to this school. If possible, they would try any way they could to transfer their child to a better school. Mr. Zhang, who was the former vice-principal and had been working for 40 years in the school, told me that every year there were at least more than one hundred students who transferred to other schools. Students were also very sad and disappointed if they knew they had to enter into No. 8 School. For example, Miss Sun, a former student in this school, shared her experience with me. When her parents told her she would be a new student in No. 8 School after she graduated from the primary school, she cried very hard and felt ashamed and hopeless for her future. For a while, she did not want to talk with her friends. She was so painful and ashamed that she was scared to look at people when she walked on the street.

Liu Jinghai, the principal of No. 8 School as well as the initiator of the experiment, described the serious situation of No. 8 School at that time.

> During the mid-1980s, there were 12 at-risk schools in the Zhabei Distract. Why did I choose No. 8 School as the target of the reform? I selected the school for success education based on four conditions: that the school has a large number of at-risk students; the school is located in a poor community; the school stands out in having poor quality of teachers and a poor facility.

After having reviewed all information, I found that No. 8 School met all those criteria while other schools might only have two or three of them. In fact, No. 8 School could add one more disadvantage: poor financing.

At that time, students' average grade in their primary schools was the bottom last three among 35 middle schools in the District. The community which the school serves is one of the most backward communities in Shanghai. The situation can be summarized as "three lows and two highs" among 128 streets in Shanghai, the average years of schooling of Zhabei residents were the lowest, the rate of college students per 10,000 people was the lowest, and so is the rate of technicians per 10,000; the rate of illiterates and semi-illiterates aged over 15 was the highest and the crime rate was also the highest.

Liu continued that 95% of students coming from low-income families lived in "the area of slum-dwellers." Their parents were usually the generation of people who lost opportunities for secondary and higher education during the Cultural Revolution. The educational conditions of parents can be described as follows: 17.6% received six years of education; 54.9% had nine years of schooling; 23.2% had twelve years of schooling; only 2% had more than twelve years of education. Most of the families were living in city slums without a good study environment and a library where people could find study materials. The parents had neither confidence in their children's education nor appropriate methods for educating their children at home.

In this serious at-risk state, No. 8 School was a response to the Shanghai government's call for educational reform to meet a rapidly developing economy in Shanghai.

THE DEVELOPMENTAL STAGES OF SUCCESS EDUCATION REFORM

In this section, I will briefly review the history of success education and examine the developmental stages of the reform. Based on the data I collected, the development of success education can be divided into three stages: initiation, expansion, and consolidation.

The First Stage: Initiating the Experiment (1987–1990)

As a new educational reform supported by the Shanghai government, *success education*, in fact, started in 1985. However, at that time, the reform was not named as *success education*, but called "The Association of Twelve At-risk Schools" established by the Education Bureau of Zhabei District (EBZD). The purpose of the association, led by Liu Jinghai, the director of the Teaching and Research Group in Zhabei Normal College, was to conduct an experimental research in order to enhance at-risk students' academic achievements. After two years of experimental research, the program received positive results. Detailed information about this will be discussed in the next chapter. To strengthen this educational reform and find ways of improving educational quality in at-risk schools, in January 1987 Liu Jinghai submitted a proposal called "Improving Students' Quality Largely through a Comprehensive Reform of Moral Education, Chinese, Math, and English Teaching in At-risk Middle Schools" to the Shanghai Municipal Committee for Education (SMCE). In March 1987, his proposal was accepted as a key project of educational reform by SMCE. Liu received a grant of $30,000 yuan from the city government to support a three-year research experiment program. In June 1987, a research group was formed which consisted of eight experts from EBZD, Normal College of Zhabei District and No. 8 School. Under Liu's leadership, the research group started *success education* in No. 8 School.

Having selected two classes of the first year students (7th grade) as their experimental samples, Liu and the research group began their *success education* program in No. 8 School in June 1987. The program lasted three years until the participating experimental students completed their junior high in 1990. How was the program carried out? What are the results after three years? The following section will give a brief review of the process.

Before the Reform

Before the experiment, the two classes the research group chose to focus on were under typical at-risk conditions. Previous interviews, school documents and books described that (Chen, 2003; Chen, 2002; Hong, 2006; Liu, 1997; Liu et al., 1993):

> Among 77 students in two selected classes, 37.7% failed one grade in their primary school years and 14.4% repeated the same grade 2–3 times. In the unified tests of Zhabei District, the rate of failure in these two 7th- grade classes was 41.6% in Chinese reading, 50% in mathematics, and 100% in English listening and speaking; 84.7% of students' total score of the three subjects were below the average grade of the Zhabei District.
>
> Because of repeated failure, students of the program had low self-esteem, low motivation, and bad study habit. Among the two classes, only 11.1% students could do their homework by themselves. Without self-confidence, more than 90% of the students did not believe they were capable of graduating from the school. Also, feeling ashamed of being a student in No. 8 School, 90% of students did not like their school at all. Most of the students came from working class families, living under poor conditions.

Conditions of Experiment and Assumptions

SMCE required that the experiment must be conducted under three conditions that:

1. The students were the original students from No. 8 School; no new students;
2. The teachers were the same teachers in No. 8 School; no new teachers would be brought in for this reform.
3. The amount of teaching time was to be controlled; no extra time was allowed to be added.

The research group was guided by the following basic assumptions:

- In the nine years of compulsory education, every student with normal cognitive ability has the potential and desire to develop his/herself. Each is capable of making progress and reaching the standard of compulsory education;
- Every student has the aspiration and potential to be successful, and is able to achieve success in many aspects in his/her life;
- The purpose of education and the essential task of teaching are to help students succeed in their study and prepare them for success in society in the future.

Alternative Choice

Since this is a research-based reform, in the early stage of the experiment, Liu and the research group had done as much research as they could on at-risk students. The literature review they edited resulted in hundreds of pages containing domestic and international theory and practice on school success and improvement of at-risk students in both Chinese and English. At the same time, in order to identify the causes of students' problems in their study and behavior, the research group also conducted investigations among these experimental students in No. 8 School as well as students in other schools. The investigations covered very broad issues such as students' IQ, study ability, the correlation between students' attention and their academic achievement, study habits, and study attitude. While Liu and the group were conducting the research and investigation, they were also trying many alternative ways to help the experimental students to achieve academic success. They conducted class observations, analyzed the data they had collected, wrote research papers and held meetings every day to exchange their research findings, all with the determination to find out what efficient ways were there to help at-risk students.

Based on the studies and hard work, the research group found that the at-risk students' intelligence was normal, but their study habits were abnormal. What caused this phenomenon? They noticed that it was repeated school failure that made at-risk students lose self-confidence and motivation. The alternative approach to these students, the research group realized, must focus on helping them to be successful in both study and life. In traditional China, there is a saying that "Failure is the mother of success," but in the *success education* experiment, they said "Success is the mother of success." Success brings more success. Therefore, in 1989 after having implemented the reform for more than two years with the two classes of students, the research group decided to call the education reform they were conducting *success education*.

What is *success education*? It is a philosophy that believes every student has aspiration and potential for success and is able to achieve success in many ways. Specifically, *success education* is an education that aims at helping at-risk students to achieve success in their study and their life through a comprehensive approach to build up students' self-confidence and cultivate their "abilities to succeed." Rather than paying attention to only the top students as the traditional Chinese education system does, the end of *success education* is to achieve success for all by developing students' full potentials. Thus, *success education* is in itself a kind of quality education for all.

Adhering to this new education belief, Liu and the research group carried out many alternative strategies in their reform. For example, they began by transforming teachers' perceptions and trained them to become successful teachers. By creating opportunities for students to experience success, they facilitated students to achieve all kinds of success in the classroom. They also worked on developing good relationship with parents in order to help them build up confidence in their children. All these strategies will be examined in detail in future chapters.

Improvements

After having conducted the experiment for three years, the project had achieved noticeable positive effects.

First, students' attitude had been improved. In the 1990 spring semester, the research group conducted a survey on "self-confidence, willpower, and motivation" among eleven middle schools in Shanghai. The two experimental classes of No. 8 School ranked second in the eleven schools in Shanghai.

School satisfaction was raised from 10% before the reform to 90% in 1990. The percentage of students' confidence in study was raised from 10% to more than 90%. The number of students willing to do homework was increased from 11.1% to 91.1%.

Second, students' behavior had been improved. Before the reform, the students in No. 8 School were known for their antisocial behavior, poor discipline, and low motivation. In 1990, BEZD did an investigation through observation, interview, survey, and meetings regarding 14 favorable student behaviors among all middle schools in Zhabei area. No. 8 School was ranked number one. One of the two experimental classes was classified by BEZD as "an excellent class," a title given only to the best class. No criminal behavior occurred during three years.

Third, student school performance had been enhanced. The scores of the two experimental classes combined together in Chinese, math, and English were raised from the bottom level to the medium level in the Zhabei District. The average IQ score of two experimental classes increased from 95.93 in 1987 to 109.7 in 1990, the greatest increase among 11 middle schools in this area. The percentage of qualified students was raised to 90% from 30% in 1987.

The Second Stage: Expanding the Reform (1990–2000)

In June 1990, after the third year of the project, the Shanghai Municipal Committee for Education and the Education Bureau of Zhabei District held a conference to evaluate the experiment. The achievements of *success education* in No. 8 School had been recognized by the governments of Shanghai. In March 1993, and March 2000, EBZD respectively held the first and second "National *Success Education* Conference." Educators from all over the country attended the conferences. The reform has been acknowledged within the country.

After 1990, the reform had been expanded to all the classes in No. 8 School. In 1994, Liu resigned as the director of the Department of Teaching and Research of Education Bureau of Zhabei District and worked for No. 8 School again, this time as the full time Principal. Under Liu's leadership, student improvements continued. For example, the rate of students meeting the requirement for compulsory education had reached 98%-100% in 1990–1994 and has remained at 100% from 1995 to 2002. The school has been rewarded as "an excellent school" three times by Shanghai city. The program had been promoted to several primary schools, the other 11 at-risk middle schools, some high schools, and vocational schools in the Zhabei District. Some succeeded and some did not.

In early 1995, the State Education Commission enacted a regulation and officially promoted *success education* as one of three successful educational reforms in the nation. From then on, the reform has been expanded to the whole country. More than 10,000 leaders, school administrators, and educators have visited No. 8 School. Many schools have attempted to incorporated *success education*. Some have achieved positive results, and some have not, indicating the need for continuing research. Since the 1990s, the school has been visited by educators from more than ten countries and areas such as the United States, England, Australia, Japan, South Korea, Holland, Austria, Peru, Chile, Singapore, Hong Kong, and Macao. The reform result has also been written up in research papers and presented at the American Educational Research Association (AERA).

The Third Stage: Consolidating the Reform (2001–Present)

The building of a branch campus of No. 8 School in the suburbs in 2001 moved the *success education* program into a new stage: its deepening and consolidating stage. With nearly 10 acres of land, the branch school is a comprehensive junior-senior secondary school. Recruiting students nationally, there were 29 junior high classes and three senior high classes with 1,270 students in 2004. Among these students, around 50 came from Beijing, Zhejiang, Hujian, Henan, Jiangsu, and Anhui provinces. Drastically different from the old campus, this is a very modern school, equipped with "four [types of] machines" (32 inch color digital TV, computer, multiple function video system, and digital projection system) and "four nets" (campus website, internet, long distant education website, and closed-circuit television) in each classroom. Students from diverse backgrounds, from working class, farming peasants, and wealthy families attend this secondary school.

Confronted with new types of students with diverse backgrounds in the branch campus, Liu developed *success education* in a new way. He explained that:

> The more research I have done, the more I found that there are obvious advantages to both the Eastern and Western educational systems. Eastern education pays more attention to knowledge learning while Western education pays more attention to ability acquisition. Western education's merits are Eastern education's shortcomings, or vice versa. Therefore, to find out and locate the point of balance between knowledge learning and ability acquisition is the key. Apparently, the convergence of Eastern and Western education is the general trend in the 21st century. For this reason, I would like to combine the best of both systems in my schools in the future.

Thus, in the branch campus, to meet the new challenges, Liu has since 2001 promoted these ideas—"The integration of knowledge, ability, and personality" and "The integration of Eastern and Western education" as his new educational goals as well as the goals for the further development of *success education* reform. The purpose of the new strategy is to facilitate students' simultaneous development of knowledge, ability, and personality in the globalization era.

"How can these ideas be implemented? What is the connection with *success education* reform?" I asked Liu during an interview. He told me about the three phases of *success education*: (1) The first phase is characterized by teachers helping with students a lot so that they achieve success; (2) the second stage is with less assistance from teachers students try to achieve success by themselves; and (3) the third stage is students become self-mastery learners and achieve success for themselves. The third phase is the ultimate goal of the reform. However, between the first and the third phases, there was a bridge to build. Liu described that, at the beginning stage of the reform, the major task the school was facing was how teachers could help students experience success. After three years' practice, Liu and the research group found that if the teachers helped too much, students would just rely on the help and did not want to give a try to achieve success by themselves. Therefore, Liu designed the second phase in which teachers were asked to give less aid but focus on creating circumstances and asking stimulating questions to make students join in the process of learning actively. In the branch school, the reform is still at the second phase of the reform. Therefore, combining the strength of Western education and emphasizing the cultivation of ability on top of the Chinese education advantage was assumed as powerful ways to achieve the third phase of the reform.

It is still too early to say if the reform is successful or not in its third stage since it needs to take a long time to measure the results. During my interview, some teachers held a different opinion that today in the new branch school it is not *success education* that is being carried out any more, since not all the students come from poor families and the community is not as poor as well. However, Liu said that the idea and methodology of *success education* are still used in the branch campus. Also, they have 30% of students from wealthy families around the country who do not want to study at all. Thus, *success education* is facing a new challenge: How can it help those "at-risk" students from wealthy families? That is also a national issue in China with the rapid increase of overall national wealth and the appearance of an upper class. In fact, *success education* is facing many other challenges as well. I will discuss them in the following chapters.

CHAPTER 6

MULTIPLE LEVELS OF LEADERSHIP SUPPORT AND THE CRUCIAL ROLES OF PRINCIPAL LIU JINGHAI

As mentioned before, instead of piecemeal reform, success education is a whole school program. Ahead of the nation, Shanghai conducted research-based reforms as early as June 1986. Success education is the product of this reform. In this chapter, I will use CSR model to interpret the No. 8 School's reform, aiming at exploring how the program has been implemented, the pattern this school-wide reform carries, and the problems and challenges the school has met with.

THE ROLE OF THE GOVERNMENTS IN SUCCESS EDUCATION REFORM

Research shows that leadership is the key to achieve the successful implementation of comprehensive school reform (Murphy & Datnow, 2003). Without exception, success education is a result of cooperation of Shanghai municipal government, the Zhabei District government, and No. 8 School at three levels. The governments at district and city levels of Shanghai played a very important role in the reform of No. 8 School. The central government also paid attention to promoting success education as a model of successful education reforms around the country. In the following section, I will examine the role played by the governments at district, city, and state levels and their impacts on success education reform.

At the District Level

At the district level, the first priority for the Zhabei government was to improve at-risk schools during the mid-1980s. This priority was set at the beginning of China's economic reform in order to catch with up the fast economic growth in Shanghai. As mentioned previously, due to historical reasons, the residents' educational level in the Zhabei District was the lowest in Shanghai before the reform. In the late 1970s, among 35 middle schools there were 12, or one-third, at-risk schools in Zhabei area with less than 30% of students passing the qualification exams for compulsory education.[1] Among the lowest quality schools, only six students out of 100 students met the criteria of compulsory education. Facing a large number of at-risk students, Mr. Huang, the director of EBZD, said that at that time we had no choice but to reform education to change our schools for the better. Therefore, the Zhabei District government attempted to enhance the quality of education among at-risk schools as early as 1979. To provide equal opportunity for all students, they abolished key primary schools and key middle schools in the district in 1980. From 1985 to 1987, to implement The Regulation on Universalizing Compulsory Education in Shanghai issued by the municipal government in 1985, and the Compulsory Education Law enacted by the central government in 1986, the Zhabei District government adopted several essential strategies on helping at-risk schools and at-risk students as follows.

First, EBZD made a clear and firm decision that EBZD will give preference to at-risk schools and will never give up on a single school; the school will give preferential treatment to at-risk students and will never give up on a single student. It called for administrators, educators, and parents to love, care, and help those low performance schools and disadvantaged students.

Second, to strengthen the leadership of at-risk schools, EBZD selected outstanding teachers from key schools and assigned them as principals to work in those schools. Also, for the first time EBZD organized principals from those 12 middle schools and sent them to other high performance schools for observation and training, with the aim of improving their leadership skills. Liu Jinghai was assigned to study in Shanghai Normal University at that time to get his second BA degree.

Third, the Zhabei District government appropriated money to these twelve at-risk schools to improve their teaching equipment. Each school received 30,000 yuan, a significant amount in 1980s, to establish and upgrade its physics, chemistry, and biology labs. This amount of money could also be invested to purchase textbooks, study materials, and computers.

Fourth, in 1985 EBZD established the Association of Twelve At-risk Schools, as mentioned above, under the leadership of Liu Jinghai. The association set up a time schedule to organize various activities such as they had teachers to conduct class observations, and the schools gathered together discussing common issues and problems they were facing, exchanging effective experiences in teaching, learning, and management. In 1987, after these strategies had been implemented for two years, the twelve schools had made great progress. The rate of students passing the qualification exams for the compulsory education had been increased from less than 30% to 85% among those schools. Some schools shed their names of being at-risk schools. This positive result encouraged Liu Jinghai who initiated *success education* in 1987.

Becoming a partner of the reform, EBZD made commitment on participative management of the project during the initial stage. It appointed Liu Jinghai as the experimental group leader and assigned another eight researchers and faculty from the Teaching and Research Group, Middle School Teaching Group, Moral Education Group of EBZD as well as from Zhabei Normal College to join the experimental team in No. 8 School. Working together, they defined crucial problems, set up reform goals, and spelled out the rules. After three years of hard work, the program achieved great success. Students' academic achievement improved markedly.

After 1990 *success education* began to be expanded. How did EBZD continue to support the reform when this three-year program finished? I asked Mr. Huang during the interview. He told me that,

> Since the first stage of success education produced positive results, we decided to extend the experiment to the whole No. 8 School and other schools in the Zhabei area. We promoted success education by three ways: First, we held a series of meetings to call for schools in the district to learn from No. 8 School. Second, we made the policy to encourage all of our schools to follow the example and conduct this kind of research-based reform. Third, we designed and offered a number of success education courses in Zhabei Normal College to train principals and teachers from other schools in the district.

What are the results? I asked curiously. Mr. Huang described that although most schools in this area have not exactly followed the *success education* model, they have run their own research-based reforms according to their school's needs. They may call them encouragement education, affective education, creative education, positive thinking education, self-mastery education, or other names. However, the core ideas of those reforms were drawn from *success education* and the ultimate goal was to make students successful.

Mr. Huang gave me some figures to indicate the impact of the *success education* model on school improvement in the district. He said that Zhabei used to be the most educationally backward district in Shanghai. However, led by the example of *success education*, schools in the district have all carried out various kinds of education reforms since the 1990s. As a result, the level of education in the district has been enhanced tremendously. For example, the enrollment in nine-year compulsory education has reached 100%. The rate of students getting into higher education in the area had increased from 20%–30% in 1984–85, to 85.3% in 2003. For their schools' dramatic turnaround, the Zhabei District was given the "two-basics advancement award" by Shanghai government in 1997, recognizing that the district had gone ahead of others in universalizing nine years basic compulsory education, and in basically wiping out illiteracy among its youth.

The support from the district government for the reform also can be seen in its willingness to give more autonomy to the school in management, teacher training and promotion, curriculum design, choice of textbooks, and student recruitment. For example, compared to other schools in Shanghai, No. 8 School can recruit students nationally. These autonomies not only increases the school's influence in the country, but also increases the school's revenue for it can charge tuition and fees to students from outside Shanghai. The Principal also can recruit teachers from around the country while most other schools in Shanghai at that time could not. The school is allowed to use the mathematic textbooks edited by themselves.

At the City Level

During the city rapid process of modernization, the city government of Shanghai realized that with only one-third of its schools qualified for compulsory education[2] in the 1970s to 1980s, the Zhabei area, the poorest part of the city, had seriously hindered the overall level of economic development in Shanghai. Therefore, the city government paid much attention to Zhabei's education development ever since the 1980s. By giving more power to the Zhabei District government, the municipal government encouraged the local district to initiate alternative approaches to improve at-risk students' education. In 1987, the Shanghai Municipal Committee for Education (SMCE) approved Liu Jinghai's research-based reform proposal. That is the initiation of *success education*. During the implementation of the reform, SMCE has given active support for the program.

Mr. Zhang, the former deputy director of Shanghai Education Commission, director-general of the Shanghai Association of Education, gave his full support for the reform and recalled during our interview:

> During the 1980s–1990s, Shanghai was getting into the stage of popularizing nine years' compulsory education. In my understanding, compulsory education is not just obligation education, more important, it is education which should be suitable for every child. Therefore, when I first heard about success education experiment from a moral education meeting at the city level, I realized that this was a meaningful exploration on improving at-risk students and very helpful to universalizing nine years compulsory education in Shanghai. Thus, we held a special meeting in Shanghai and decided to promote No. 8 School's reform. After that, we run a series of citywide and countrywide research conferences on success education in the Zhabei District to fully support this new education reform.

Under strong support from the SMCE, the EBZD held two national conferences on *success education* respectively in 1993 and 2000, receiving 122 papers and publishing 107 papers in professional journals. They also published 14 books on the reform. Some stories have been written as novels and a 7-series TV play. Also, supported by funding from the SMCE, the Shanghai Institute of Success Education was established in 1997, located in No. 8 School. Its journal, *Success Education Research*, publishes teachers' research papers on their teaching experience, learning, and class management using the principles of *success education*, aimed at facilitating teachers' professional development.

At the State Level

The result of *success education* had even attracted attention of the Chinese central government. In the summer of 1994, after listening to the report about *success education* at a meeting attended by leaders from provincial bureaus of education, the Vice Prime Minister of China, Li Lanqing, made a speech and called for all schools in the country to learn from No. 8 School. In the same year, the Vice Director of State Education Commission (SEC), Liu Bing, visited No. 8 School several times and acknowledged the achievements made by the school. In 1995, *success education* was promoted by SEC as a successful education reform model to the country. Under such a strong support, *success education* reached its peak in 1996, attracting educators from the country and other countries. In September 1997, Director of SEC, Chen Zhili, also visited No. 8 School and pointed out that *success education* represented a new and significant step toward Chinese educational reforms.

THE CRUCIAL ROLE OF PRINCIPAL LIU JINGHAI

Research shows that the principal is viewed as a primary agent of change (Fullan, 1992). During the investigation, I found that Principal Liu Jinghai, who created, led, and persisted in success education, is the heart of No. 8 School reform. If one wants to study success education, he or she cannot ignore this single, most important person. Thus, in this part of my research, first I would like to examine Liu's background for initiating the reform. Then, I will explore his thoughts on, actions of, and strategies for the reform. The feedback from people will be discussed as well.

Background

Why did Liu Jinghai initiate *success education*? In my research, I find the motivation behind is not only the need for school changes in the Zhabei District during the mid-1980s, but also related to his own unique experience. Liu has spent more than twenty years at No. 8 School since 1980, serving as vice principal, researcher, and finally principal in March 1994. The reason he created the *success education* experiment to facilitate at-risk students could directly be related to his job experience as an educator. Since 1974 Liu has been working in underperforming schools in the Zhabei District right after his graduation from East China Normal University. In his daily work, he had been busy dealing with many at-risk students.

A story about one of his students could be seen as a catalyst for his decision to devote the major part of his life to improving at-risk students. During the period from 1980–1983 when he was the vice principal of No. 8 School, he had a student who impressed him with his politeness. Liu had several very nice conversations with the student and felt he was an active and smart student. However, one day he was shocked by bad news: This student was sentenced to death by the local court because he was found guilty of murder. After investigation, Liu learned that the student's father had died when he was very young. He lived in poverty with his mother. Liu felt that poor home background and

Photo 6.1 Principal Liu Jinghao (photo provided by No. 8 School).

lack of attention from home and school were the major causes behind the reason why the student committed the crime. Liu thought that this tragedy was the result from the failure of the traditional education model. Why does our exam-oriented education system only allow a small number of students at the top to succeed while making most other students to fail? He felt strongly that he had to do something to help those problem students.

Another factor that influenced Liu's interest in improving the educational experience for at-risk students can be traced to his beneficial experience obtained from his two elementary teachers. He was a clever but naughty boy in his primary days. As a fast learner, he began to make trouble in the classroom after he quickly understood the points the teacher was teaching. He even made some teachers cry because they could not continue their class due to Liu's mischievousness. However, there were two teachers who were very original in dealing with his problems. Ms. Wang gave him a picture-story book to read just before he started to be troublesome during the class. He was attracted by those interesting stories and the class could continue smoothly. When he was in 5th and 6th grade, another teacher, Ms. Yang, assigned him to take responsibility for painting pictures for the class' newspaper and through this helped him to be more patient. This was an honor job for students and to draw better, he set out to work very hard and drew very carefully. Through this experience, he became a good student willing to service the class and became very enthusiastic about learning. These experiences illuminated him, in a sense, to teach students in different ways according to their different characteristics.

In 1983, in order to do more research on this worldwide issue of school failure, he went to the Department of Education Administration of Shanghai Normal University to get his second bachelor's degree. During his two-year study, he concentrated on the solutions to helping academically failing students and collected data about this problem.

In 1985 Liu was appointed as the Vice Director of the Department of Teaching and Research of Education Bureau of the Zhabei District in charge of 12 at-risk schools in this area. After two years, he became the Director of the Department, continuing his work to improve at-risk schools. Based on the study and investigation he had done for years, in January 1987 Liu submitted his research proposal, later developed as the program of *success education*, to SMCE. Under the city and local governments' active support, Liu started his journey to reform No. 8 School by applying *success education* in 1987.

Thoughts, Actions, Strategies and Challenges

During my investigation in No. 8 School, I had two interviews with Principal Liu Jinghai, each lasted two to three hours. Drawing from my interviews and other collected documents, we can see how and what Principal Liu has done to innovate the school program.

According to Liu, as a principal, there are several things he has to do if he wants to successfully conduct a school-wide reform. First, he has to form a profound philosophy on the rationale and missions of running and reforming a school in accordance with the features of this school; second, he needs to be informed of educational reform in a globalization era. More important, he has to turn them into common goals among all staff and get them all to commit themselves to the new visions. Further, he has to enhance the quality of teachers greatly to meet the needs of the change. Finally, he has to not only have a vision on the trend of curriculum innovation but also promote curricular and instruction reform.

Specifically, he told me that:

> As a principal the most important thing is that he has to be in the forefront of the whole education science in today's reform era. He must have an insight into the development of the whole society and the role of education toward the future. He must be willing to take the lead to reform. To do so, he has to continuously study education theories, analyze ongoing educational practices, and think about ways to help the school, teachers, and students to improve. He also needs to design a model of reform that is suitable for the school. Only in this way can teachers potentials be developed and the reform be carried to a higher level.

After making a decision to change, the next step is to select the area for reform. Thus, I asked Liu, "Why did you choose at-risk student education as your research topic?" His response was:

> I found helping at-risk students is a meaningful subject to research. As we have known that the issue of at-risk students is a worldwide issue. Based on my research, even many advanced countries such as the United States, Canada, Japan, and England, have a high rate of at-risk students. Although nations in the world have made great efforts to help at-risk students, successful stories are few. In China, because of the problems generated by the exam-oriented system, most scholars and educators focused just on the top students. I was the first person who conducted a project of helping at-risk students within the country in the mid-1980s. This is really a pioneer research and reform. Just like love is an eternal topic in arts, improving at-risk students is an eternal topic in education. I love this career and have a passion on helping those children.

Liu's remark indicates that a principal's vision, aspiration, and enthusiasm are critical to achieve the success of a comprehensive school reform.

Liu was 44 years old when he became the Principal of No. 8 School in 1994. He promised his staff that he was planning to put all his energy for the next 16 years on *success education* before he retired at 60 years of age. According to his staff, Liu not only just said it, he earnestly practiced what he advocated. He worked extremely hard and put all his life into the reform, Chen (2003) wrote in his book, *Liu Jinghai and Success Education*, that Liu might have this or that shortcomings as an ordinary person in daily life, however, as a principal, what he thinks about all the time is school improvement and he sacrificed himself to help students make progress (pp. 13–14).

In his book, Chen gave several moving stories about Liu. For example, at the beginning of the reform, Liu worked so hard that he often forgot to pick up his little daughter who was in kindergarten. Always the last one to be picked up, his daughter was scared and cried very hard. The teachers in the kindergarten did not believe that Liu was her real father. Other stories were recorded as well: One year, instead of celebrating the Chinese New Year with his own family, Liu visited at-risk students' families and spent time with them. Liu persisted on working and teaching when he was ill with a high fever. Although suffering from several diseases such as urgent nephritis, duodenal ulcer, erosion gastritis, and high blood pressure, etc., he never thought about himself and worked very hard.... Many moving stories like this were told by teachers, students, and parents during my interviews.

"How many hours did you usually work a day during the early stage of the reform?" I asked. Liu told me that it is hard to say. At the first stage, he was the Director of the Department of Teaching and Research of EBZD while he also conducted *success education* in No. 8 School. Working on two jobs and assuming two leadership roles, he had a very heavy work loads:

> As a Director, I was in charge of the standard tests of Chinese, Mathematics, and English in the district, including test design, assessment, and analysis. It was a lot of work. In my other spare time, I was responsible for success education reform in No. 8 School. During those days, I often went back home very late and had no weekend. Since the reform occupied all my time, I could not take care of my wife and daughter and do my duty at home. I got into conflicts with my wife for a while. Of course, eventually she understood me and supported me.

Liu's dedication set up a good example for his staff, teachers, students and parents. That eventually helped him to implement many measures for the success of the reform.

"What are the main strategies you have used to promote the school reform?" I asked. He answered that although there were many strategies, they can be summarized as three aspects: helping teachers, helping students, and helping parents to achieve success. These three aspects are an interlocking network. Lacking any one part, the reform cannot succeed.

104   *Success for All*

For example, Liu believed only when teachers achieve high standards in their professional development can students' academic performance be improved. This was the key to and the prerequisite for students' success and the school's success. Therefore, a school should first become a place in which teachers can achieve success in their career and their life. As a result, Liu gave top priority to teachers' training. Helping teachers to be successful is a principal's required duty, Liu said. In so doing, many strategies have been initiated by Liu to improve teachers' professional development. More details will be explored later.

Harboring a big dream Liu wanted to run a school in China in which all staff, teachers, and students can achieve success. All those aspects are very important factors in the successful implementation of an educational reform.

"What are the main challenges you were facing when you implemented *success education*?" I then asked. "I was facing a lot of challenges," Liu said, "however, the main challenges for me were two: one was from my work and another one was from my research."

With respect to work, according to Liu, the most difficult time was the beginning of the second stage of the experiment after 1990. At the first stage, the experiment was implemented only in two classes. However, three years later, because of positive outcomes from the reform, the experiment had been expanded to include the whole school. The first major challenge faced by Liu was how to educate all his staff and the teachers to accept the idea of *success education*. Another difficulty Liu was coping with was financial problems. Because of decentralization of educational funding as we have discussed previously, the city government had reduced its investment in the schools. Liu had to find the resources to support his school. To generate money, Liu ran factories, opened stores, and sold breads, steamed stuffed buns, spring water, etc. Liu said:

> In order to get enough money to pay teachers' premium, I sold spring water on the street under the scorching sun, earning merely 0.20 yuan per bottle. In all, I did struggle very hard to solve many problems on my own. Sometimes, I felt upset and sorrow for myself. However, I never thought of giving it up.

As to the challenge in research, what Liu thought of the most was how to make a breakthrough in this experiment. Liu recalled:

> Every time when I could not figure out what to do, I would be lost in thought for a long time to think of all possibilities. For example, to identify a theme for the experiment, I pondered so deeply that my nervous system was not normal for half a year and I could not clearly comprehend what people said when they talked with me. Eventually, I found every strategy we had adopted

was linked to helping students to experience success. Thus, we summarized our reform as success education.

According to Liu and the research group, there are three phases of *success education*: The first stage, to help students experience success; the second stage, to get students to try to succeed; and the third stage, to help students master learning skills to make themselves successful. At every stage, Liu put in a lot of energy and time to find the logical link to connect all elements of the reform. Especially, Liu said, the second phase, to get the student to try to succeed, is a bridge to connect the first and the third stage. It is a very important concept for *success education* in both theory and practice. I will examine this issue in a future chapter.

Transforming the School Culture

The literature on school culture makes it clear that school culture and climate are essential to achieve school success (Mackenzie, 1983). A principal plays a central role in shaping and reconstructing school culture. Leithwood and Janzti (1990) also state that the successful principals can effectively improve the school culture. In my research, I found that Liu is the person who changed his school culture by discarding old values and beliefs of No. 8 School as a low performance school which was full of failing students. In order to establish a new culture of success and confidence, Liu defined his school culture as a "dreamy culture," an "introspective culture," and an "open-minded and lenient culture." Reflecting upon the implementation of the idea of *success education* over the years, he realized that to successfully implement the reform, the school has to develop these three elements of school culture as a well-defined set of goals for all members of the school to value, promote, and follow.

Specifically, he explained why his school culture consists of three elements. "Dreamy culture" means that we have to help teachers and students set up a big goal to be successful in life. A confident person is a person full of dreams. Only when one has dreams and ideals can he or she change himself or herself, and eventually the classroom dynamic with these students are changed.

"Introspective culture" refers to helping teachers and students reflect on their actions and discover the problems they need to improve. Liu said:

> Since reform is always a new thing, it is inevitable for people to make mistakes. However, if we reflect often, we can modify our mistakes in time. In that way, we can make progress every day and our school can be improved continuously.

The purpose of "open-minded and lenient culture," Liu explained, is to create a harmonious learning environment for teachers and students. He stated:

> The process of reform is full of difficulties and we are facing many challenges. Only when we have an open and lenient mind, can we learn from each other, support each other, and help each other. Under these circumstances, we can achieve success for both individuals and the school.

By having worked on the improvement of the school culture for nearly twenty years, students in today No. 8 School did not feel ashamed of themselves any more. During my interview, I found that students who have graduated from the school and those who are still in school, are both very proud of their school. Also, the teachers who are working in the school were no longer looked down upon by people. Rather, they find it easy to find a job in other schools if they want to move. From this phenomenon, one may say that principal Liu's conceptualization and putting into practice of a unique and powerful school culture provide a positive environment for the reform.

Feedback from the Teachers, Students, and Parents

Research reveals that the principal as an active and ongoing supporter as well as the collaborative leader is the key to the reform (Datnow & Castellano, 2001; Fullan, 1992). How has Principal Liu Jinghai been viewed and accepted? With this question, I explored Liu's image in people's minds in the school. Most people including staff, teachers, students, and parents answered yes to the question that asked whether their principal was a good leader. The following data is based on my interview.

"What do you think about Principal Liu as a school leader and a reformer?" I asked.

Ms. Jin, the vice principal, who had worked with Liu for four years, responded:

> Liu has very strong character. He is a person who dares to think, dares to speak and dares to act. He has done many things which people thought were impossible. That is why our reform is still ongoing today.

"What are the impossible things done by Liu? Would you please give me some examples?" I am curious.

Jin described,

> For example, in order to reform our traditional teaching method and catch up with the advanced technology in the classroom, Liu promoted teachers to use a computer and powerpoint to give their lessons to students. Under our circumstance, it was deemed impossible because our teachers for their lifetime had given their lectures to students by blackboard and chalk. They never touched a computer. How could they do a powerpoint? They were so scared of Liu's reform. However, Liu only used six months to train our teachers. Right now there is a computer in every classroom and two thirds of teachers are enjoying powerpoint teaching. Is that incredible?

Ms. Lou, a head teacher, who took part in *success education* reform since the beginning, said:

> I admired Liu very much. He has been working for the school and for success education conscientiously all the time. You never know how difficult it is for Liu to persist in the reform. Some people misunderstood him, others swore at him and contradicted him. However, Liu never cared about what people said about him and tried to overcome all the barriers on the way to reform. He strongly believed that whatever he has done is just for the benefit of the children.

Ms. Zhou, the director of the department of logistics, who has had experience in working in both an old and new schools since 1994, commented:

> Liu loves at-risk students and cares for them very much. He thought this world is not fair that some children can live in wealthy families while many children live in poverty in Zhabei distract. Although we cannot change the environment, we can change children's fate through success education. Liu tried very hard to make his dream come to true. He has indeed changed many children's destinies in this school, especially those disadvantaged children. For that, many people, in particular those students' parents, were full of gratitude for Liu. He is a great educator, I truly believe. His thoughts and reform are very helpful and efficient for the working class children. Success education made at-risk students believe that they can change their future through studying hard. That is very meaningful.

As to students and parents, Mr. Chu, a student who graduated from the school in 1996, and his father Mr. Chu Hujian, a worker from Shanghai Bike Factory, impressed me very much. The father told me that his son used to be an at-risk student with a very bad academic record and serious behavioral problems. He failed many subjects while in primary school. No school was willing to keep him. He was arrested by the police because he smashed a big glass door of a public building before he went to No. 8 School. The father recalled:

Before No. 8 school, my son Qingshen studied in another district in Shanghai. I was so worried about him since he was not a good student in school. The teachers phoned me all the time to report his bad behaviors. I was scared to pick up the phone. When I heard success education, I decided to transfer my son to No. 8 School and give it a try. After my son went to No. 8 School, Principal Liu talked with Qingshen once a month and encouraged him whenever he made any progress. Also, he encouraged me to have confidence in Qingshen every time I met him at parents meeting.

Through teachers' hard work, Qingshen made progress very quickly. Under Liu's and other teachers' help, he passed the entrance exam and was accepted into the Shanghai Police Officer School after he graduated from No. 8 School. Now a police officer, he is enjoying his career and life. "I am a beneficiary of *success education*. I really appreciate Liu reform," he said.

"Studying in No. 8 School is a turning point of my life," Qingshen told me:

If I continued to study in my previous school, my life might be totally different. Today, I am a police officer who is in charge of taking over prisoners. Without success education, maybe I am the prisoner who is put under surveillance. Moreover, I am using the idea of success education to encourage prisoners and they made progress every day. I am very happy about that. I am grateful for success education to give me an entirely new life.

In terms of his relationship with teachers, many teachers told me that Liu always pays attention to his staff's benefits and needs. He cares for every staff member very much. Ms. Lou said:

For example, from time to time Liu asked for information about the staff's needs: Whose child needs help from the school? Whose child has not found a job, or might need help? Whose family members are ill in the hospital? ... Any kind of needs, if Liu can help, he will put his full energy to do it.

However, some teachers felt pressure to work in the schools because Liu always pushed them to go forward and continuously learn new things. No matter what people think about Liu, one thing is in common, that is, all the interviewees thought Liu did a good thing helping at-risk students. In summary, Liu plays an essential role in the whole process of initiating and implementing the experiment.

FORMING A RESOURCEFUL AND SUPPORTIVE MANAGEMENT SYSTEM

My data reveals that although leadership at all levels, especially at the school level, to a great extent, determines whether change is blocked or

Multiple Levels of Leadership Support and the Crucial Roles of Principal Liu Jinghai **109**

promoted, the reform design cannot be implemented without a strong supportive, cooperative school management system. Therefore, in this section of my research, I will examine how the school management system collaborated to implement the reform model after it was put into effect by the principal.

First, let's look at the management system of No. 8 School (Figure 6.1).

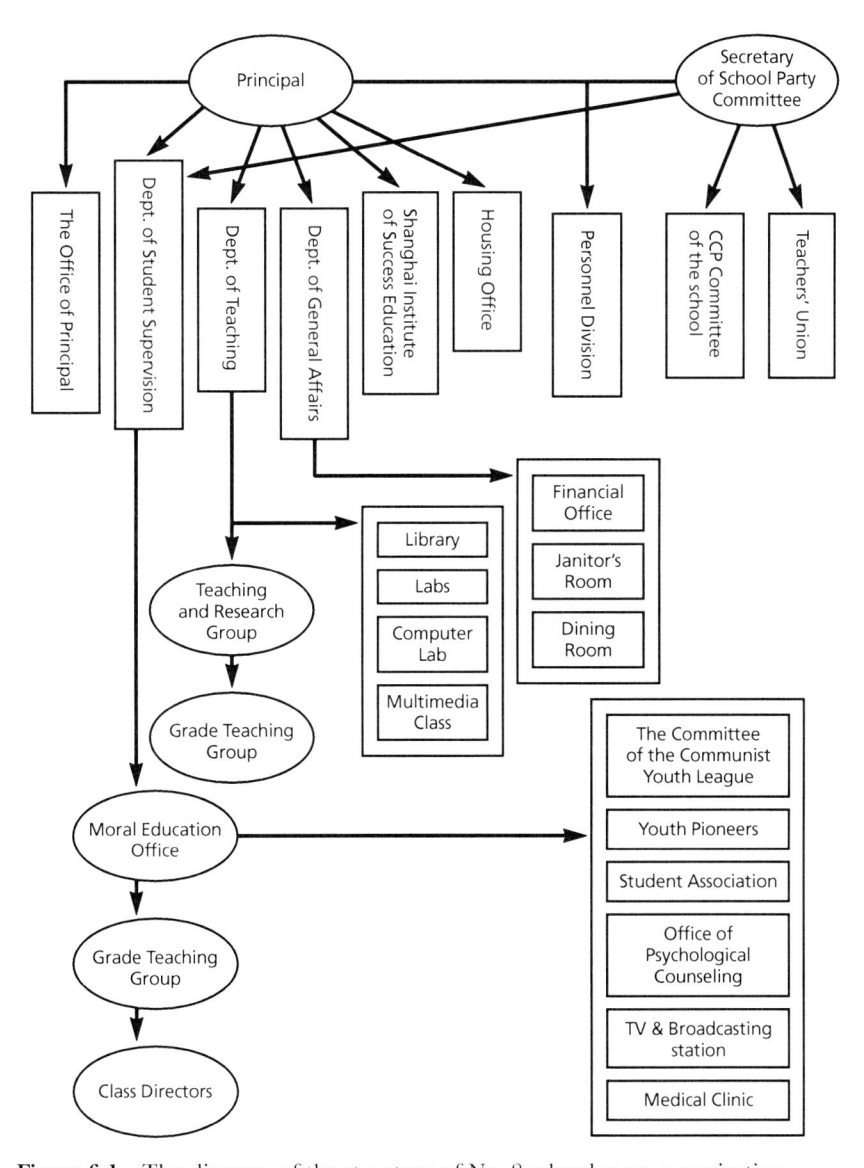

Figure 6.1 The diagram of the structure of No. 8 school as an organization.

From Figure 6.1, one can see that No. 8 School carries out a principal's responsibility system, meaning the principal takes full responsibility for the school's management, teaching, and learning. The school leadership team consists of principal Liu, the two vice principals—one is responsible for teaching and another is responsible for general affairs, and the secretary of the CCP committee of the school who is in charge of teachers and students' ideological work. Under the principal's leadership, the middle level leadership is composed of directors of different departments such as the Office of the Principal, Department of Student Supervision, Department of Teaching, and Department of General Affairs, etc. These two levels of leadership form a network and play a very important role in implementing the reform.

How could Liu and the research group shape a shared goal of *success education* and bring the two levels of leaders to make a commitment on the reform? Liu explained that the first thing they did was to help school administrators build up three beliefs:

1. Believe that every teacher has the potential to succeed;
2. Believe that every teacher has a desire to be successful;
3. Believe that every teacher can achieve success in many aspects.

With these "three beliefs," the administrators of the school are made to understand that the purpose of school management is to facilitate every teacher to be successful and eventually help every student achieve success in their study and life.

Under this guideline, they had conducted all kinds of activities to help teachers be successful. For example, the school Party committee offered a program called "Everybody Striving to Become a Successful Star" among members of the Chinese Communist Party (CCP) in the school. In this program, the committee designed a form which helped teachers find their own strong points by designing a three-year self-development plan. In the form, every teacher is urged to find his/her own merits, shortcomings, potential merits, potential shortcomings, and new growth point. After submitting their forms, the committee holds a CCP member's meeting to have a group discussion on these forms one by one. Through the group discussion, the committee helps every teacher design his/her three-year personal development plan. To support this activity, the school evaluates the teacher every six months. Based on the assessment, the teacher who made progress would be rewarded.

To set up a motivational mechanism in the school, Liu and his team reformed the salary and personnel system. Aimed at stimulating teachers' enthusiasm with *success education*, the school leaders altered the salary system by giving mobile salary to award those teachers who make more progress in their teaching and more contributions to the school. This policy broke the rule of "everyone eating in a big bowl," a policy of egalitarianism which had been carried out since the 1950s to pay all people the same amount regardless of their efforts and abilities. To implement this policy, the school evaluates teachers once a semester, based on both students' and parents' surveys on their satisfaction with the teachers' performance. These efforts aim to establish a fair system for the teachers and to inspire them to work hard to help bring success to the experiment.

As for the personnel system, the school advertises job openings around the country in order to hire the best teachers possible. To motivate teachers, the school has reset the rule of promotion. According to the new rule, the teachers who are not qualified will be moved from a higher level to a lower level of professional position,[3] based on their performance. In this way, teachers were encouraged to continue to improve themselves and work more efficiently.

During my investigation, I had a chance to attend school administrative meetings in both the old and new campuses. That provided important experience which helped me understand what was the way the principal communicated with his subordinates and how the school system functioned. Usually, once every other week the principal calls an administrative meeting. Besides using the occasion to convey directives passed down from various levels of government, the main purpose of the meetings is for administrators to report school work, identify existing problems, find solutions to the problems, and discuss short term and long term future plans.

Here I would like to describe an administrative meeting which was held on April 30, 2004 as an example to illustrate how the school leadership worked and in what way they collaborated. Lasting two and a half hours from 9:00 a.m. to 11:30 a.m., the subject of the meeting was about teaching reform. For the first part of the meeting, all middle level leaders from the departments reported their work and presented a number of problems existing among the students. In the second part, school leaders including the secretary of the school Party committee and the two vice principals described what they were doing and what should be done in the future. For instance, Ms. Li, the secretary of the school Party committee mentioned how several class directors (*Banzhuren*) who are teachers in charge of all aspects of students' learning and life besides teaching had come together and shared their experiences on how to help at-risk students by overcoming many difficulties.

Finally, spending one hour, Principal Liu summarized the meeting and gave guidelines for the future. He emphasized the importance of reforming the classroom and enhancing the quality of teaching. He suggested that the head of the Teaching Department should seek out those teachers who have excelled in their work and analyze their experience and at the same time figure out where problems persist. To improve at-risk students' academic achievement, Liu especially stressed that it was essential to cultivate their good study habits and maintain discipline in the classroom. The school should establish a system that after every examination, the teachers would analyze the results of the test and find out where students had done well and where there were problems. Liu paid a lot of attention to promoting powerpoint lessons to the classrooms for the following semester. He planned to invest money in the summer to encourage teachers to learn how to use technology in the classroom. Liu even discussed with his colleagues on how effective teachers could use powerpoint to design a circumstance for students to learn from the very beginning of a class, how the teacher should ask questions to his/her students during the class, and how to predict students' reaction at the end. The meeting ended with a clear expectation for all as to what they should do. I felt this was a very productive meeting.

In summary, *Success education* is a product which has been jointly designed and support by Shanghai governments at all levels. It aimed to meet the need of educational reforms toward universalizing nine-year compulsory education and carrying out quality education in China and Shanghai broadly. It is clear Shanghai city government has made efforts to create an open environment, provide guidelines and financial support for the experiment to come into being and succeed. The district government gave an active support by participating in the reform as a partner, through organizing a research team and providing funding for the reform. Without the support from the various levels of governments, the reform could not have been implemented, not to say to have significant success. However, it is clear Principal Liu played an essential, pivotal role in the reform. He initiated the reform, led the experiment, and has been putting his heart and soul into improving and developing the program. Liu's ambition, determination, hard work and carefully crafted strategies to build a school culture of success, to motivate teachers, to be innovative in teaching approaches, demonstrated that he has functioned as a primary agent of change. Under Liu's leadership, the collaboration of school management system provided a supportive resource for the success of the reform.

NOTES

1. According to the regulation on education in Shanghai, a student must meet the following requirements to be allowed to graduate from middle school: (1) finish four years schooling, starting from 6th grade; (2) pass the examinations of all subjects (over 60 for each subject), or mainly pass Chinese, Math, and English with a maximum of two other subjects below 60; and (3) pass the moral education evaluation and have good behavior. These requirements are also the basic criteria of compulsory education.

2. The Ministry of Education of the People Republic of China stipulates that the qualifications of universalizing nine years compulsory education in urban areas should reach the following rates before 2000: (1) 100% of the rate of enrollment of both primary and middle school; (2) Below 1% and 2% of the rate of dropouts in primary and middle school; (3) Ninety-eight percent of the rate of graduation from middle school among students at age 15; (4) the rate of illiteracy among 15-year-old students should be controlled within 1%; (5) more than 90% primary teachers and 80% middle school teachers should meet the required education levels; and (6) the principal should be trained and certified.
3. In the middle school in Shanghai, there are three levels of professional title: preliminary, middle, and advanced. The qualifications for three levels of position are as follows: (1) the preliminary level of teaching title: one year teaching experience after graduating from college and passing the school evaluation. (2) the middle level of teaching title: becoming the preliminary level teacher for four years, undergraduate or equivalent diplomas, good quality in teaching, 2–4 years experience as a class director, two academic paper publications at the school and district level, and at least one public class. (3) the advanced level of teaching title: five years experience as a teacher in the middle level, passing the unified English and computer tests offered by the city government; more than three article publications in professional journals at city level, outstanding teaching performance, and a key teacher in the field.

CHAPTER 7

PROFESSIONAL DEVELOPMENT IN *SUCCESS EDUCATION* MODEL

Professional development is regarded as the key to achieving school success since teachers play a central role in student learning in the classroom. In No. 8 School reform, success education demands a dramatic shift of teaching from a traditional way to an alternative way that can improve students' individual and specific strengths. Therefore, the school leaders rated professional growth as the most valuable work to do during the whole process of the reform.

As mentioned before, located in a high-poverty area, one of the toughest tasks for the school to face at the beginning of *success education* reform was the poor quality of the teaching forces. Poverty and problems of the neighborhood district made it difficult for No. 8 School to hire high-quality teachers. Moreover, many good teachers in the school jumped to better places as soon as opportunities presented themselves. Having lost many good teachers, qualified teachers were often in short supply. Sometimes, 30% of the teachers in the school were borrowed from other schools. Most teachers could not meet the criteria of teacher qualification. In China, to be a middle school teacher, one has to graduate from a university with a BA degree or equivalent academic credentials. However, in 1987 only 80% of the teachers in No. 8 School were qualified. Among them, only 20%

graduated from university and 60% hardly met the teachers' qualification's through in-service training. No teachers of Chinese, math, and English, three core subjects, had university degrees. With only junior high and senior high education, the school's Chinese and English teachers eventually upgraded themselves and reached the teaching standard through on-job training. Moreover, the math teacher graduated from the Nanjing Agriculture College, majoring in veterinary medicine. In terms of professional titles, at that time in No. 8 School, none of the teachers had an "advanced teacher title," the highest among primary and secondary school teachers who are selected based on an outstanding teaching performance record. Sixty point eight percent of the teachers had the middle level teaching titles while 39.2% were in the entry level position. There was not a balance of senior, middle aged and young teachers, as only 23.9% of the teachers were less than 35 years old. This situation, to a great extent, seriously hindered the school improvement.

To facilitate teachers' professional development, the school adopted external and internal measures to provide ongoing learning opportunities for teachers. In terms of external measures, the school created a culture that values lifelong learning by encouraging its teachers to go back to school and obtain university degree or more advanced degree in their spare time. They called this kind of training "academic credentials training." Since 1996, the Shanghai municipal government required a teacher in the secondary schools to take 240 hours of class work in his/her field per five years in the District Normal College to get his/her middle-level professional title and 540 hours for his/her advanced level professional title, and this is dubbed "The 240 or 540 Training Program." This kind of training is related to teaching capacity training or professional promotion training. The courses offered by the District Normal College include new trends in teaching contents and methods in different fields, advanced teaching methods, and research methods etc. The school actively supported those teachers who were taking this kind of course by providing leave and tuition for them.

Mainly, teachers' professional training occurred within school, called "school-based training." Since 1987 when the reform started, the school leaders have been paying serious attention to creating the conditions for the continuous professional growth of teachers, and staff. The following are a number of strategies that were used.

SUCCESS EDUCATION THEORY AND METHODOLOGY TRAINING

Liu and the research group realized that the process of reform was in fact a process of transforming staff's values and concepts. Success education was a very new educational philosophy which attempts to dramatically shift the paradigm of traditional education. Unless the majority of teachers believe in and actively support success education, this school-wide reform effort would fail. All the teachers and staff must be involved in the experiment at the very beginning in the decision-making process. Only in that way can the school keep teachers focused on essential goals of the reform. Therefore, success education literacy training has been the first priority for professional training in the school, especially in the early stage of the reform.

To do so, school leaders were aware of the importance of changing teachers' concepts and attitude toward themselves and toward at-risk students. For a long time, teachers in No. 8 School felt inferior and shameful to work in this school ridden by a bad reputation of low achievement and students' disciplinary and criminal problems. Under this situation, many teachers had no motivation and passion to improve their teaching and tried to find other jobs. The teachers who stayed in the school were not because they were willing but they had no choice. Also, they had no confidence in students. Feeling hopeless, they generally thought that it was impossible to improve the academic achievement of those at-risk students. Failure had become the prevalent tone of the school culture and was deeply ingrained in the teachers' mind.

To achieve the reform goal, the school leaders made the decision to promote *success education* by rebuilding the teachers' mindset with a new spirit and culture. That is to say, the school would educate the teachers and staff in understanding the basic tenets of *success education* and help them to build up "three beliefs" as the essential principles of *success education*:

1. To believe that every student inherently wants to succeed;
2. To believe that every student has potential for success;
3. To believe that every student has the ability to be successful in many ways.

In order to create a climate of reform, school leaders conducted all kinds of activities to introduce the new educational approach to their teachers and staff. For example, the topics on how to integrate *success education* into student learning and teachers' teaching practice tended to be the major contents for weekly staff meetings. Seminars, symposiums, and conferences at district, city, and national levels were held to campaign for the experiment. They also ran classes during weekends and holidays to coach and train teacher, leaders and administrators.

More impressively, I found that all the departments of the school collaborated to make the reform effort a success. For example, in 1991 when the experiment was initiated in the whole school, the school Party committee held a school-wide discussion under the title of "*Success Education* and

Me" for two weeks. Through discussions, most teachers realized that since the first stage of the reform was successful, every teacher should be responsible for getting actively involved in the whole school's reform to make it a school-wide success. A survey showed that after all kinds of training, 89.4% of teachers regarded *success education* as the right direction for the school to take and it was necessary to be carried out.

Some teachers recalled that, at the climax of *success education*, namely the second stage, almost everyone and every department were actively involved in the reform. Mr. Chen (1993) who worked as a carpenter for the school, wrote of his experience:

> Our school is carrying out success education. All the work in school should provide service for success education teaching and learning. Therefore, I should involve myself in success education seriously. What can I do for the reform as a logistical worker? I found that desks and chairs in the classrooms have been worn and students' myopias have increased in recent years. I thought to myself, why don't I alter these desks and chairs to reduce the rate of children's myopias? ... to save money, I used the old desk as materials since our school is a poor school. After hard work, I finally designed and made new kinds of desks with chairs together for our students, replacing all the old desks and chairs. Not long after, I produced multiple functional office desks for our teachers. Everyone is very happy to use my production (pp. 47–49).

Those stories indicate that after school leaders' hard work for years, the idea of success education was becoming a shared goal among all staff and teachers and the idea of success for all has been transformed into a new school culture.

In 1997, under the support of both the district and the municipal governments, Shanghai Institute of *Success Education* was established in the school. The function of the Institute is to act as a teaching and research base to study the theory, methodology, and development of *success education* as well as to train teachers, staff, and administrators from its own school and other schools around the country by using the ideas of *success education*. So far, the institute has continuously given two courses—*the Theory and Practice of Success Education* and the *Teaching Models That Enhance Success*. The teaching materials of these two courses have been published in two books. Introducing the new educational reform comprehensively, the *success education* courses provide rich and in-depth content about the rationales, history, methodology, strategies, and evaluation of the experiment. Especially, the second book reflects on the new development of *success education* in instruction and curriculum reform.

It has been said that the courses are helpful and popular. In 1997, more than 230 teachers from No. 8 School and Tian Jia Bing Middle School attended the training courses. Up to 2003, the Institute had offered *success education* lessons to more than 1,000 teachers in its own school and the district as part of "The 240 Training Program," the required hours for professional training for teachers in Shanghai. Also, more than 40 principals and teachers from the country took these two courses. The feedback from attendees was quite positive.

MAKING DEVELOPMENTAL PLANS

The school works out a teacher development plan every three years and develops a special teacher training program. The first step of the training program was to help teachers make their own developmental plan. The school leaders contended that any good training program will not work well unless teachers are motivated. Also, the school leaders believe that the theory of success education can also be applied to teachers. It means that everyone can become a successful teacher. Liu and the research group organized the teachers to learn education theories, analyze their own teaching techniques, and share their successful teaching experiences. They conducted a program called "Everybody Striving to Become a Successful Star" to motivate teachers to participate in the reform. As mentioned in the previous chapter, this was an initiative for everyone from CCP members to every teacher and staff. Based on the personal developmental plan, the school leaders held group meetings to discuss everybody's plan, analyze his/her advantages and shortcomings, find the resources to support them and connect accountability to teachers' goal. Upon the personal developmental plan, the school will set up professional files to record the teachers' performance. A school-wide assessment takes place twice a year about the fulfillment of the teachers' plans. The assessment is linked to teachers' promotion and their salary. The ultimate objective of this training is to develop a self-motivated mechanism so that teachers will be productive without requiring constant monitoring and supervision.

The focus of the training program varies based on different teachers' situation such as age, experience, teaching level, and teaching style. For example, for those new teachers who have presently graduated from universities, the training may emphasize job orientation, qualification, teaching methods and teaching skills while senior teachers may need more computer technology training.

After having carried out the reform for more than a decade, the quality of the teacher force in No. 8 School has been improved greatly. For example, in 2001, all 92 teachers in the school achieve professional qualifications in correspondence with their professional levels. Fifty percent of teachers received a BA degree while 28.2% with college education were pursuing higher level of degree. They had 14 teachers with an "advanced teacher" title, accounting for 18.6% of all teachers, and 54.3% received held middle level professional teaching titles. Fifty-four or 58.7% teachers in the school were less than 35 years, an improvement perceived to be needed to have a fresh workforce to work with middle school students.

SEEKING FOR PATTERNS OF OUTSTANDING TEACHING AND TRAINING TEACHERS TO ADOPT THEM

During the reform, Principal Liu was often absorbed in thinking about these questions: How can we improve the quality of teaching? Why some of our teachers teach so well? How can we raise teachers' teaching skills? Liu realized that to improve the quality of teaching, the school needs to find out where problems exist and take efforts to summarize the teaching experience of outstanding teachers in order to identify the patterns of outstanding teaching and promote them for teachers to follow.

To do so, the school purchased video cameras through borrowing money from the bank and made video recordings of every teacher. Generally, a teacher's class was recorded once a semester while those outstanding teachers had all their classes videotaped each semester. For years, they have recorded more than one thousand videotapes. The purpose of making teaching videotapes is twofold: as a reference for each teacher herself/himself, and as a model for other teachers to learn from.

The videotapes were given back to each teacher by the school. Through watching his/her own tape, the teacher was able to get a clear picture of his/her teaching. By reflecting on the classroom experience, the teacher could analyze what was working and what was not working in his/her own teaching, and learned how to improve it. A teacher went to Liu's office and told him that after he watched his own teaching tape, he finally figured out why his teaching was not efficient. That was because every time the student asked a question, he always repeated the question again. Since this happened many times in all his classes, it bored the class. Having identified his problem, the teacher's teaching skills were improved.

More important, teachers' videotapes, in particular those outstanding teachers' tapes, were watched by groups of teachers and by experts as examples to be emulated and analyzed. For example, the school used to organize a research group, which consisted of several graduate students from local universities, assistant principals, and math experts from the city, to study the video lessons given by a head teacher as well as an outstanding math teacher in No. 8 School. They found that the teacher's math classes had a clear structure, provided clear and relevant knowledge review, and the teacher adopted dynamic class management skills and used vivid and heuristic languages, etc. After analysis and discussions, the school decided to promote this math teacher class as a model to all other math teachers in the school. Consequently, teachers in the field of math teaching learned the new methods very fast and received very positive results. Through nearly two decades of reform, the teaching level in math in No. 8 School has been enhanced rapidly. The average achievement of the experimented school students in math has been raised to #2 among the public middle schools in the Zhabei District. The school in math ranked at #35 in 1987 before the reform took place.

TEAM TEACHING TRAINING

Wiles and Bondi (2001) define team teaching as:

> Team teaching (or teaming) is a type of instructional organization in which two or more teachers pool their resources, interests, expertise, and knowledge of students and take joint responsibility for meeting a significant part of the instructional needs of the same group of students. (p. 61)

In No. 8 School, team teaching is incorporated in their method of teaching. Team teaching in fact is integrated throughout the whole process of teaching: From teachers' preparation for lessons, to classroom instruction, and to feedback after class. Team teaching happens not only among the teachers, but also between teachers and students.

First, let's look at team teaching among teachers. Figure 7.1 is a diagram of the school teaching process.

As shown in Figure 7.1, the pattern of teaching in No. 8 School indicated the following process: Individual teachers prepare their courses independently based on textbooks, teaching materials, and guideline from the city educational bureau. Then, Lecture Preparation Group has a two-hour meeting weekly to discuss individual teachers' draft of the lecture while the Teaching and Research Group meets once every two weeks. The group meetings provide opportunities for teachers to share ideas, make comments, and exchange student information. After revising their lectures based on the opinions from the group meetings, teachers feel more confident giving their lectures. The classes are open to every teacher all the time. The school encourages teachers to observe each other teaching at any time in order to improve the quality of teaching.

From time to time, the school will have classes open to experts and all teachers in the same field from other schools, districts, and cities. After

122 *Success for All*

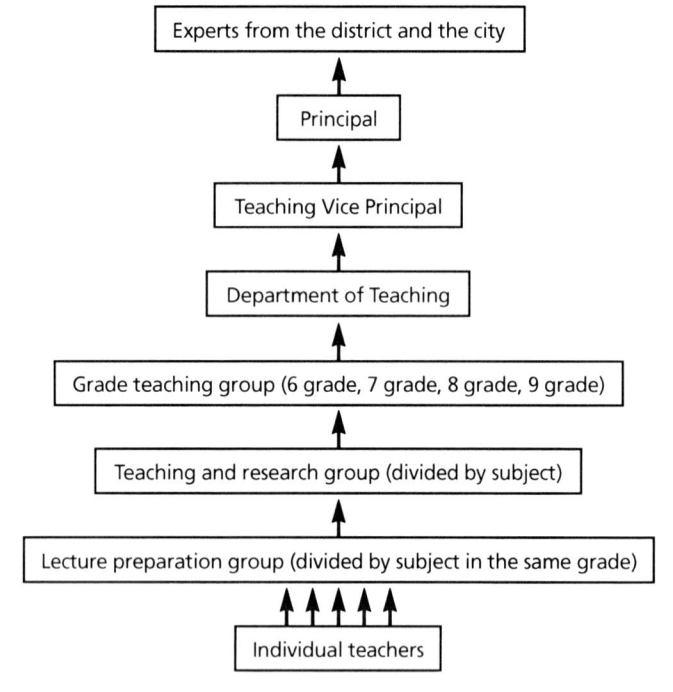

Figure 7.1 The diagram of teaching process as an organization in No. 8 School, Shanghai, China.

the class, all the teachers and experts will have a meeting to provide their feedback to the teachers who gave the public class and point out the strong part of their lectures and the part needing improvement. Also, the public class, to some extent, is used as setting a criterion for evaluating a teacher teaching quality. If a teacher can lecture a public class, it means that his/her teaching has reached a certain level that other teachers can learn from him/her as a good example.

During my investigation, I attended both subject group meetings and the public classes in Chinese and math. For example, I took part in a math-teachers' group meeting at 8th grade in the old campus and found that it was very dynamic and helpful. At the beginning, the teachers presented what they had individually done to prepare for the subject that would be taught the following week, then, they gave suggestions and comments to each other, and explored better ways to teach in the classroom. They also exchanged student information and discussed how to help those low performance students. The meeting lasted about two hours. It impressed me as a very efficient meeting.

In the new campus, I attended four Chinese teachers' public classes that lasted for the whole morning. Some experts from the district and city were invited to have classroom observation. About twenty people including principal Liu, the vice principal, the Part secretary, the head of the Institute of S*uccess Education*, all the school's Chinese teachers, and experts sat in back of the classroom. The group leader (or department head) of the Chinese subject distributed an evaluation form and a notebook to everyone. After class, we were asked to fill out the form and send it to the group leader. For the whole afternoon, Principal Liu held a meeting with all attendees. I observed that everyone listened seriously to the experts' advice, discussed the classes one by one, and figured out what they could do for the next step.

After the meeting, I asked Ms. Mei, a young Chinese teacher who gave a public class in the morning, "Do you think these kinds of team teaching activities help you with your teaching in some way?" "Definitely," she said. In her words:

> It really helps me a lot. The first version of my lesson was totally different from the one I gave today. I felt I made progress after my colleagues helped me through group meetings. To prepare for today's class, it took me more than one month to write my lesson plans and revised again and again. In fact, our teaching is always a product of team work that combines our group wisdom.

As the school set to introduce new technology into teaching, the period of preparing the class lecture for a teacher is longer than before and needs more team work. In the new campus after 2001, instead of using only chalks and the blackboard which had been used for a century, Liu promoted the application of a computer powerpoint in the classroom. "We usually prepare our classes three months ahead since we use powerpoint presentations for our classes." Ms. He, the director of Department of Teaching, told me. "Our teachers have to work in summer and winter holidays to prepare our courses," she continued and described how a class would be prepared.

According to Ms. He, a powerpoint presentation is much more complicated than using the traditional methods of instruction. One has to learn computer skills, search for information through the web, and read more books and material to prepare for the course. As soon as the teacher finishes his or her powerpoint, the group will have meetings and pull their heads together to revise the draft. Some powerpoint presentations are group projects that need everyone to participate in. Once the project is done, they will invite experts to come to the school and evaluate it. After achieving a common understanding the powerpoint has met all criteria for a good class, they can use the powerpoint in the classroom.

As to the function of this kind of training, Ms. Jin, vice principal of the school, shared her opinions with me:

> The process of doing the powerpoint presentations is the process for our teachers to grow. It is in the process of preparing the powerpoint for the courses that teachers can learn from each other, collaborate with each other in their job, and help each other. That is the way we create a professional community and a network for communication within the school.

Another kind of team teaching training is designed for students' participation, called "case teaching." The cases can be selected in many ways. They may be nominated by school leaders who identify good teaching experiences or problems from their classroom observations. Or they may come from a teacher's own teaching experience. Also, the cases can be identified from very important issues and problems arising from teachings in the school.

"Case teaching" refers to a process in which the teacher designs a circumstance in the classroom that creates a problem to be dealt with. The teacher asks the students to join the discussion and find solutions to the problem with the teacher. In this way, teachers and students learn from each other. The case teaching model enhances student-center learning, breaking down the rigidity and passivity of teacher-center learning, a system that has been adopted for thousands of years in China. Also, "this student-teacher interaction fosters students' sense of human interdependence, responsibility, and citizenship. These areas have particular importance at this stage of child development" (Wiles & Bondi, 2001, p. 61).

Furthermore, the school made videotapes for those case teaching classes and organized teachers to watch together, analyze, and discuss the cases. For some good cases, they repeatedly watched the tapes and identified good teaching and learning practices. Through these kinds of team teaching activity, teachers were able to get a clear picture of the teaching and learning process, and eventually improve their teaching skills. Teachers in No. 8 School responded that the case teaching training effectively facilitated their teaching.

MASTER–DISCIPLE TEACHING TRAINING

The school paid special attention to young teachers' professional training since these teachers lack teaching experience and need training the most. The school established a master–disciple system to help new teachers with their teaching and class management. Each new teacher is assigned two teachers by the school as his/her mentors or masters: one for teaching and another for managing students, to start his/her new journey as a teacher. The following section will focus on the master–disciple mentoring system.

What kind of teacher can be a master teacher? Liu explained that a master teacher must:

- Love students;
- Be knowledgeable in his/her field and excellent in teaching;
- Be actively involved in success education reform;
- Have moral and ethical qualities to become a model of life for young teachers.

The period of time for master–disciple relationship training is one year. Within the year, the master teacher is in charge of supervising and facilitating the disciple teaching. For example, the master teacher must assist the disciple with the preparation for his/her lectures. The disciple is required to listen to his/her master every class and conduct classroom teaching when the master schedules to observe his/her disciple's class. After the class, the master teacher has to discuss with the disciple about his/her lesson. The school suggests that the disciple imitates and understands his/her master's class first, then he or she can develop his/her personal teaching style later on. That is a fast way for a new teacher to learn how to teach.

To support this master–disciple system, the school made some special policies that allow the master teacher to be paid a working subsidy worthy of six hours per week (with a payment of 11.6 yuan for an hour). Also, the master teacher's promotion and reward are linked to the disciples' progress. In the past, outstanding teachers usually taught many classes because they were skillful in teaching. After the reform was started, school leaders changed this practice. In order to help more young teachers, the school allowed the master teachers to have fewer courses, or even no course and put all their energy on assisting new teachers' professional development. For instance, they have several outstanding teachers who have no class and their major job is to specially facilitate new teachers in enhancing their teaching quality.

In addition, to strengthen the master–disciple system, starting in 2000, every year the school has held events called "The Series of Activities of Report on Young Teachers Growth" for all teachers and staff. They invited leaders from the Zhabei Education Bureau, Zhabei Normal College, and the Committee of Street and Community to attend the meeting. They also invited the parents of new teachers, master teachers and student representatives to participate in the activity. The activity was very dynamic and diverse. For example, they had new teachers demonstrate their class activities and exchange their teaching experiences. Also, the school let the disciples express their gratitude for their mentors' wholehearted help with their professional growth while the master teachers praised their disciples' progress. Through this activity, the new teachers were encouraged by their achievements and felt confident in their future. At the same time, the parents were very proud of their child's progress and in return supported their child's work more actively. In this way, the school created and maintained a sense of trust between the teachers and the community, and strengthened the support and help for the new teachers. This activity received positive feedback from school teachers, parents, and leaders from the district.

After the school has adopted this system for more than a decade, the master–disciple system has been reported as an efficient approach toward training new teachers. For example, at the beginning of the reform, school leaders selected ten outstanding teachers as the masters and 20 young and middle-aged teachers as disciples to learn from each other. Several years later, the school found that the system worked very well and that the disciple teachers were helped to become key teachers in their fields quickly. As a consequence, the master–disciple system has been developing not only in the school but also outside the school and even spread to other provinces. For example, from 1996 to 2000, they had trained 152 disciples, among them, 77 teachers from the school, 36 from other schools in the district, and 39 from other provinces.

In my study, I conducted one-on-one interviews and group interviews with 30 young teachers from both the old and the new campuses. When I asked these questions: "Do you think the master–disciple system is necessary? Did the system help you in any way?" All of the young teachers answered that "yes, it is definitely necessary"; "the system really helped me tremendously in terms of my professional development."

Ms. Gao, a 25-years-old math teacher, shared her experience as a disciple during 1999–2000. Gao said, "My master teacher taught me very seriously and I had learned a lot from her."

"Would you please describe how your Master helped you with your teaching?" I asked. Gao recalled:

> At that time, I attended her classes every day and she also listened to my classes every day. My class was always behind her class one day so that I could first learn from her. I took part in her classes during the day and practiced my class during the night. My master also came to the school in the evening and listened to my class rehearsal. She not only helped me to prepare for my classes but also analyzed my lectures and told me what I needed to improve.
>
> My training was not limited to my master and I could learn from other teachers as well. The school created such a good learning environment that I could enter and observe any math teachers' classes. Thus, sometimes I participated in six math classes a day. That assisted me a great deal to shape my own teaching style and improve my teaching quality.

In particular, when I did group interviews, I noticed that the relationship between the master and the disciple was very close, natural, and smooth.

Ms. Jin and Ms. Wu were still the master and the disciple when I interviewed them. Ms. Jin, a well-known math teacher in No. 8 School, praised her disciple that "she is such a smart girl and a quick learner." Ms. Wu admired her master's teaching skills that "my master's teaching language is very precise. She taught the important and difficult points of math knowledge very clearly so that the students comprehend them easily. Also, she manages the classroom very well."

In all, it seems to me that the master–disciple system in No. 8 School was beneficial to the young teachers. As many teachers told me that although many schools around the country also have this system, not all the schools practice this system as seriously as this experimental school. That may make a big difference.

GOING-OUT AND INVITING-IN TEACHING TRAINING

This strategy makes teachers' training mobile, diverse, and dynamic. "Going-out teaching training" means sending teachers out to study in other schools while "inviting-in teaching training" refers to inviting experts to come to school and train teachers. The school leaders understood that since we are living in changing times, many schools are carrying out all types of effective educational reforms. Therefore, they are alert to the success of other schools and send teachers to gain professional training or learn about those schools' advanced educational theories and practices. Especially, for those young teachers who have aspirations and potential to be successful in their career, school leaders will select those schools which are known to excel in teaching a subject and provide opportunities for No. 8 School's teachers teaching the same subject to get special training there.

In the afternoon of May 19, 2004, near the end of my investigation, I had a chance to experience how this "going-out teaching training" was going. On that day, Principal Liu organized his middle level leaders to go to Jiaowan Middle School, a private high school in Shanghai, which was carrying out a reform called "Developing Potential Education." With the purpose of learning from other schools, Liu invited Mr. Xi, the Principal of the visited school, to give a two-hour presentation on their new educational reform and the accountability mechanism they had put in to improve their students' academic achievements. After Mr. Xi's presentation, they toured the classrooms in the school one by one and got a picture of how this school functioned. In the end, Liu gave a brief speech and gave his colleagues homework for the following week's staff meeting, that is, they would discuss what they had learned that day. Although this activity lasted only three and a half hours, the teachers shared their feelings with me that they were very impressed with the school they had visited.

With respect to "inviting-in teaching training," this is another kind of activity to facilitate teachers' professional development. That is to say, Liu often invites leaders and experts from the district, the city, and universities in Shanghai to guide and give advice to his teachers. The reasons to do so are: (1) To garner more resources from the society; (2) to get ideas on how to enhance educational reform; and (3) to help teachers improve their knowledge and teaching quality.

During my two months of field work, the school organized three teaching activities for which the leaders and experts from the district and city were invited. The following is the list of these three activities.

1. On April 14, 2004, a public class in Chinese. Mr. Huang, a well-known expert in the subject of Chinese as well as one of the main figures who design Chinese standard tests for the National Entrance Examination in Shanghai, was invited to come to the school with other experts in Chinese. After listening to four Chinese teachers' courses, the experts gave their comments and suggestions to those four young teachers. They also provided guidelines on how to teach Chinese according to new emphasis in the National Entrance Examination.
2. In the afternoon of April 14, 2004, powerpoint presentation demonstration. The leaders and experts from the Shanghai Superintendent's Office came to school to examine the quality of math and English powerpoint classes.
3. In the afternoon of May 11, 2004, math group activity for preparation for the class. Mr. Zhang, the leader as well as a math education expert in Zhabei Educational Bureau, was invited to give a lecture on how to prepare a math class.

From the above three events, we can see those activities may play an important role in maintaining a momentum of continuous growth for teachers.

RESEARCH-BASED TEACHING TRAINING

As a research-based reform, while having emphasized training teachers' teaching skills, the school also stressed developing teachers' research capability. In traditional Chinese education, the major task of teachers in secondary schools is to disseminate knowledge and help students to pass the national examinations. With an attempt to transform this traditional role of teachers, success education assists teachers to be successful in both teaching and research, and in practice and theory. Therefore, the school leaders created an effective research environment and built a support system for teachers to improve their academic level.

How do they encourage and help teachers to do research? First, the school stimulated teachers' enthusiasm in research by identifying problems in their teaching and summarizing their personal teaching experiences. The school leaders found that a major challenge for middle school teachers to do research is that the teachers found it difficult to identify topics and methods. So, the school organized teachers to do classroom observations, analyze the class videotapes, especially to collect outstanding teachers' teaching experience and compile their stories in order to find a research subject. Furthermore, teachers were guided to read books, search for information, and form into research groups by subjects. Many topics were identified which originated from teachers' own stories and experience. For example, the book, *One Hundred Examples of Success Education*, is based on teachers' teaching experience. Published on campus, *Success Education Research*, a journal sponsored by Shanghai Institute of Success Education, provides a major forum for teachers to publish their research papers.

Also, the school compiled information pamphlets such as *The Guide to Enhancing Success Education Research*, *The Guide to "Trying for Success" Research*, and *The Gist of Teaching Model in the Classroom*, etc. to help teachers to do research. Under these programs, they designed almost one hundred research topics which teachers could choose to do study. Moreover, the school invited teachers from the other 18 middle schools in the district (most of them used to be at-risk schools as well) to collaborate on doing research. Also, the school set up a key research team, which comprised researchers from Shanghai Institute of Success Education, several assistant principals in the district, and middle school principals from other provinces who took part in *success education* training programs in the school, to do research.

Since 2000, No. 8 School has been focusing its research on "The Teaching Model of Trying for Success in the Classroom." Chinese, math, and English groups have set up their research subjects and positive results have been published. Other groups such as physics, chemistry, biology, are following the model established by Chinese, math, and English groups to carry out their reform.

Second, the school encouraged teachers to actively attend all kinds of conferences. For example, in 1990 SMCE held "the Conference on Exchanging Experience of *Success Education*" in No. 8 School. The papers submitted to the conference by the school leaders and teachers were published in 1992, becoming a very important research in the first stage of the experiment. In 1993 and 2000, SMCE and EBZD held two national conferences on *success education*. Many teachers in No. 8 School presented their papers in the conferences. Their conference papers have been published in two volumes, *Collectanea of Expanding Research on Success Education*, vol. 1 and 2.

By 2003, the teachers in No. 8 School had published 326 papers in a variety of professional journals.

Third, enhancing teachers' teaching quality through editing and writing textbooks, learning materials, and DVD class powerpoint presentations. After having practiced the reform for years, Liu and other school leaders wished that *success education* should not only have its own educational ideology and philosophy, but also have characteristics of its own curriculum, textbooks, and teaching model. As early as 1987 when the reform started, EBZD suggested Liu and the research group to study and reform math courses at the junior high level as a key project. Therefore, emphasizing the importance of math reform, they began to edit their math textbooks according to at-risk students' study pace and characteristics in late 1980s.

Based on outstanding teachers' teaching, Liu organized a team of 18 middle schools in the Zhabei District to write and edit their own math textbooks, study materials, and drill exercises. Aimed at strengthening math teachers' professional training, the team used the following procedure: learning—studying—writing and editing—practicing (in the classroom)—finalizing (the text), to do their research (Liu, 2001). The team also met together once every two weeks to prepare their courses and discuss the problems they were facing in the classroom. At the same time, they summarized their teaching experience and found the solutions to the problems. Combining theory and practice together, the textbooks and other study materials were made suitable for at-risk students to learn. Under the support from the governments at district and city level, these textbooks and materials had been used by 12 middle schools with nearly 4,000 students in the district in 2000. All those students' academic achievements had been improved greatly. Today No. 8 School's math course has been one of the best in the district.

In summary, to enhance the teachers' quality, No. 8 School has put in great efforts on teaching method reform. To build a teacher work force to make *success education* a great success, they have initiated a variety of alternative teacher training programs. Especially, team teaching, pattern teaching, and master–disciple system teaching training were regarded as very efficient methods to facilitate teacher professional development. By establishing a teaching and research base on the campus, the school has provided an environment for teachers to have continuous improvement. Through all these efforts, today the quality of teachers in No. 8 School has been raised to a new level, from the bottom position before the reform to be among those at top in terms of overall school achievement.

CHAPTER 8

THE QUIET REVOLUTION IN THE CLASSROOM

Approaches to Help Students Learn and Succeed

This chapter will examine efforts to improve teaching in the classroom. Specifically, it will touch on the core ideas of success education and the main strategies adopted by No. 8 School to improve at-risk students. It will explore the teaching and learning revolution as a result of the experiment in the school. Further, the chapter will examine how the philosophy of success education is reflected in the components of classroom instruction such as teachers' expectations, school curriculum, criteria for student evaluation, and teaching models in the classroom.

TRANSFORMATION OF TEACHERS' EXPECTATIONS

Good teaching starts from teachers' expectations for students. It may be regarded as a "hidden curriculum." It has been documented that there is a very close correlation between teachers' preconception and students' performance (e.g., low teacher expectations lead to low student outcomes regardless of the student actual ability) (Foster, 1992; Smith et al., 1998). Research also shows that teachers' high expectations for students' academic achievements are a key component of many efficient programs helping at-risk students (Sanders & Jordan, 2000).

Through their research and investigation, Liu and the research group at the early stage of the *success education* reform found that one of the main factors that caused students' academic failure was a negative learning environment that, to a great extent, was influenced by teachers' low expectations, complaints, and blaming, all of which started in their elementary schools. Since teaching in the school was associated with a bad reputation, teachers in No. 8 School did not enjoy working in the school. Also, because they had taught at-risk students for a long time, teachers in No. 8 School had lost confidence in students' success. Thus, when students had troubles with their study, instead of providing them encouragement, teachers usually criticized and blamed them. That reinforced disadvantaged students' low self-esteem and made the situation even worse.

To augment teachers' high expectations for students, school leaders helped teachers identify certain behaviors demonstrating their low expectations for at-risk students and helped them analyze the negative impacts of those teachers' behaviors on students' performance. Liu noticed that, drawn from his own classroom observations, teachers' expectations were different for the high achieving students and at-risk students. For example, one day he listened to a teacher's class. He found that when the teacher asked questions to students, his response to a high achieving student was more patient than to that of a low achiever. Liu said usually a situation looked like that: When a high achieving student could not answer a teacher's question, the teacher would patiently offer hints to him because he believed that the child would understand quickly and give a right answer. As a result, the student did and the teacher had satisfied his expectation. However, when a disadvantaged student failed to answer the question, Liu lists three ways teachers had habitually used to blame those students: "XXX, you just stand up and observe how other classmates answer the question"; "I have already known that you will not be able to answer this question"; "If you can answer this question, everybody in the classroom can." This kind of negative feedback hurt the at-risk students who gradually lose interest in learning. By analyzing these kinds of examples, teachers reflected upon their own teaching and realized how important a teacher's high expectation for students are.

Also, the school organized its teachers to learn the theory of *success education* and tried to develop their confidence in students. Further, the school guided the teachers in learning other kinds of theories from the international field on the impacts of teachers' expectations on students' performance, such as Rosenthal and Jacobson's "Pygmalion effect" (1968), "role theory" created by Mead (1934), and Good and Brophy's (1984) teaching method model. All those theories emphasize that teachers' expectations for students play a significant role in their teaching. Based on learning, study, and practice, gradually the school leaders and the teachers established their own teachers' expectation's theory of *success education* by combining long-term expectations and short-term targets.

"Long-term expectation" refers to the "three beliefs" mentioned before while "short-term targets" are the specific goals for students to reach. That is to say, in theory, teachers must hold a belief that, from a point of view of long-term development, every student will achieve a variety of success in their life because he or she was born to have desire and potentials to be successful. In practice, based on individual students' features and levels of knowledge they are at, teachers can design some easy goals for them to achieve as the first step, then gradually set a more difficult goal for the students. For example, Liu said at the early stage of the experiment they taught new equations in math classes very slowly since the children lacked much basic knowledge for understanding them. "Our math teachers repeated some old knowledge again and again until our students completely mastered this point."

Combining "long-term expectation" with "short-term targets," according to *success education,* there is no student we cannot teach if the teacher knows how to teach that child. Everyone is unique and has his/her advantages. The essence of teaching is to find the specific method to fit the particular person. Therefore, at-risk students' difficulties in learning are temporary since they also have the potential to achieve success. In this way, a teacher should never lose his/her confidence in students. Liu even believes that having high expectations for students is an essential qualification for one to be a teacher in *success education*. Thus, he requires his teachers to never blame their students but always to encourage them.

To assist teachers in developing high expectations and goals for students, the school required teachers to build up a profile for all students and analyze each at-risk student's advantages, disadvantages, and characteristics. Especially, teachers are encouraged to identify students' merits. To train teachers on how to dig up students' merits, the school collected successful teachers' stories, then promoted them through staff meetings, symposiums, and conferences. Some good examples have been published in books.

Through these efforts, positive attitudes toward at-risk students have been built up among teachers. Ms. Lou, who was a teacher for thirty years in No. 8 School, shared her story with me during our interview:

> I used to be a tough teacher and students did not like me at all since I always tried to catch their dark sides and blamed them. For example, when I talked with my students I often asked them to answer such questions: "How many

bad things have you done during your elementary school? How many times did your primary school teachers criticize you?" Also, when I asked student questions, I always wanted to know their history of behavioral problems and poor academic records. If a student made a mistake, I would say to him/her that I have long known that you were a bad student starting from elementary school. My students were very much embarrassed and hated me for repeating all the bad things they had done. Because of that, I usually had a very tense relationship with my students.

After we implemented *success education,* Principal Liu suggested I change my attitude and my method to treat students by using a positive approach. I gave it a try. I remembered that before our new students entered into No. 8 School, I visited their elementary teachers, their families, and their classmates to get their information. This time, rather than collecting all the bad things they did, I wrote down all the good deeds they had done.

At the first day of the new semester, I asked my students to write an essay under the title of *Introduce Myself.* In the essay, I required them to report all the talents and interests they have, all the good things they had done for people, and all the happy experiences they have had. Then, we had a class meeting to read their papers. It really surprised me that every student had many good attributes. A boy reported he could sing very well while a girl said she could pin a coat button by herself. Some said they helped their mother to do house work, others said they were good in sports.... Everybody was happy during this class. Not only my students but also myself were full of confidence in our school and in our future. As a result, three years later when my students graduated, we had become an advanced class in the school, and everyone made great progress.

Other teacher's transformational stories such as what Ms. Lou experienced, were quite common in my interviews. Also, I tried to explore teachers' changes in their expectations from the students' perspective. When the students answered my questions: "Are the teachers in this school more patient to you than that in your previous school? Do they encourage you when you get into troubles in your study?" Most of them said "yes." Drawn from the collected data, the research definitely finds a positive result in teachers' concept of at-risk students. While enhancing teachers' expectations for students, the next step for the school was to create opportunities for students to achieve success.

INVENTING ALTERNATIVE APPROACHES IN CURRICULUM AND TEACHING METHODS

Based on five months of research and investigation (May-September, 1987), Liu and the research group found that although at-risk students had many problems such as discipline problems, not doing home work, playing truant, or even joining a gang and participating in criminal behavior, the major problems were low self-esteem and lacking motivation for learning. The causes of these problems were students' repeated failures in school and the constant blames they received from teachers and parents. These negative experiences rendered students to have no confidence in themselves and no interest in school work at all. To deal with these problems, the research group realized that, rather than taking a partial approach, that is, in their own words, treating the head when the head aches, treating the foot when the foot hurts, or simply treating the symptoms but not the cause of the disease, they would apply a method in the traditional Chinese medicine for improving at-risk student education. This method focuses on treating a disease by building up one's resistance to disease—that is, in success education, they need an internal way to build up students' self-confidence. In other words, the fundamental thing for the school to do was to create all kinds of opportunities to help students succeed in their study and restore their confidence in learning.

How can they reach this goal? Traditional teaching treats learning as an external task to students, aiming at helping top students pass the National Entrance Examination. Therefore, the teaching outline issued by the city set very high requirements for all students and they were too difficult for at-risk students to reach. To a great extent, traditional education itself has contributed to students' failure. Thus, Liu and the research group started their alternative approaches by reforming the curriculum to match at-risk students' actual level of the knowledge. The school attempted to change a rigid and unrealistic practice adopted in most Chinese schools, that is to say, schools usually complain about students' low performance, but on the other hand, they teach students by following an inflexible curriculum.

Moreover, the way of improving at-risk students in traditional education was a pullout model in which teachers worked with only one student at a time, by teaching them extra hours and monitoring them all the time in order to increase their chance of passing the National Entrance Examination. Teachers became very tired, and felt much pressure, but the change was minimal. Thus, the school leaders decided to alter the entire curriculum and teaching methods to make school-wide improvements. However, in China, the reform in the curriculum did not mean changing the terminal targets of the unified city teaching outline, but it means only adjusting the requirements and speed in the procedure of teaching, namely to slow down at the beginning and to speed up later on when students are motivated to catch up with the regular class.

According to the school leaders, the essential part of the curriculum and instructional reform is to help students achieve success so that they can transform the need for learning as an external pressure imposed on them, to cultivating an internal motivation to learn in the students. Only when students are highly motivated and enjoy study can their academic achievement be improved. In this sense, Liu said that is the nature of *success education* instruction.

In addition, the school intended to be a pioneer in modifying the educational system in China, through implementing *quality education,* and creating a culture that values lifelong learning. Therefore, the main purpose of the innovation of *success education* is to train students to foster a set of comprehensive quality that integrates the following four aspects: (1) Improved morality and behavioral habits; (2) firm mastery of basic knowledge; (3) development of basic learning ability; and (4) perseverance and positive mentality.

The development of the *success education* teaching model has experienced three phases.

The First Stage: Teachers Assist Students to Succeed (The Helping-for-Success Model)

This strategy was adopted very much at the first and the middle of second stages of the reform. The aim at this phase is to attract students to participate in learning activities. Teachers helped students achieve success by designing a flexible curriculum. They might reduce and cancel some contents if the requirements are too high for students or the knowledge is not relevant to students' life. In the meanwhile, they might add some classes to the curriculum, which are basic knowledge and necessary skills for students to succeed in the future, although those contents are not included in the standard subject requirements. For example, in Chinese subject, they put calligraphy, dictation, reading (fast reading), and speech etc., useful skills in students' life, into the regular curriculum.

Also, the school regards that in their alternative curriculum, it is very important to strengthen the learning ability and social adaptive ability of children. Throughout the reform, the school has been paying a lot of attention to cultivating students' good learning habits which is considered as the foundation of success in the future. For example, they have greatly emphasized fostering students' good habit in doing home work, and regarded this as a way to train students to be responsible.

More important, after years of practice and with great efforts, the school eventually created a realistic, effective, and a dynamic curriculum that takes into consideration of the characteristics of at-risk students and is fitted their learning. Liu described this strategy as a "Low starting point, strict requirement, small pace, more activities, and quick feedback," or simply called "low, small, more, and fast" measures. It means that according to students' knowledge level, the experimental classes adjusted their regular teaching contents to fit each individual student's learning pace and style so that the students would feel that they were able to learn. Since these strategies have become the most effective teaching methods of *success education*, I will describe them in more detail in the following section.

"*Low*" stands for the low level of starting. In order to provide opportunities for students to succeed in the classroom, this strategy requires teachers to obtain a clear picture of and basic information about students such as their actual level of knowledge, capacity, and mentality before they prepare their lectures. The school employed a variety of methods such as survey, interview, questionnaire and test to obtain first hand information of students. In this way, teachers are able to set a comparatively low learning requirement which can integrate both new and old knowledge. For instance, a Chinese subject group at the first stage of the reform lowered their teaching by going back to contents students learned in grade 4 of elementary education while math and English groups also began by teaching some basic knowledge from the primary school level. The strategy of starting at a lower level ensured that students would achieve success in the classroom quickly and easily. It has been reported that this strategy tremendously stimulated students enthusiasm for academic learning.

"*Small*" refers to small paces. In terms of teaching contents, the experiment suggests that teachers develop their lectures from easier learning materials and gradually proceed to more difficult subjects in accordance with students' acceptable level. When students confront any difficulty in their learning, teachers will reduce the requirements to guarantee their success. The strategy of a small pace reduces the possibility of failure. Because the students have experienced achieving success again and again, they enjoyed the process of learning and become more and more confident and motivated to learn.

With positive results, many teachers in the school wrote their experience of using this teaching method. Ms. Yu, an outstanding English teacher in Shanghai and the head teacher of the English group in the early stage of the experiment, shared her teaching experience with me. She said that students' academic achievement in English in No. 8 School was at the bottom among all public schools in the district at the beginning of the reform. For example, the ability to listen, speak, and write in English was zero. To teach English efficiently, by applying the "small" teaching strategy, they divided each listening and speaking training class into six stages: watching slides, listening to the tape, imitating the voice, learning how to speak, compiling and extending the sentence, and speaking fluently. If students had any difficulty keeping up with the teaching pace at any stage, the teacher would repeat again and again until students could fluently speak the sentence. After three years' experiment, the average of English academic achievement in

No. 8 School had reached the middle level among all public middle schools in the district.

"*More*" means more activities. In the traditional Chinese education model, teachers play a central role in the classroom throughout history. The school transformed the traditional teaching model by creating more activities for students during teachers' instruction. They found that this alternative approach was particularly suitable for disadvantaged students since they have a short memory span and are easily distracted. Usually, in a *success education* classroom, instead of lecturing all the time as was done in the traditional classroom, teachers would lecture for only about ten minutes while the rest of the time was devoted to students' learning activities. Students in the experimental class were encouraged to get involved in all kinds of activities such as cooperation learning, group discussion, one-on-one conversation, team work projects, and so forth. This student-center teaching method not only helped students to concentrate on their learning, but it also efficiently helped solve the school's discipline problems; furthermore, students developed other abilities such as social and communication skills during the process.

Mr. Chu, who was an at-risk student in 1993 with very low scores (16 for Chinese, 20 for math, and 30 for English) when he entered the school, described his living experience in the classroom. He recalled,

> We did have a lot of activities during the class at that time. For example, we had the interaction between teachers and students by asking and answering questions. Sometimes we did class exercises independently, sometimes in a group. I particularly remembered that in math class, we could learn mathematics knowledge and skills by all kinds of methods: Oral questions and answers, written calculation, mental arithmetic, calculation with an abacus, evaluation by myself or by other classmates.... It was a lot of fun. Through these activities, I found that I could learn not only from my teachers but also from my classmates. In that way, I made progress very fast.

"*Fast*" represents fast feedback. This strategy requires teachers to promptly respond to students about their learning or leave a block of time in each class to check students' learning situation. In traditional education, students' learning problems would be caught through their homework or examinations. It takes a long time for teachers to remedy the knowledge and skills' students missed and lacked. Usually, if this happened, the school would hold make-up classes after the school day or during the weekend. In the *success education* model, teachers check students' learning all the time. If students make progress, teachers will encourage them promptly so that students savor their success in a timely manner. This timely feedback may arouse them to have more interest in future study. Also, this strategy allows teachers to find students' existing problems in the classroom, and immediately adjust their teaching speed and requirements, and figure out ways to solve students' problems. One of the direct results of this strategy was that the school has avoided having many class-wide remedy classes later. That was impossible before the reform.

Besides the four strategies summarized above, I found the school also adopts two other measures, that is, the school provides students concentrated help from teachers after class and the school facilitates cooperation among teachers. In the old campus of No. 8 School, there were many slogans posted on the school walls encouraging students in their study. One of them has become a well-known quote that is drilled into students' minds: "Do not be scared by learning difficulties to achieve success, teachers are

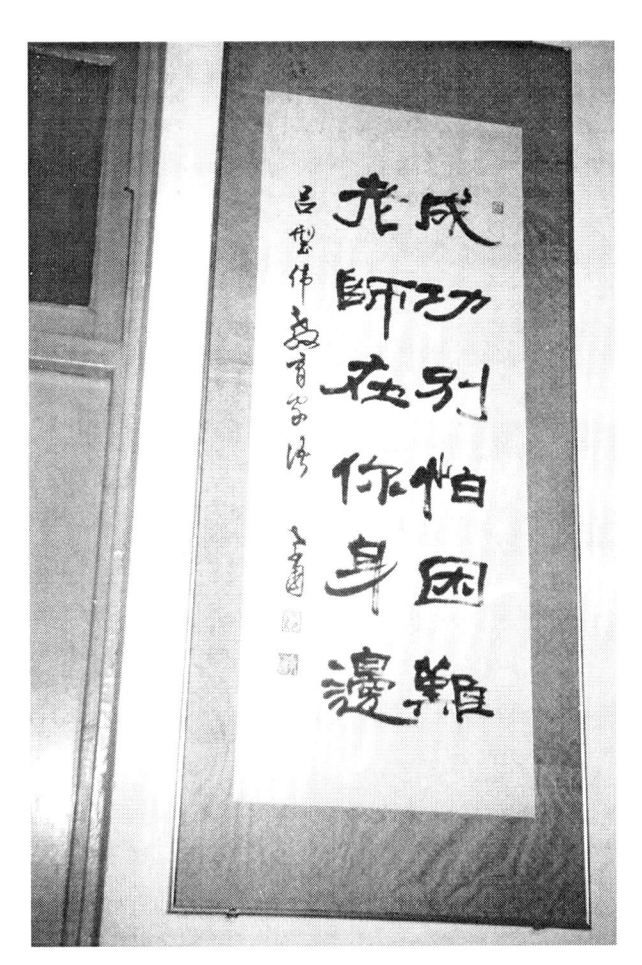

Photo 8.1 A slogan on the wall in old campus: "Do not be scared by learning difficulties to achieve success, teachers are just around you"—willing to help you, 2004.

just around you"—willing to help you, The slogan made students and their parents feel warm and strong support from the school. Many students and parents I interviewed shared such feelings.

The slogan was put into action by many teachers. Thanks to active support from the city and district governments, *success education* became a common and noble goal for all the teachers and staff. School teachers helped students not only in the classroom but also outside of the class. Professional accountability requires teachers to make sure every student master the courses they taught. If not, the missed part will be remedied after class or at other time such on a weekend or holidays. Since at-risk students missed learning much basic knowledge in their elementary schools, teachers had to make sure they learned the basic knowledge to catch up with the class. For those students with the most difficulty in learning, teachers usually let them stay in school after class and taught them individually for several hours for free. I asked them how many hours a day they worked in school at the early stage of the *success education* reform? They told me around 10–12 hours (from 6:30 a.m. to 5–7:00 p.m.). Some of them even worked to 9–10 p.m. When I visited the school in 2004, every day I could find teachers who stayed in their offices to give students individual help. A few teachers sometimes did not go home until 9 p.m. Although teachers might be tired because of working the extra hours, their help was crucial for those at-risk students whose parents were working class with a low level of education. Many students I interviewed told me that they benefitted very much from the individual help from their teachers.

Another effective approach for improving at-risk students is teachers' collaboration in their work. At the early stage, teachers' enthusiasm with helping students was very high. They tried many ways to build up a collaborative network among themselves for assisting students. If a teacher found a child who had a problem, he or she would tell other teachers and see if there was any way for them to cooperate together, to create a learning atmosphere and help that student. Sometime the student's learning problem might not be in that teacher's field, but the teachers would still try to help.

These strategies helping students learn brought in positive results. Students' academic achievement was enhanced tremendously, from having only 30% students passing qualification exams for Compulsive Education before 1987, to 100% in 1990. Through experiencing all kinds of success in study under teachers' help, at-risk students had gradually developed their self-confidence. The school culture has been changed to a positive one: Students were motivated, teachers had high expectations, and the school had a supportive climate. Its implementation having turned the school from a trouble-ridden school to a successful school, *success education* has been promoted in the district, city, and even around the country since the early 1990s.

However, from 1995 school leaders found that there were some limitations of the "Helping-for-Success Model" which had been carried out since 1987. The most obvious problem was that students relied too much on teachers' help. In other words, teachers assisted students too much that without teachers' aid and push, the students would stop and fail to make much progress. Also, the teaching model at the first stage was characterized by basic knowledge remedy, and it did not meet the need of improving student competence and other aspects of personal development. Therefore, since 1998 the school has pushed its reform forward to the second stage.

The Second Stage: Students Trying to Succeed (The Trying-for-Success Model)

Since the "trying-for-success model" is the major reform undertaken by the school, I will examine this particular teaching model in detail in this section. Mainly, I will discuss this issue from three aspects: initiation, implementation, and result.

The initiation of the trying-for-success model.   To deal with the problem of students' motivation, Liu and the research group tried to find the solutions. During his observation of classroom teachings, Liu noticed the phenomenon that outstanding teachers were always able to make the class interesting and stimulate students to actively participate in class. One day when he listened to a math teacher's lesson on the angle in a circular segment, he observed that this teacher did not teach his students any math theory, but created a presentation which involved all kinds of pictures, then asked students to recognize, compare, and explore what is the angle in a circular segment. Throughout the class, students were encouraged to ask questions, discuss, and finally find the answer by themselves. Liu was inspired by the class and realized that involving students in a learning experience might be the new teaching model of *success education* in its second stage.

Under strong support from the district and city governments, the school leaders organized a research group consisting of experts from the district and city level to make videotapes for outstanding teachers' classes in No. 8 School. Then, they analyzed the tapes one by one from multiple dimensions such as the teachers' oral language, posture language, blackboard writing, the questions' teachers asked and the reactions from the students. They also studied the important processes of a class, including background knowledge review, new knowledge learning, students' exploration, and teachers' guidance. Furthermore, through comparing education in the West and the East, they found that while Chinese education emphasizes the knowledge learning part, Western education features capability training and development. In today's globalization era, there is a tendency toward

142 *Success for All*

integrating Western and Eastern education. With the aspiration of becoming a pioneer, the school attempts to reform its classroom instruction by combining the advantages of both Western and Eastern education. Thus, based on theory studies and practice analysis, the research group eventually formed a new teaching model of *success education* at the second stage as the "trying-for-success model." At this stage, teachers' assistance was reduced and the students were encouraged to achieve success more by themselves.

What are the differences between the traditional model and the new model? The following are two diagrams comparing these two models.

Figure 8.1 shows a typical Chinese teaching process modeled after the Soviet Union model in the 1950s. From the diagram, seven procedures can be seen in this traditional teaching model: (1) Information delivery; (2) memory-based and rote learning; (3) three centers instruction: classroom-centered, teacher-centered, and textbook-centered; (4) a single-direction stimulation and single teaching milieu; (5) isolated work; (6) passive learning; and (7) isolated and artificial context.

To meet the needs of ongoing social changes as well as enhance at-risk students learning, the new educational model—"trying-for-success model" features the following, as shown in Figure 8.2.

Specifically, there are five procedures in the "trying-for-success model." "Preparation excises" is the beginning of class to review the background knowledge that students have learned and closely links to the new lesson that will be taught. Instead of instructing in the traditional manner, students are stimulated by doing a series of interesting exercises that are easily done. Through asking questions or creating an activity, teachers lead students to get into new contents of learning. In an inspiring and positive learning environment, students start their exploration in the new world of knowledge. Feeling more involved and interested, this approach differs from the past model in which teachers explain the textbook and give examples to students in a top-down, linear interactional manner. In the new learning model, under teachers' guidance, students learn knowledge in the textbook by themselves. Through a variety of class activities, students are motivated to be actively involved in the process of learning. They might

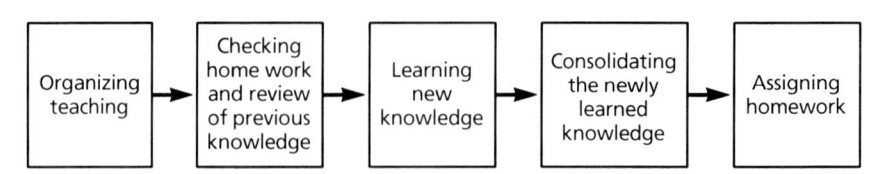

Organizing teaching → Checking home work and review of previous knowledge → Learning new knowledge → Consolidating the newly learned knowledge → Assigning homework

Figure 8.1 The diagram of traditional Chinese teaching process.
Source: From a collected school document by Liu Jinghai. "The Teaching Model of Success Education.", p. 123.

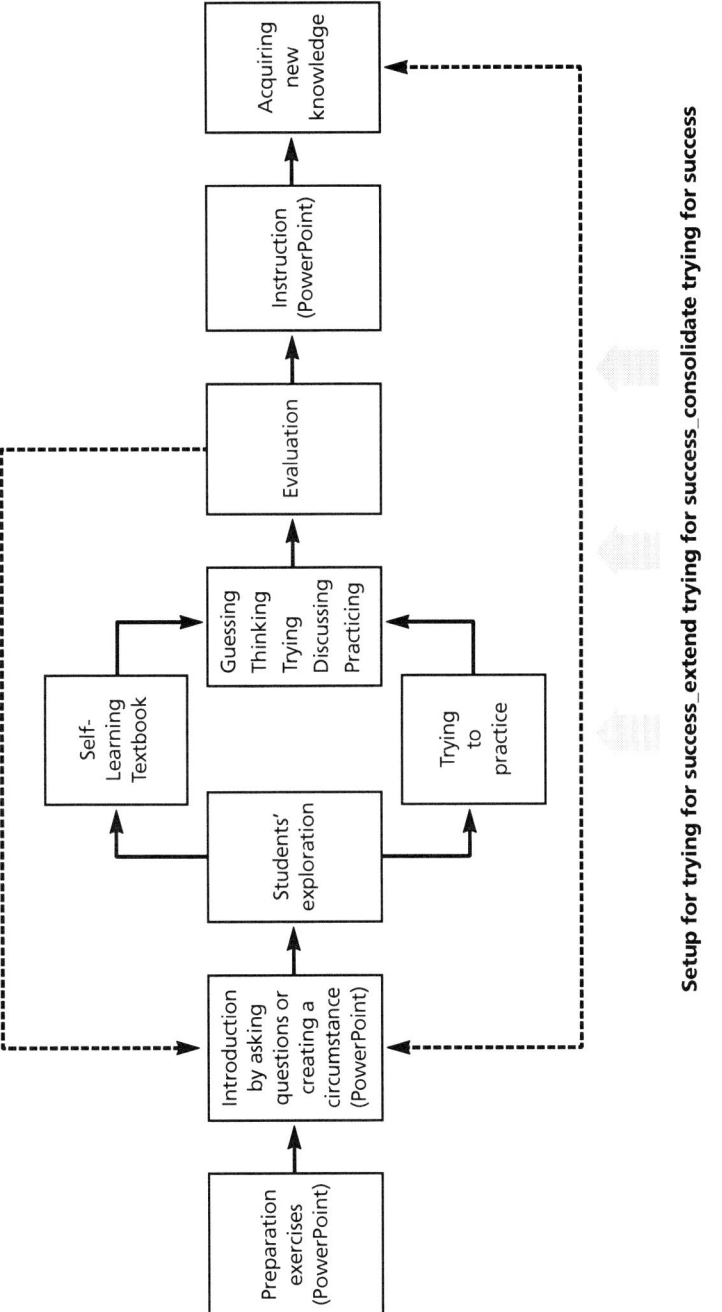

Figure 8.2 The diagram of the "trying-for-success model" in No. 8 School in Shanghai, China
Source: Chen, D. (2002). *The Theory and Practice of Success Education*. Shanghai, China: Shanghai Education Press, p. 192. The author added the words in parentheses.

deduce the results or think of an original way to deal with a problem; they might learn in a group, or just simply practice by him/herself.

More important, not being a passive learner anymore, students are encouraged to try to find the answers and principles behind the phenomenon by themselves. Making their contributions to the learning process, students feel that the new teaching method provides more opportunities for them to achieve success in learning. In this open and dynamic learning environment, students are inspired to pour out all their ideas. In their exploration, some students may get a right answer while the others do not. Instead of a single solution to the question as expected in the traditional learning environment, students may come up with multiple answers from taking widely different angles. Teachers focus on assessing students' progress and encouraging them for their active participation. In the end, teachers summarize for the class and clarify the new knowledge learned through the process. This is basically how the second stage of a *success education* class functions.

From the above diagram, one can see that a quiet revolution in the classroom has been happening in No. 8 School. China is a country which views teachers as the primary authority of knowledge and the classroom has been teacher-centered for thousands of years. In response to the needs of modernization and globalization, the *success education* classroom is transforming from a traditional one to a modern one. According to school leaders, this new educational learning environment can be contrasted with the older, more traditional environment in a number of ways: (1) It offers student-centered instruction; (2) it is characterized by "reducing knowledge imitation and delivery while increasing interactive participative, experience-based learning"; (3) it focuses on fostering students' quality helping them build a mentality of success, nurture strong self-learning ability, and bring about high learning efficiency; (4) it provides multi-sensory stimulation and multimedia; (5) it is exploratory, inquiry-based learning; (6) learning is linked to authentic, real-world context; and (7) it fosters cooperative learning and student involvement in the learning process.

In all, compared to the conventional class, in the new learning system the teacher acts as a facilitator, rather than just as a dispenser of knowledge, to create a learning environment for students to be active learners. They teach much less than they would do in the traditional instructional model, but guide, supervise, and lead students to explore most of the time.

The implementation of the new teaching method. From a "helping-for-success model" to a "trying-for-success model," a milestone has been reached in both theory and practice in *success education*. How did the school get teachers to implement this new teaching approach? First, it prepares teachers for the reform. At the beginning, teachers did not believe that at-risk students were able to achieve success in the classroom by themselves since they missed so much background knowledge in their primary schools because of repeated failure. The school leaders made efforts to change teachers' concepts by setting up outstanding teachers' teaching as good and viable examples. They arranged time for teachers to observe those outstanding teachers' classes, then, encouraged them to follow the new model in their own classes.

Another challenge faced by the school was that teachers worried that the new method might not be as efficient as the traditional one in terms of knowledge acquisition for students since it would take more time for students to explore in the classroom. To bring confidence to teachers in the change, school leaders took the responsibility if a class had a slow start and did not show immediate results. By measuring the positive results in a small scale, the school gradually extended the new model to the whole school.

In practice, teachers felt one of the largest challenges was how they could control the classroom when students expressed all their ideas, answers, and solutions thereby trying to achieve success by themselves. In the old instructional model, teachers had gotten accustomed to using one textbook that would give only one answer for a situation. In using the new teaching method, teachers felt uncertainty as well as pressure to handle a much more complicated classroom situation. Some of them even lost their sleep when they were driven to reform. The school leaders regarded it as a good opportunity to facilitate teachers' professional development. For example, the school adjusted the criteria for evaluating teachers' teaching and build in flexibility in the criteria, such as not criticizing teachers when they could not answer students' questions [in the traditional classrooms, teachers are expected to know all the answers]. They also assisted teachers to prepare their lectures more fully so that teachers could make their classes more predictable. As a result of changing the way teachers are evaluated, a student's active involvement in learning and new ways of thinking are encouraged. Likewise, the school enhanced teachers' professional growth by using a more flexible, more diverse way of teacher evaluation.

Also, it was felt that it was important to modify textbooks to meet the needs of at-risk students. Although the textbooks have been improved a great deal during the reform, they generally serve the average students. To assure at-risk students to achieve more success, the school edited their own textbooks. Especially, the school organized teachers and experts to modify their math textbooks. The new textbooks are made suitable for at-risk students to follow the "trying-for-success model." For example, for each learning unit, the modified textbooks are divided into four parts: "Preparation," "sorting and layering," "students' exploration," and "self-learning." This change makes it much easier for at-risk students to succeed in the classroom.

The major change was applying new technologies in teacher teaching. The computer industry has probably been the fastest growing industry in human history. The new technology has made a tremendous change in traditional education and schooling. Liu and other school leaders became aware of the importance of new technology and started to take advantage of it in education at an early stage. Since 2001 when the new branch of school was established, the school invested a large sum of money on building a technology system. They have more than 300 computers on the campus with three computer labs and there is a computer in each classroom. The school spent money and time to train teachers in their computer skills and encouraged them to use multimedia and powerpoint in their classes. So far, their DVD products of math and English courses have been used in more than 100 schools in Shanghai and other provinces.

The new curriculum using technology has made a great contribution to the implementation of the "trying-for-success model." By using powerpoint, VCR, DVD, and other kinds of multimedia, teachers can provide a vivid, colorful, resourceful, and imaginative learning environment for students. The new instructional system emphasizes designing innovative, interesting, meaningful, and visual methods that can attract students' attention at the beginning of a class and maintain their interest in the middle of class. For example, a song, a picture, an episode from a film, a story, or animated cartoon, can enhance and improve students' learning. New technology plays an essential role in achieving these teaching goals.

The results of reform. After carrying out the "trying-for-success model" for years, the new learning system has reportedly achieved positive results. One of the direct results is that the reform has enhanced the quality of teaching and learning. A survey on the situation of math learning conducted by the school, which involved 928 students, shows that most of that students indicated that they love math and have made more progress in their learning than before. They also felt that their teachers taught less and let them have more activities than before (Chen, 2003).

Moreover, a voice from a student meeting reveals that:

"In the past, teachers usually taught the theory and principles first, then, they gave us some homework to do. Because we were just passively receiving information from the teachers, we could not remember the contents we had learned in the class. In the new learning, although teachers lecture to us less in the classroom, we have more exploration by ourselves. Instead of learning by rote, today we are more learning by doing. Thus, we learn everything in the classroom much faster than before. More importantly, we felt that we are the owners of our learning and will not be scared of learning any more." (Chen, 2003, p. 151)

Through my research, I do find some advantages of this alternative approach. During my investigation, I observed more than ten classes in both the old and new campus, covering the subjects of Chinese, math, English, physics, art, geography, politics, history, and psychology. In particular, I observed two 8th-grade classes, one in the old campus, the other in the new campus, and each lasted a whole week. In addition, I participated in a number of activities run by the school to demonstrate their powerpoint courses to teachers, experts, principals, and administrators from the city and other provinces. I also watched all DVD tapes I collected of outstanding teachers teaching and read all documents, books, and articles on this reform.

While taking part in all the above activities, the most impressive thing for me was that students in No. 8 School were very active and confident in joining all kinds of activities in the classroom. I am a Chinese and received my education from primary to graduate level in China. Comparing the new teaching method in No. 8 School to that in my days, I felt strongly that the traditional classroom in China has been changed tremendously. The teaching model in *success education* is much more flexible, dynamic, resourceful, and varied than the one in the old system.

For example, I watched a Chinese class videotape made by the school and was impressed by the rich contents and teachers' approaches for multisensory stimulation. In this class, the teacher taught students how to use imagination in their writing. She presented a powerpoint of a beautiful butterfly picture to create a learning environment at the beginning, then, she asked the students to use their imaginations. After summarizing students' ideas, she played part of a film to stimulate students and had them discuss imagination writing skills in a group. Students asked and answered questions. She did a summary again. Then, she played another video tape for students to recognize a new imagination skill. Finally, she distributed some study materials to students and asked them to do exercises in the classroom. The whole class was very active and multidimensional throughout.

In addition, I noticed that the new model can enhance teachers' teaching quality as well. Ms. He, an outstanding math teacher, told me that in the "helping-for-success model" at the early stage of the reform on the old campus, teachers assisted students with their study by using a pen, a blackboard, chalks, and a piece of paper. However, in the "trying-for-success model" on the new campus, with the availability of new technology, it is possible for teachers to teach students by using computers. That makes it totally different from the traditional classroom. At the beginning, she was very scared since she did not know anything about the computer. However, after having received training, she had learned not only computer skills but also much more. She said that in order to prepare a class she had to spend a lot of time reading all kinds of materials from the website. Before, she only read some entertainment stuff in the web but never wanted to read professional articles. However, after Liu required teachers to adopt technology in the classroom, she started to read research papers in her field. She felt she learned a lot and was very happy when she achieved success in her classroom instruction. For example, through the internet she has learned that in the world there were more than 400 methods to prove the Pythagorean Theorem. One of the former U.S. Presidents had proven this theorem. She said that if she has not had to prepare the powerpoint for the class, she would never know these things. Therefore, the new model truly helped her with her professional development.

On the other hand, my research also found that although the instructional reform has made great progress in the school, problems existed. Generally, there were three aspects of disparity, that is, there is a gap between the public lecture class and regular class, between the class recorded in videotapes and the real class, and between the outstanding teacher's class and ordinary teacher's class. After I got permission from the school to do my class observations in two particular classes, I sometimes went into the classroom to observe randomly. I found that the effect was not as good as shown in the tapes or in the public lecture class. In regular class, students were not as active as those shown in the tapes or in the public lectures, while the teachers' lectures were not as dynamic either. Second, in terms of teaching quality, a disparity existed between young teachers and older teachers. Most young teachers in this school were more willing to use new technology in their classroom than the older teachers. That made their classes more attractive and better received by the students. I saw that most older generation teachers still used the blackboard and chalks to teach their classes although their teaching methods had been changed greatly. It may need more time to help senior teachers to master computer skills in order to innovate their classroom. Third, between the old and the new campus there was a big gap in terms of the use of technology. While many teachers applied computers to their classrooms in the new school, the teachers in the old campus still taught mainly in the traditional way.

The Third Stage: Students Master Skills to Achieve Success Actively (Self-Mastery-for-Success Model)

This is the highest level as well as the ultimate goal of *success education*. At this stage, students would have already developed a positive and stable self-image. The concept of success has been internally instilled into students' consciousness and they could motivate themselves and educate themselves. In other words, under teachers' guidance, students in the "self-mastery-for-success model" were able to have their own learning plans, schedules, and pace of learning, and eventually reach the education goal required by the school. In this stage, students mainly learn by themselves while the role of a teacher is as an advisor. Specifically, according to Liu, the "self-mastery-for-success" can be explained in the following four aspects (Chen, 2003).

First, students can choose learning content. That is to say, in this highest teaching model, within the required teaching outline, students can decide what they want to learn and in what way they want to learn. Because these students are highly motivated, they may learn some lessons by themselves. In this way, students can have more free time to select outside readings in accordance with their own study interests. In order to meet these students' needs, the school curriculum can be arranged in a flexible way.

Second, students can choose their learning schedule and location. One of the drawbacks of the traditional education is its highly controlled learning schedule and location. Under the old system, students are deprived of having their own choice in learning time and location. In many ways, this inflexible system is not suitable for everyone as individuals are unique beings. In the new learning system, students can flexibly decide when and where their learning will occur, based on their own learning situation. Thus, their enthusiasm in leaning will be enhanced.

Third, students can arrange their own learning pace. In the traditional classroom, the purpose of education is to cope with all kinds of standardized tests in order to help students pass the National Entrance Examination. Therefore, all students are required to learn in basically the same way and at the same pace regardless of their different knowledge levels, their different learning styles, and their different pace. As a result, some quick learners may feel that they are wasting time, since the current school system cannot meet their curiosity to learn new knowledge; in contrast, other students may think that the learning speed is too fast for them. The "self-mastery-for-success model" allows students to choose their learning pace and content. That is very important for those at-risk students to improve their academic outcome, who can decide their own learning pace in accordance with their reality.

Fourth, students can evaluate their learning effectiveness by themselves. Under the conventional educational system, the teacher is always the authority to evaluate students' learning. Students' examination score is regarded as the only criterion for assessing if a student is a good student or not. In this highly competitive model, at-risk students usually become the victims of the exam-driven system. To change this situation, *success education* alters the evaluation criteria by giving the power to students, that is, let students evaluate themselves. This way, students can understand themselves better, then can educate themselves and adjust themselves. As a consequence, students will establish self-expectation and self-confidence. Furthermore, the evaluation can also be conducted among students so that they can learn from each other and feel more authentic and more persuadable.

Liu used three words to describe this model as "self-education, voluntary learning, and self-regulation." Liu and the research group designed this highest teaching model of *success education* based on an attempt to overcome the disadvantages of the modern Chinese exam-oriented educational system. This third model is an educational model that is way beyond any orthodox educational models, Liu explained. "But how can you implement it?" I asked. According to Liu, it needs students who have a very clear direction to go, teachers who are knowledgeable and know educational principles very well, and a very open and advanced education system. Especially, it relies on a highly advanced technology system, a new learning environment, which can make learning occur across space and time. The new learning will employ integrated systems and interactive learning systems such as the Internet, web school, web class, and long distance education. It should be a totally opened and multidimensional learning.

"So far, how is this system going? In what way does it work? What is the result?" I asked Liu. Liu replied:

> Currently, we are mainly carrying out the "trying-for-success model." We only have some ideas about the third model and did some small experiments on that. Maybe many conditions are not ready yet. Our teachers also are not ready yet. Some of them even did not understand the second model. There are many questions we still need to do further research.

To verify Liu's comments, I asked teachers what is this new model during my interview. All of them did not have a clear picture.

Ms. He was one of the teachers who did an experiment on this new idea. She told me that she applied the new teaching model to her two math classes. However, she said she might not dare to do this kind of new thing any more since she worried that her students might not be ready yet. She described how she did her experiment:

> I asked my students to do their homework and review all the things they had learned on that day after school at home. Then, they were required to read the textbook for the second day's class. After reading, they were supposed to do a ten-or-fifteen-minute test for the new class. On the second day, at the beginning of the class, I took a couple of minutes to review all the tests the students did and knew what part they had already understood and what part they did not. For those unknown parts, I organized students into groups to discuss, ignoring those knowledge students had known. After group discussion, each group sent a representative to present their learning in front of class. Finally, I summarized the learning. That was all I did. The thing I worried about the most was that only a few students presented their ideas during the class while most students did not get a chance to share their learning. I am not sure if they really understood their lessons. Especially, for those at-risk students, since they lacked much background knowledge, this kind of class is difficult for them.

Ms. He's experience indicated that the school is facing some challenges to implement its highest level of teaching reform. This may be a dream for No. 8 School to reach. In particular, China still has the National Entrance Examination. Within this highly competitive context, it is still a long, long way to go to achieve their goal. However, my research told me that after 2000 the school has been advancing to a new ideology as the deepening of *success education*: "The integration of knowledge, ability, and personality," and "the integration of the strength of Eastern and Western education." In other words, to catch up with the movement of globalization, the school set up its aspiration that attempts to combine the best parts of Western and Eastern education together. Also, from a holistic perspective, the school tries to train its students as a whole person that integrates moral, intelligent, physical, emotional, and social development together. To some extent, this may be a meaningful exploration to arrive at the goal of "self-mastery-for-success model."

Liu explained why he promoted these "two integrations" within the school. The nature of *success education* is to foster students' success mentality, self-confidence in learning, and ultimately help them become a self-directed learner and achieve success through self-efforts. In the exam-driven educational system, because of the overemphasis on knowledge acquisition, students' abilities and personal development have been neglected. Therefore, instead of teachers teaching all the time as in the old learning system, Liu suggested that his teachers only teach students "the optimized knowledge" and leave more room for students to develop their abilities and personality. Liu thought that since today we are living in an era of knowledge explosion, it is impossible for us to teach all the knowledge needed to our students. The best way as a teacher is to train students with those qualities which will enable them to acquire knowledge for themselves in the future. Facing a highly competitive society, developing students' abilities and character traits are even more important than learning knowledge itself. Therefore, what is the nature of education? Liu insisted that education is not simply to deliver information any more. The meaning of education today, according to Liu, is to facilitate students' "harmonious development of knowledge, ability, and personality." It is also "the integration of Eastern and Western education" since we are living in a globalization era. Only by running a school in such a comprehensive way can our students be trained to achieve success by themselves.

To implement these new reforms, Liu and other school leaders have adopted various strategies. For example, to develop students' abilities, the school is continuously carrying out the "trying-for-success model" in which teachers teach less, so that it creates more opportunities for students to explore. Also, the school asks students to manage their own classes and run all kinds of extracurricular activities by themselves.

152 Success for All

Liu thought that self-confidence is the core of personality. Therefore, to nurture students' high self-esteem and self confidence, *success education* insists on three principles in their classroom, that is, a class must let students: (1) have more success than failure; (2) experience success; and (3) deal with failure positively. To have accountability on that, the school requires its teachers to never blame their students and always be positive in the classroom. Furthermore, they modified and invented their own textbooks, study materials, and homework books, which fit students' learning pace. In this way, students have the opportunity to achieve success.

To integrate the strength of Western and Eastern education, Liu introduced a "party culture" to the campus. He proposed having a party once a month in the school. The party is to be organized and hosted by one class at a time, open to all students in the school if the program is good. The purpose of hosting a party is to train students' abilities in many ways such as their leadership skills, communication skills, problem solving skills, and other kinds of social skill. Preparing the party seriously, all in the class will be involved.

For example, I attended a party during the time when I was in No. 8 School. The party was conduced by a 7th class, titled "Worshiping star idols is not good." Two students (a female and a male) hosted the program which lasted for more than an hour. All classmates were divided into different groups and acted as different roles (such as parents, teachers, children, stars etc.) to demonstrate the theme: Entertainment activities such as watching

Photo 8.2 The party: "Worshiping star idols is not good," 2004.

TV and films, singing, and dancing are a good relaxation after class, however, if one is addicted to star idols, it will negatively affect students' study.

Other reforms influenced by Western education can be seen in the campus. For example, instead of only having required courses as it was in the past, they have more elective courses opened to students. Purposefully, Liu even trains his students to combine the Eastern and the Western system together through a small daily routine like morning exercises. Usually, all schools at basic education level in China have morning exercises, gathering all students in a big sports ground to start their learning day. In the past, like any schools in China, students in No. 8 School were always trained to line up like an army troop, entering into the sports ground in proper order. Liu thought that there was too much uniform behavior training for students. Thus, he transforms this practice in a half-Chinese and half-Western way: Students can get into the sports ground freely with the pop music and line up in the end to go to their classrooms. Even though many teachers and some school leaders have different opinions, the new practice has been implemented much to the pleasure of the students.

In summary, the school has been trying any possible ways to train students to achieve success. They have explored the different stages of the development of *success education,* indicating progress from the lower level to higher level. Using an analogy of how a child learns to walk, Liu described the relationship between three models vividly as shown in Figure 8.3. The diagram clearly shows that the end of *success education* is to cultivate independent learners, free beings who can achieve success for themselves.

THE INNOVATION OF EVALUATION CRITERIA

Evaluation is an essential element that directly influences at-risk students' mentality and performance. In regular Chinese schools, educational excellence is only measured by a series of standardized academic tests and scores. This placed great pressure on students and teachers and damaged many at-risk students' self-esteem and self-confidence. Also, labeling students only

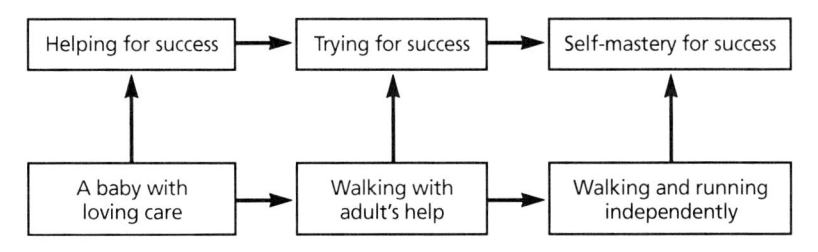

Figure 8.3 Diagram of the different stages of the development of *success education.*

by measuring the result of learning and not by looking at the process at all, the traditional evaluation method itself has become one of the main factors putting students at risk. Under this evaluation system, those students who failed again and again could not find their potential and eventually lost the motivation in learning.

Thus, while reforming the teaching method, *success education* has altered the school evaluation system simultaneously. Called "evaluation with encouragement," the new assessment system was characterized by consideration for at-risk students' starting points in learning (not the end of learning) and a focus on students' progress. Therefore, the research group replaced the unitary testing standard with dynamic, multidimensional, and diverse methods to evaluate students' performance. Specifically, the main strategies taken by the school were the following (Liu, 2001).

First, changing the function of evaluation from ranking students from top to bottom, to that of helping students recognize themselves and develop themselves. In traditional education, to achieve the goal of helping students pass the National Entrance Examination, all kinds of examinations and tests from teachers, school, district, and city are conducted from time to time. In those assessments, based on the scores they got students are labeled and their names posted on the wall, making them felt like they were commodities to be sold. Under this circumstance, the relationship between teachers, school, and students is tense. The huge stress has made a large number of students scared and tired of learning.

To stimulate students' enthusiasm for learning, instead of having unified exams as required by the outline of teaching issued by the Ministry of Education, the school tested students based on their real knowledge level so that they could succeed after making an effort. For example, at the first stage of the reform, students' Chinese only reached grade 4 level of elementary school. After analyzing the easiest objective students could achieve, the research group designed examinations in such a way that matches students' actual situation. As a result, students were excited about their grades and for the first time felt that they were able to learn. Other courses such as math and English followed the same strategy.

Also, another obvious feature of *success education* evaluation system is not just to test what students have learned but rather assist them to identify their own strengths. Liu pointed out that the difference between the traditional model and the alternative one is that in the old system, everyone was perceived to have disadvantages so he or she needs to learn; however in the new model, everyone is deemed to have strengths, and everyone can be successful. In this sense, the nature of evaluation in *success education* is to help children find their strengths, evaluate themselves, and develop themselves.

Mr. Xia, an outstanding Chinese teacher, shared his experience about how he helped a 9th grade student who had difficulty in Chinese to improve his writing skill. According to Xia, this student never got any good grades in writing in his entire learning history. He lost his hope in that. In one test, the student's composition was not good except for the beginning part. Xia keenly praised his progress shown in the beginning part of his writing and made copies of his paper for everyone in the class. Xia asked all his classmates to read the first paragraph of the article, then, analyzed why it was good. Having received positive comments from the class, the students' interest in writing was greatly enhanced. Eventually, he not only improved his article, but also made a great deal of progress in writing in his studies.

Second, changing the method of evaluation from giving uniform tests to designing individualized assessment. Wiles and Bondi (2001) expect that in the twenty-first century the new American middle school should shift from a comprehensive evaluation system to an individualized assessment model. As early as the mid-1980s, No. 8 School noticed that because of negative life experiences, there existed a big disparity among at-risk students in their learning. It was impossible for teachers to use the standardized tests which set very high requirements to evaluate those students who have suffered failure for long at the beginning. Otherwise, it would even worsen the situation. Hence, the school made the decision to replace the unified examinations by a multi-level assessment system. As long as students showed any progress, they would encourage them.

In greater detail, the school divided student evaluation into four levels (A, B, C, D) and allowed students to select a level they could reach. When students achieved a certain level, they could attend the test set for that level. In daily homework, teachers gave different levels of exercises to different students. They allowed some students to not do some homework that may be too difficult for them, but which was required by the outline. For students with the most difficulties, the school even designed individualized tests for them. For example, in the math course, a student at the first experimental class was getting into big trouble in geometry. The teacher flexibly used his score of algebra to replace his grade in geometry (Zhang et al., 1993). But in the meantime, the teacher tried many ways to make up his knowledge in geometry. Finally, the student passed the examinations in both geometry and algebra with the teacher's help. There were many such kinds of stories during my interview.

Third, changing the contents of evaluation from one simple written form to multidimensional tests. In regular classes, teachers usually only use a written test to evaluate students, whereas writing is usually the weakest part of at-risk students. The research group realized that if the old format of assessment was used continuously, it would reinforce the failure of at-risk students. In fact, students have multiple intelligence and abilities, and it is not fair to only use one method to evaluate them. Also, in real life, our society needs all kinds of talents, why does our school only provide such narrow training for our students?

Thus, the new evaluation model broke the old rule by having a variety of examinations. For example, in Chinese language classes, teachers designed two kinds of tests for students: One was a comprehensive exam, the regular exam form used by most Chinese schools, accounting for 50% of the total score, and another 50% was designed which consisted of reading (speed reading), listening comprehension, speech-giving, and calligraphy (pen & writing brush). These components are useful in real life but are not included in the national examination (Wang, 1993). Also, in the math class, they added students' performance in the classroom to the contents of evaluation. For instance, to foster good study habits, teachers widened the assessment to evaluate how seriously students took their classes and how actively they participated in the classroom learning. In terms of homework, the evaluation included whether students asked teachers for help if they had a problem, whether the students could finish their task independently or not, and even whether their formats of homework could meet the requirements. To encourage students, teachers saw detecting any progress students have made as a necessary part of evaluation. For those most difficult students, as long as they took any serious actions in their learning, the teachers would praise them (Zhang et al., 1993).

In addition, to encourage students to make more progress, the school created many kinds of awards. For example, since the "three excellent prize" (excellent in morality, intelligence, and physical education), a highest level award in Chinese schools, is only given to a small proportion of students, the school set up a "progress award in study habits," "class service award," and a "progress award in academic achievement" and so forth, to give most students a feeling of success. Also, they increased awards for students who took part in extracurricular activities in order to attract more students to engage in learning after school. Through enriching the contents and methods of assessment, students felt that they had more opportunities to achieve academic success.

Fourth, changing the method of evaluation from the teacher-centered model to a system of multiple evaluation channels. In the past, teachers were seen as the single authority making decisions on students' tests. Lacking a positive interaction between educators and learners, the rigid system turned students into passive learners. To create a dynamic learning climate, besides teachers' assessment, *success education* encouraged students to have self-evaluation and group evaluation. Some teachers even invited parents to participate in the process of evaluation.

In this new system, students were required to set up their goals in learning, formulate their own strategies to achieve their goals, and finally evaluate their learning by themselves at the end of the semester. In that way, students became an active partner in their own evaluation. Moreover, sometimes teachers in No. 8 School regarded student peer evaluation as more powerful and more efficient than that from teachers. Therefore, in classrooms, student group evaluation has often been used to form an active learning atmosphere. For example, Mr. Xia, the head teacher of Chinese in the first stage of reform, described his experience of practicing this method. He said that to make students experience fun in Chinese learning, after examinations, sometimes he distributed students' compositions, speeches, works of calligraphy to the class, asking students to evaluate them. By having this kind of activity, students confirmed that their progress praised by teachers was true since they got other opinions from their classmates. As a result, they might develop more self-confidence in their success (Xia, 1993).

Fifth, evaluating students' failure with encouragement. Although *success education* has always tried to provide many opportunities for students to improve, failure for students is still inevitable. In the traditional instructional pattern, teachers simply made an error mark when students gave a wrong answer in their tests. However, in *success education* system, teachers have to carefully analyze students' failure, aiming at encouraging at-risk students by finding any tiny success factors in their examinations. Becoming students' spiritual fort of support, teachers in the school are required to never criticize students in the classroom and always to be positive toward students. Rather than blaming students as in the past, teachers should help students figure out the reasons why they made the mistakes and how they can remedy those errors.

During the experiment, to restore students' self-esteem and self-confidence, the teachers made every attempt not to give students a low score. If students failed to pass the exams, the school would allow them to retest. Also, instead of giving a precise mark, teachers usually offered students an indistinct score such as "good" instead of 60 or "excellent" not 100 on their exams. That is because students have many other qualities that could not be evaluated by quantitative standards.

In No. 8 School, teachers believe that they will never give up on any students, no matter how much difficulty they are having. There is a well-known story in the school, which told us how teachers encouraged a student to increase her score from 7 to 74. A girl only got 7 points on her physics examination at the beginning of the reform. She felt hopeless in learning this subject. Mr. Xue, a teacher who was in charge of managing her class, talked with her and encouraged her if she could increase her score to 8 or 9 on the next exam. She promised him she would since she would only have to increase her scores a little bit, 1 or 2 points more. On the second exam, although she worked very hard, she obtained only a score of 37. She cried about her failure. However, Xue told all her class that jumping from

7 to 37, was a miracle. Therefore, he awarded her "the biggest progress in the class." The girl was so moved and the encouragement stimulated her interest in physics learning. On the third exam, she got 54, still failing to pass the exam. She utterly lost her confidence in this subject since no matter how hard she tried she just seemed to not make it. Xue encouraged her again and said that she was such a clever girl that she only needed to earn 6 points more to pass the exam. The student smiled and was motivated again. The fourth time the exam was a unified test at district level. The girl got 74 points. She was so excited that she told everyone that the happiest time she has spent were those she spent in No. 8 School (Xue, 1993).

In all, by adopting an alternative evaluation system, the school helped at-risk students experience remarkable success in their learning that inspired dramatically their enthusiasm in schooling. This has been said as a very effective strategy to enhance at-risk students' academic achievements used by No. 8 School in its early stage of experiment. However, in the new campus, I did not observe this strategy was continuously applied to ar-risk students. The important reasons, to a great extent, may be because the school became a key school at district level and students were not at-risk students anymore.

SUMMARY

To enhance at-risk students' self-esteem and self-confidence in learning, No. 8 School has made tremendous efforts. They started their teaching reform by raising teachers' expectation for at-risk students. They initiated three teaching models to meet students' needs in the different stages. The "helping-for-success model" was the first effort they adopted to improve students' academic learning; it had been proven to affect students positively. When the practice had moved forward, the school expanded the teaching method to one called the "trying-for-success model," to fit students who had made progress and needed to learn independently by themselves. As the highest level of the teaching model, "self-mastery-for-success" was designed to help those students who are totally transformed from being at-risk students to outstanding students. The school not only changed its teaching methods, but also altered its evaluation criterion. Instead of the uniform testing standard used in the past, the new evaluation system, called "evaluation with encouragement," used multiple ways and dimensions to encourage students to achieve success. All these efforts had resulted in very promising effects on at-risk students' academic learning.

Photo 8.3 The class in the old campus of No. 8 School, 2004.

CHAPTER 9

THE NEW FUNCTION OF MORAL EDUCATION IN *SUCCESS EDUCATION*

A Network of Developing At-Risk Students Self-Confidence and Ability of Self-Education

Throughout Chinese history, in both literal meaning and practice, education has been regarded as having two functions: Teaching children knowledge and cultivating their moral character (*jiaoshu yuren*). In previous chapters, I have examined the teaching innovation carried out in No. 8 School. The following three chapters will discuss the other important part of Chinese schooling and address this question: How success education has reconstructed its function of nurturing at-risk students' personal development in today's reform era? Therefore, three aspects that are relevant to facilitating students' personal development: Moral education, student management, and parents' and community's involvement will be explored.

This chapter starts with the study of moral education reform through *success education*. Besides student learning in Chinese, math, and English, moral education was the fourth aspect of reform, originally shown in Liu's

---

Success for All, pages 161–186
Copyright © 2008 by Information Age Publishing
All rights of reproduction in any form reserved.

research proposal in 1987. Mainly, the chapter will define moral education from a Chinese perspective, how the school changed its traditional function of moral education, how those moral education activities helped at-risk students with their personal growth and academic outcomes, and the results they have achieved.

AN OVERVIEW OF MORAL EDUCATION

China is a country which values moral virtues throughout its history. In ancient Chinese philosophy, a person is essentially viewed as a moral being. All human activities should result in the moral good (Wu & Ginsberg, 1986). Accordingly, the Chinese conceive that the highest level of education is to teach children how to become a moral being. Thus, moral education has always been an indispensable part of the curriculum in China from K–12 to the university levels.

Unlike Western schools, moral education (*Deyu*) in China is not just a course, but rather it includes course taking, values development through student management and behavior training. The aim of moral education is to cultivate children to be good citizens. Therefore, moral education in China is a high priority involving teachers and leaders, and it is institutionalized in the form of a Moral Education Office. Figure 9.1 is a diagram of moral education as an organization.

Figure 9.1 shows that moral education as an organization for students' management in No. 8 School is a complicated system which requires many departments to collaborate. Since the nature of moral education is students' ideological work, at the school level, the secretary of the school Party committee takes the main responsibility for this task. Although every staff and teacher plays a role in shaping students' morality, the major forces of moral education are those teachers who are in charge of classes, the Committee of the Communist Youth League, Youth Pioneers, Office of Psychological Counseling, and Youth Protection Organization. The Student Association, and TV & Radio Station are mainly run by students under the leadership of the Committee of the Communist Youth League and Youth Pioneers. Moral education as a course is taught in elementary schools. However, in middle schools, it primarily impacts students through schools conducting all kinds of activities that are suitable for adolescents. In the experimental school, as a part of moral education, psychology is a popular course, helping students to adjust their mind-set on many issues. Also, the doctor working in the Medical Clinic gives some lectures on physical and mental health education to students through a school broadcasting program at lunch time. This is a brief description of moral education in No. 8 School. However, according to the teachers whom I interviewed, moral education for at-risk students,

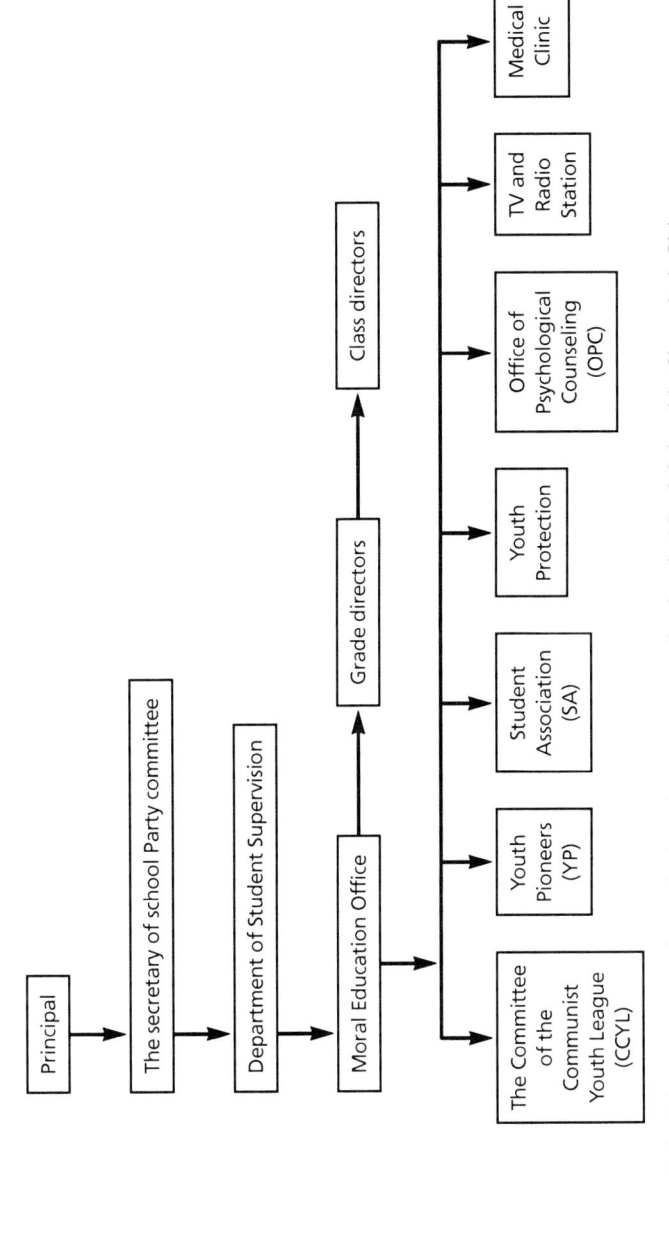

The New Function of Moral Education in Success Education **163**

Figure 9.1 The structure of moral education as an organization in No. 8 School in Shanghai, China.

particularly, is difficult, which is, in fact, permeated throughout the whole process of schooling.

CALLING FOR REFORM IN MORAL EDUCATION

When Liu was asked to answer the question, "What have you done regarding moral education reform," he said that he has paid special attention to three aspects in student management: (1) Training students to abide by disciplines; (2) cultivating good study habits; and (3) helping students build up self-confidence in success. By reviewing the data, I found that there existed some serious problems in the above three aspects before the experiment was carried out in No. 8 School. These problems were the primary motivation for Liu to call for moral education reform.

In terms of discipline, called a "garbage school" or a "hooligan school," No. 8 School had serious problems with students' misbehaving for a long time. Located in a high poverty area, the school had the highest rate of crime in the district. Stealing, robbery, fighting, and criminal gangs were common among students. Offenders from outside the school often lured and colluded with students to commit crimes. The discipline problems in the school were so severe that moral education teachers acted as policemen to force students into the classroom when the class began, or got them back from the game rooms on the street during the lunch time for the afternoon class. Without a safe and quiet learning environment, students had many problems in learning.

In terms of study habits, students in this school had low motivation for learning. Living in "the area of slum-dwellers," most No. 8 School students came from low income and single-parent families. Two thirds of the parents had lost their jobs. With a low educational background, many parents had low expectations for their children's education. Many children lived with their grandparents due to their parent's divorce, or that their parents were too busy to take care of them. Lacking support from families and community, the students had not formed good study habits. They did not want to do home work, did not want to read and write, and even did not want to go to school.

In terms of self-confidence, the research group revealed that low self-esteem was the major problem that existed among students in No. 8 School. Through several months of investigation, the research group found that in terms of intelligence, the IQ test they applied showed that students' scores in this school were not lower than the average level in other regular schools. However, research in other non-cognitive factors such as self-esteem, self-confidence, willpower, interest in learning, and affection, presented a much lower level than other students. Low self-confidence in learning resulted in students' continuous failure. They felt that at home their parents did not like them; in school they were the students teachers disliked; and further, the school they attended was the worst school in society. They were forced to go to No. 8 School. They did not like themselves nor did they like the school. All these negative factors made them lose hope in their future and lose control over their behavior.

Based on their research findings, Liu and the research group figured out that the main problems of at-risk students in learning were not problems of cognition or intelligence but non-cognitive problems, namely the problem of motivation. The strategies taken by the school to deal with this problem should then focus on strengthening students' non-cognitive training or enhancing students' self-motivation, a task that is generally carried out by moral education. However, the traditional way of moral education did not meet the new needs of students.

Generally speaking, moral education in China is an ideological and political education. As a political tool, the contents of the teaching materials are set out to be consistent with CPC ideology. The fundamental task of moral education in secondary schools is to cultivate the young generation to become successors of socialism. The goal of moral education at junior high level is to nurture "three loves": love of the motherland; love of the Communist Party of China; love of socialism and become a good citizen with culture, knowledge and discipline. Therefore, activities with themes of patriotism, collectivism, and socialism are often assigned to schools from the district and city. With obvious political purpose and rigid forms, students often feel they are extra burdens to add to them and sometimes even became tired of these kinds of moral education activities. For all of the above reasons reform in moral education was called for so Liu and the research group undertook the task of innovating moral education in 1987.

THE STRATEGIES OF MORAL EDUCATION REFORM IN NO. 8 SCHOOL

To achieve its reform goal, a moral education group, which consisted of experts and teachers from the district and the school, had been organized to begin an innovation in this field in 1987. Liu states that the purposes of moral education in success education are: (1) To stimulate students' motivation to get to know themselves in a correct way, evaluate themselves properly, and develop an ability to educate themselves; and (2) to cultivate students a success mentality that can enable them to develop a sound attitude in both learning and life. In other words, the nature of moral education reform in success education is to rebuild students' inner world that eventually will enable students to become a self-regulated learner. The following are some alternative measures undertaken by the school to reform its moral education (Chen, C. 1993).

1. Building up a New Relationship between Teachers and Students

For a long time, educators have extolled the benefits of a positive relationship between teachers and students (Bradley et al., 2005). The quality of teacher-student relationships is regarded as the corner stone for all other aspects of classroom management. Research shows teachers' interpersonal behavior is an essential facet of the classroom learning environment and is associated with enhanced cognitive and affective outcomes such as motivation, self-esteem, and learning engagement (Fraser & Walberg 1991). Particularly, a caring teacher-student relationship is extremely important to improve at-risk students' academic outcomes (Baker et al., 1997; Piania & Walsh, 1996).

China has a long tradition which values teaching moral ethics. In ancient China, a teacher is a person who can transmit wisdom, impart knowledge, and resolve doubts. Thus, the teacher is usually viewed as a moral model to shape students' mentality through his/her words and behaviors (*yanchuan shenjiao*). What is the relationship between teachers and students in No. 8 School before the reform? Within a poor living environment, the students had serious discipline problems. Teachers had tried very hard to solve the problems. However, by following the traditional model, teachers had generally taken coercive measures to control students from top down. There is a saying to describe this situation: "When I (the teacher) teach, you (the student) listen, then do the way what I told you." Within such a context, teacher-student relationship was very tense. Also, under the exam-orientated education system, teachers paid a lot of attention to students' scores, criticizing those low achievers all the time. Consequently, students were scared of teachers and did not want to communicate with them. Isolated from teachers, students' academic achievements went from bad to worse.

In the revised moral education approach, the school educated teachers in the philosophy of *success education*. They conducted all kinds of meetings, classes, and conferences to train teachers to respect at-risk students, love those disadvantaged students, be patient with problem students, and try various ways to help them. The school realized that although the requirements of teaching ethics are varied, the core of the training is to educate them to "love students," especially, to "give special attention to at-risk students." Therefore, the school formulated its requirements of teaching morality—"Six 'nots' in treating students," as follows:

1. Do not punish students or use corporal punishment in disguised form;
2. Do not mock and abuse students;
3. Do not discriminate against at-risk students who have drawbacks, make mistakes, or fail exams;
4. Do not infringe upon students' rights of privacy;
5. Do not randomly deprive students' rights of taking the class as a punishment;
6. Do not criticize any students in a parent's meeting.

On the contrary, teachers were advised to always recognize students' strengths, and encourage them when they made progress. After this training, many teachers modified the way they taught and the methods they used to manage students. Gradually, the idea of *success education* was embraced by the teachers in school.

Also, in the new learning environment created by the reform, students felt they were respected, cared for, and appreciated and they developed a sense of trust in their teachers. A more equal and caring teacher-student connection has been established. For example, when asked the questions "how do you think of your teachers? Are they good?" All the students I surveyed answered "yes." Many alumni students said that teachers in No. 8 School were like their parents, who took care of them, respected and understood them.

2. Managing the Class by Students Themselves

Another effective measure used by the school, with respect to moral education reform, is to emphasize classroom management. That is to say, the class is the main vehicle to carry out the reform. In China, a "*class*" is not just a lesson but more a unit of learning in which a group of students in the same grade are assigned to a classroom where they are taught and conduct all kinds of activities together throughout the whole primary school or secondary school. In other words, from the beginning to the end for four years in junior high, students in a class will take all courses together in the same classroom, forming a cooperative group under the leadership of a class director—a teacher who supervises the class not only in academic affairs but in all matters related to the children. Also, the class is the main place where peer influence occurs in school. Therefore, creating a positive learning climate in the class is very important for students to grow and develop.

As mentioned before, students' discipline and study habits were big problems faced by teachers in No. 8 School. How did they deal with these problems? The school leaders found that the reason why the traditional model did not work well was that it employed a coercive and authoritarian way to restrain students externally. The rigid approach made the adolescents disgusted with the school regulations. S*uccess education* attempts to explore an original and internal way of communicating with students. By sharing power and responsibility with students in the process of classroom management, an equal relationship between teachers and students has been built up. Becoming a collaborator in the administrative system with teachers, students started to learn how to serve the community, and how to manage themselves.

According to Ai (1993), the student management forces consisted of three groups: the Student Supervision Team, Student Association, and the Committee of Class. Selected from student leaders at different grades, the Student Supervision Team participates in the implementing of moral education directly under leadership of the Department of Student Supervision in school, responsible for submitting student information to the director of the department. The Student Association comprises student leaders chosen by the classes, functioning as a bridge to communicate between school leaders, teachers and students. The Committee of Class is the basic but essential students' organization at the class level. Selected by classmates, the Committee of Class performs the major management tasks of a class under the class director's supervision.

Specifically, the school has been running a program called "Building up the star class" to reform its moral education since the 1990s. This is a comprehensive reform in student management, covering children's total performance in schooling. To be selected as a star class, a class has to be excellent in discipline, behavior, and learning. The objectives of conducting the project are to develop students' ability to educate themselves, to correct their behavioral problems by themselves, and to experience success in school life. Every semester, Moral Education Office awards those star classes based on their comparative performance with other class and the weekly assessment. The program consists of three aspects—"The evaluation of students' daily behavior," "the construction of standardized classrooms, and "weekly duty management." Under the teacher's supervision, students engaged in all three processes. The following section will provide a clear picture to explain how students are involved in the school's management.

"*The students' daily behavior regulation*" consists of a list of basic requirements issued by the school, which a student is expected to follow. The regulation includes ten expectations covering items such as students arriving and leaving school on time, being neatly dressed and adorned, wearing required symbols (Youth Pioneers, the Communist Youth League, etc.), being well mannered in daily life, being quiet during the rest hours (lunch time), caring for public property, doing physical exercises seriously, maintaining cleanness in public areas, getting to class in two minutes before the class starts, and maintaining good discipline in class and other activities. All these requirements are evaluated daily by teachers and staff from the Department of Student Supervision and Moral Education Office, as well as

Photo 9.1 Students' daily behavior: Morning exercises, 2004.

Photo 9.2 Students' daily behavior: Eye-protection exercises, 2004.

three student groups mentioned above. The evaluation scores are posted on the school bulletin board. If a class does a good job, it will be given the "flowing flag of excellence." Four classes will be selected every week and ranked 1, 2, 3, 4 by excellence. Every Monday morning when the school holds the flag-raising ceremony, the school leaders will award the flowing flag to those selected classes. If one student has any behavioral problem, the class will not be selected. It has been reported as an effective way to improve students' behavior and discipline.

In terms of "*the construction of standardized classrooms*," although there are a few janitors who do the cleaning in the school generally, students still need to clean their own classes, the teaching building, and the campus, all these activities aimed at training students to take responsibility, be able to do hard work, and cultivate a good attitude toward labor. The regulations of a standardized classroom require students in a class to keep their room clean, neat, dustless, and beautiful. To do so, students have to clean their classroom twice a day, put their desks, chairs, and other things including curtains, books, and cleaning tools etc. in order. To implement "the construction of standardized classrooms," the Committee of Class will have a meeting to work out a plan at the beginning of each semester, then, have student names on duty every day. The committee will watch all the time to make sure everything is fine. In the meanwhile, student groups at different levels will check the implementation every day, fill out an evaluation form, and report the situation to the Department of Student Supervision. The results of the assessment will be amalgamated as evidence of qualifications for being selected the star class at the end of the semester.

In terms of "*weekly duty management*," every class in No. 8 School takes turns to be responsible for cleaning the campus, arranging the flag-raising ceremony, and checking all the students' behavior for a week. Starting at 6:30 a.m., students in the class on duty are divided into groups to do their tasks. Twenty children are arranged to clean the campus and teaching building while four students are assigned as inspectors to check the whole areas. What impressed me was that early every morning eight students, who wore a school uniform with a red scarf, CYL badge, and a long red sash crossing the shoulder, stood up straight in front of the school gate to be on duty. They saluted and greeted every teacher who came to school: "Good morning, teacher!" In the meantime, they checked every student and saw if he or she wore uniform, a red scarf, CYL badge, etc. and if he or she behaved properly to teachers and classmates. If not, they would write down the student name, grade, and class number, submitting all this information to the teachers in the Moral Education Office. In the teaching building, another four students in front of the gate and two students on each floor did the same thing. It seemed to me that teachers in this school were respected very much.

Photo 9.3 Students on duty, 2004.

The flag-raising ceremony on Monday morning at 7:30 a.m. is always the most solemn moment for the school. All the teachers, staff, and students gather together on the sports ground, and while the national anthem was being played, all salute to the national flag while four student flag-raisers hoist the flag slowly. The whole ceremony is hosted by the class which is on duty. The two main flag-raisers are not selected randomly from the class on duty, but purposefully chosen as the model for all students to learn from. They are the persons who have made great progress in behavior as well as in learning during a period of time. After raising the flag, the host will introduce two main flag-raisers' stories to all participants. The principal or other school leaders may give comments and call for all students to learn from them. The whole ceremony lasts 20 minutes.

During the day, the students on duty need to check students' daily behaviors and see if any problems occur. Also, every day after class, two students will go to the class one by one and check if the doors, and windows are closed, and the lights and fans are turned off. The shift will be passed to the next class at noon time on Friday. After finishing the duty, the class is required to submit a summary to the Department of Student Supervision

172 *Success for All*

Photo 9.4 The flag-raising ceremony in Monday morning, 2004.

Photo 9.5 Vice principal awarded two main flag-raisers in Monday morning flag-raising ceremony, 2004.

over the weekend. In all, every student in the class on duty is involved in the activities. It has been reported that to some extent, the program facilitated students to develop their management abilities and other qualities.

Except for the above three kinds of activities, to achieve the goal of the star class, other qualifications such as study habit, academic achievement, prizes winning from all kinds of school competitions, the frequency of going to the library, and the amount of participation in interest groups after class and other social activities are also evaluated. Indeed, this is a comprehensive program that requires students to work hard. As a result, through students' engagement in the management of their learning and campus life, the students discipline, study habits, and behaviors are greatly improved.

3. Reconstructing Students' Self-Confidence through Moral Education

The fundamental task of *success education* is to help at-risk students change the way they look at themselves by applying an entirely new, confidence-building self-concept system. How does moral education function as a tool to achieve this goal? The school worked hard to increase students' self-esteem through stressing a non-cognitive approach, in particular, at the early stage of the experiment.

First, finding the starting point that could combine the requirements of moral education with students' needs. As mentioned above, traditional moral education serves a political purpose. Viewed as extra tasks imposed on them and its use far from their real life, students were not interested in these kinds of activities. After launching *success education*, the school worked on combining moral education with students' needs, trying to find all possible ways to transform at-risk students' mind-set from a passive and failure-oriented one to a positive and hopeful one. Based on research of students' psychological characteristics and through analyzing their problems in schooling, the research group designed different programs of moral education for students at different grade levels.

For the first and second year students, the school had a program, titled "Everyone was born to have unique talents to serve society," to develop their self-confidence and foster their good study habits through an affective approach. Newly coming out of primary school, new students entered No. 8 School with frustrations, as their classmates passed the exams and confidently started a new life in key middle schools. Feeling depressed, they had no interest in this at-risk school which was looked down on by society, no confidence in learning, and no hope in the future. Also, facing new teachers and new classmates in the new school, they had to deal with a wholly new environment with uncertainty.

To help students transform these negative feelings, the school organized many activities for new students. The aim of the program was to assist students to love their new school and new class, respect teachers, and care for their new classmates. For example, the school held a welcome party to all students and parents, presenting the achievements the school had gained and the school aspiration to build a better school under the idea of *success education*. At the beginning of the new semester, instead of dealing a blow to the students at the first encounter which many teachers did in the old model, class directors organized many ice-breaking activities for the students to be familiar with each other. For instance, they conducted a survey on "my merits and my strong points" as well as a class introduction meeting with a similar theme. They also conducted a series of projects like "I love my class," and "I love my school." Through these activities, students' enthusiasm with their class and the school continued to grow. They started to enjoy the new life in school.

For the third year students, the school conducted a moral education project with a title "Our motherland needs the person with strong willpower," focusing on students' willpower training. During middle school years, students enter the stage of adolescence, which often features risk taking and volatility in student behaviors and emotions, because of a change in hormones. Also, the curriculum designed for students at this level is much more complex than previous years. Many students are not fully prepared for a harder learning task. As a result, a large number of students lose their motivation and become low academic achievers. Thus, the school educated students to purposefully reinforce their self-training in terms of building stronger willpower. At the same time, teachers taught students learning skills to enhance their efficiency in study. Practicing the *success education* idea which tells students: "Do not worry about your study, teachers are willing to help you at any time," school teachers took much responsibility for students' daily learning. If they found any problems, they would help students after school until they understood what they were supposed to be learning.

Especially, the school paid much attention to arranging good examples for students to emulate in their moral education. From time to time, they invited moral models from outside to come to school and give speeches to encourage students. For example, the school used to hold an activity—"The Report Meeting of Tiantian Zhou's Story, One of Ten Excellent Youths of the County."[1] Zhou was a female deaf-mute child who became an outstanding student in a regular school with her father help (Zhou had many academic achievements, and studied in the United States as a graduate student). The school invited her and her father to come to school and shared her story, aimed at encouraging students to strengthen their willpower like Zhou in learning. The school also identified examples between their own students and called for students to learning from those student role models. For example, they held activities of learning from Ms. Jianhua Hu who had overcome extreme poverty to achieve academic success, and Ms. Zhang who stayed at home because of a serious illness, but, because she worked hard learning by herself she passed the qualification exams with top scores. During my interview, I experienced such kinds of moral education activity in person. The school invited four disabled people who had achieved various kinds of success in their career and their life to give speeches to all students. Principal Liu expected all students to learn from them and made greater progress in their learning. Those four speakers became students' tutors in moral education for the school.

For the fourth year students, a program called "The motherland is in my mind" was held, aimed at training students' motivation for career achievement. Students in the last year of their junior high must make choices on whether to go into senior high school, or a vocational school, or to go to work directly. Many students' aspirations for career achievement were low while some students hesitated to make their decisions. The school continuously encouraged students to believe that they have potentials to achieve any success they desired, urging them to set up a higher and bigger goal and become a lifelong learner in the future. Meanwhile, they guided students to make better choices, helping them to analyze their strengths and weaknesses. They held parent meetings and after the meeting discussed with them their children's future decision individually. The school collected as much information as possible about vocational schools for those students who may not be eligible to go to a regular senior high school or who wish to join the work force earlier because of their family's financial condition. In all, they intended to make every student leave the school with hope and joy.

Second, designing a psychology course to adjust students' mind-set. In China, a psychology course is supposed to be taught at the university level. As early as 1987 when *success education* experiment started, the moral education group decided to set up a psychology course as an alternative approach to aid students in mental health, and, especially, in the formation of success mentality. In this sense, No. 8 School was a pioneer in introducing a psychology course to Chinese education at the middle school level.

Different from the regular psychology class, which emphasizes teaching students only psychological knowledge, the course designed by No. 8 School served to solve students' problems and meet their spiritual needs. For example, to help students throw away the sense of inferiority, they designed a series of classes such as "Value and Enjoy Yourselves," "Change Yourselves," "Become a Happy Youth," "Be the Master of Your Mood," and "Show Disdain for the Frustration," etc.

176 Success for All

I observed one public psychological class and watched several videotaped classes. I found that in the psychological class the teacher acted as an actress to maintain a joyful and interesting atmosphere. Teaching in a dynamic way, the teacher adopted multiple methods in the classroom. For instance, she might tell some stories which could encourage students, share famous sentences from eminent people, sing a song with students, apply psychological testing, play a game, put on a play, lead a discussion, or simply teach some psychological knowledge. The whole class seemed very interested and responded very actively.

There were 10 psychology classes for each semester. Without a textbook, the teaching and study materials were designed by the teacher. The topics of the class were flexible to reflect the issues and problems that students were facing at that time. Besides the class, the school also provided psychological consultation service to students and parents.

The documents I collected show that, having become one of the most popular classes, the psychology class has received positive results. In 1992, a survey conducted by the school with 168 students, who took the psychology class that year, revealed that more than 70% of the students liked this class. Ninety percent of the students felt that the course helped them get to know themselves better and their self-confidence had been enhanced. Some students wrote that before they took the class, they thought a person was born to be clever or foolish. However, after the teacher gave many stories that contested the belief, such as the story of Edison who failed 10,298 times

Photo 9.6 The psychology class in the new campus of No. 8 School, 2004.

before he invented the materials for the light bulb, the students felt they could also succeed. Also, 70% of the students felt that they could concentrate better in class and had formed new, good habits (Chen, 1993).

Third, integrating moral education into regular teaching. Since at-risk students were vulnerable due to having experienced many failures, the school was aware that moral education must be embodied in the whole process of teaching to improve students' self-esteem, and it should not only be limited to students' activities outside of class. Liu advocated that every staff and teacher in the school, to some extent, should be a moral educator. They have guidelines to do so: "Nurture students in school management, in service, and in teaching." Therefore, the school required teachers to take advantage of all possibilities to cultivate students' moral character. For example, they suggested teachers to identify any element that can build up students' spirit and inspire students in learning in textbooks and other study materials. In the classroom, teachers were expected to use positive and encouraging language to ask student questions and evaluate students' answers. When students confronted any problems in study, teachers would stress the importance of perseverance and help students cope with any difficulty in their academic learning.

In particular, teachers were expected to train students to have good study habits through their teaching. At-risk students generally could not discipline themselves and form good study habits because they lacked the support of their families. That is one of the main factors that contributes to students' failure. Principal Liu has paid major attention to dealing with this problem for he thought that a person's habits decide his/her pattern of behavior. The task of education is to correct students' bad habits and foster good ones. Liu noticed that if a teacher could cultivate students' good learning habits the class she/he taught usually had high academic achievement.

Thus, from the beginning of the reform, the research group put a lot of energy into teaching students how to review the knowledge they had learned, how to do assignments correctly, and how to prepare their classes for the next day. For example, Mr. Xia, the head of the Chinese subject teaching group in the early stage of the experiment, concentrated on training students to improve in three areas: (1) Clear and neat handwriting; (2) the correct format in composition and other homework, and (3) the correct usage of punctuation. After three years' training, positive results were reported. The number of unqualified students was reduced, 78.8% in the first item, 82.9% in the second item, and 84.2% in the third item respectively. Other statistical figures from the whole Chinese subject group show that in those two experimental classes, there was an increase in students' good learning habits. The rate of students who could have class preparation was enhanced from 14.9% before the experiment to

74.3% while the rate of going over the learned knowledge was increased from 16.2% to 86.5%. In particular, the rate of students who could do their homework independently increased the most, namely from 11.1% to 91.1%. Interviews indicated that there is a close link between students' good study habits and academic achievement and raised students self-confidence (Xia, 1993).

Fourth, developing students' potentials through elective courses and extracurricular activities. The traditional education model limits students' talents to only demonstrating cognitive abilities which help with their passing the National Entrance Exam, hence the majority of students failed. *Success education* advocates developing students' multiple intelligences which reflects the human reality of the diversity of talents and attributes. Therefore, to develop students' self-esteem and rebuild their confidence, the school conducted as many activities as they could to provide all kinds of channels for students to identify their potentials and build up their advantages to achieve multiple successes.

For example, in the Spring semester every year, the school holds a science and arts festival, and in the Fall semester organizes an athletic meet. In the science and arts festival, students were encouraged to participate in all kinds of competitions in knowledge, calligraphy, painting, art performance, blackboard newspaper, speech, and many kinds of scientific and technological activities. In the athletic meet, students not only took part in sports at the school level but also had much success in the matches of martial arts, sports fencing, swimming etc. at the district and city level. Through these activities, students learned skills of cooperation, interaction, communication and self-evaluation. Through this variety of successes, students grew proud of themselves, their classes, and the school (Liang, 1993; Zhou, 1993).

Moreover, besides those once a semester's activities, in regular programs the school also organized many extracurricular interest groups and set up more elective courses for students, aimed at providing more opportunities for students to develop themselves.

Liu and the research group noticed that although some at-risk students might not be good in the traditional form of academic learning, they had other talents to be developed. Therefore, the school decided to reconstruct students' self-esteem through organizing all kinds of extracurricular activities. At the first stage, the school formed 26 interest groups and 84% students participated in those groups. By taking part in the activities, students discovered their niches and for the first time found that they did not have to always fail; rather, in some areas, they could achieve success. For example, being from the bottom of the society, students never thought that they had the ability to compete outside of school. However, under teachers' encouragement, students in the first experimental classes participated in the student electricians' competition, called "Golden Hammer Prize Competition" conducted by the district and Shanghai city. Unexpectedly, they won the team title as well as the second and third position for individual events for two years consecutively. The prizes made students excited and had positive impact on their confidence in learning.

With more and better technology and improved conditions, the extracurricular activities in the new campus are playing a greater role in facilitating students' learning and personal growth. In my observation, I noticed that the school had nearly 30 interest groups mainly located in the vast basement of the teaching building under a beautiful name—"The Dream Factory." These groups cover a variety of fields such as arts (e.g., pottery art, painting, television, photography, computer cartoon, etc.), sciences (e.g., robotics, math, model-making, etc.), social sciences (e.g., mimic court, logical training, English drama, etc.), and sports (e.g., martial arts, football, ping-pong, etc.). Each group is supervised by one or two teachers, having an hour activity once a week in the afternoon on Thursday. I observed that students were very active and participate seriously in these activities.

During the noon time on May, 14, 2004, the school TV station broadcast for the first time a program with an imaginative name called "Dream Flying." I was in the classroom with the students and teachers to watch the students' first effort to do a TV program by themselves. What impressed me was the interview of Principal Liu on TV was carried out very skillfully by two student journalists. The whole program might be improved in order to have more colorful and dynamic contents. However, it was a good try for the students. After the program, Mr. Qu, the director of the Moral Education Office, told me that the TV station was wholly managed by students with teachers' guidance. They were responsible for designing the programs, making the films, and getting the feedback.

In terms of elective courses, the school has had more than twenty subjects for students to choose from. According to Liu, those courses mainly focused on the application of information and technology, including computer music, computer and robotics, website design, computer painting, and computer and audiovisual manufacturing. In the future, Principal Liu said that, to meet students' vocational needs, they would plan some more practical courses such as computer and writing, computer and furniture design, computer and decoration design, and computer and fashion design. The purpose of all these activities and elective courses conduced by the school is to train students to be more knowledgeable, capable and confident.

180 *Success for All*

Photo 9.7 The extracurricular activity: Computer learning, 2004.

Photo 9.8 The electronic organ class, 2004.

Photo 9.9 The works of pottery art made by students, 2004.

4. Enhancing Students' Ability of Self-Education

Another goal of moral education in *success education* is to help students develop the ability to educate themselves. It should be the ultimate goal of education as well, since a real education occurs only when a student actively takes actions to monitor their own learning. Liu said that the reason why we are teaching today is that for tomorrow we will not need to teach. The intractable problems faced by No. 8 School before the reform were that at-risk students were not aware of their latent abilities due to the experience of longtime failures, and that their behaviors were, to some extent, out of control. Therefore, the school attempted to create an alternative moral education system that would help students internalize the goal of *success education* (Liu, 1997).

The first strategy adopted by the school was that they guided students to understand and recognize themselves. Through teaching the psychology course, students got to know the psychological characteristics of adolescents and gained a better understanding of the way they were thinking, the pattern in which they behaved, and the measures they could use to help themselves. Especially, by participating in all kinds of activities organized by the school such as summer camps, karaoke competitions, ping-pong games, homework exhibitions, and so on, students were surprised at the talents they possessed and become very inspired. The success helped them to see a totally new person in themselves, whom they did not recognize before. As a result, students have gradually built up their self-confidence in schooling and in their future.

Secondly, assisting students to establish goals to change themselves. To help at-risk students overcome their problems, the school supervised them in setting a goal that consists of three stages: Long-term goals (3 years), short-term goals (a semester), and present time goals (one month). They talked with at-risk students individually, analyzed their advantages and disadvantage, and discussed the goals students wanted to achieve. Similarly, like the strategies applied to teaching methods, the goals set up for students in moral education also followed the "low, small, more, and fast": measures. That is to say, students' goals should be practical, not too difficult, and it should not be too low as to lose the function of inspiring the students. For example, teachers might aid students to set up a current goal as "I hope I can concentrate in the class and do not do anything that may distract me"; a short-term goal as "I hope I can pass my Chinese exam this semester"; and a long-term goal such as "I would like to be an excellent student in three years." Moreover, teachers also checked on how students were doing with their goals, and evaluated the results. If they could not accomplish the goals, the teachers would help them develop a new strategy (Chen et al., 1993).

Thirdly, assisting students in educating and adjusting themselves through classroom activities. As mentioned before, the class is the basic unit for students to grow. In traditional teaching, in order to discipline at-risk students, teachers taught too much and tried to control too much in the classroom. Since this external measure did not work well, the school tried to create a resourceful environment that could stimulate students to educate themselves.

One efficient approach toward students' self-education adopted by the school is to fully promote the function of the Committee of Class (CC). CC is the head of a class, playing a major role in classroom management. In this part, the research described an example of how students changed themselves through classroom activities. The program is called "Today I am the Master," conduced by a class in grade 6 at the second stage of the reform in the mid-1990. The purpose of the activity was to offer more rooms for students to develop their latent abilities and achieve success. Concretely, the program asked each student in the class to act as a monitor to manage the class for a day. With eight parts, the activity is a comprehensive program that aimed to train students' to be a self-learner, a self-manager, and a self-evaluator.

For example, in "Shining Pearls," the student was required to read a meaningful paragraph from a famous person, or some aphorism, to all classmates in the morning before the class started. The student had to also explain the meaning of the sentences, then, lead everyone in reading together loudly. After running the program for one year, students in the class had read more than one hundred books and magazines to select the well-known sayings. The wisdom students derived from the learning encouraged and guided students to hold a higher goal toward learning and life.

The project of "Ten Minutes Morning Meeting" opened a forum for students to discuss constructive solutions for existing problems in the class. For example, these questions were discussed: "How can we improve our English learning?" "How can we overcome our discipline problem when our teachers are not in the classroom?" "Why did we lose three points yesterday for the evaluation of our weekly duty?" "How can we help these four classmates who have serous problems in their learning?" Through these meetings, many problems had been resolved by the students themselves independently.

The student who is in charge of enforcing the school regulations was responsible for collecting homework, helping classmates arrive in class on time, and inspecting any other daily regulation required by the school to be carried out smoothly.

The most joyful program is "the entertainment at noon time." After taking all the morning classes, the master student organized all kinds of interesting activities such as games, concerts, dances, story telling, puzzles, intelligence competitions, etc. to all classmates for having an opportunity to relax.

In the afternoon, before students went back home, the "Daily help" program made the commitment to reviewing all the knowledge they had learned in the classroom during the whole day. Four classmates organized as a group to discuss the questions and problems they did not understand in the class. They tried to get the answers by themselves; if not, they would ask the teachers who came to help them until they made sure that they could do the homework at home by themselves. Through helping each other, those students with learning difficulty found they could catch up with their classmates.

Other parts of the program such as "Daily Writing," "Daily Evaluation," and "Weekly Remarks" were related to the evaluation given by the class to the students who were the master for that day and for that week. Ending a day's work, the student was asked to keep a dairy to record all the things that happen during the day. If a master student did a good job, he or she would be selected as the best master for that week. In all, students in this program received sound training in their moral abilities (e.g., responsibility, discipline, helping others) and intellectual and leadership capacities (e.g., oral expression, knowledge learning, leadership skill, and communication skill). This program was promoted within the school. It was reported to have generated very positive results.

Fourthly, supervising students to learn how to evaluate themselves. In China, as important as students' scores in academic subject, students' evaluation in moral education will be shown on the school report card. Thus, how to assess at-risk students' moral education challenged the old system in which the teacher was the only authority whose evaluation mainly focused on students' political attitudes and academic achievements. Through *success education*, the evaluation of moral education in No. 8 School was replaced by a new model which employs multiple channels to evaluate students and evaluation comments from teachers are full of encouragement.

In regular schools, the standard of assessing students' moral education may follow a rigid political doctrine passed from the top to down. However, according to the reality of at-risk students, the school adjusted their own evaluation criteria in five aspects, looking at if students:

1. Respect teachers, love their classmates, love school, and love the class—in terms of students' positive and healthy feelings;
2. Increase outside reading, and participate in extracurricular and social activities—in terms of the width and depth of students' interests;
3. Concentrate on learning in the class, do exercises after class, and comply with the school discipline—in terms of their conscious attitudes and strength of students' willpower;
4. Do homework independently, have good study habits, and be honest and sincere in life—in terms of students' personality;
5. Maintain strong self-confidence in learning, try one's best to achieve academic excellence, and become a "three good" student (morally good, physically good, intellectually good)—in terms of students' motivation.

The above qualifications for moral education were made to suit at-risk students' situation in No. 8 School. The standards can be achieved after students have make efforts. Also, in practice, to improve at-risk students' behaviors and reconstruct their self-esteem, the school added students' advantages to the evaluation.

Under a supportive and flexible system, teachers helped students to do a self-evaluation first by finding their own merits and strengths, then, the students did their assessment in their learning groups in the same encouraging way, and finally the class director who was in charge of the class, provided an objective evaluation of the students. The evaluation must make both the student and the teacher feel satisfied. For those students who made great progress in their learning and behaviors, the school would post them on the "honor roll" with their photos, and hold a meeting to honor them as good models for other students to learn from. In this way, at-risk students who used to be a failure mentality were highly encouraged and their confidence was greatly improved.

5. Establishing a Network of Helping At-risk Students

After practicing *success education* for nearly two decades, the school has set up a network to help at-risk students through moral education at all levels of class, grade, and school with multiple methods and resources. At the class level, a student with learning and behavioral problems will be arranged to sit with a high achieving student so that he or she can have access to assistance at any time when he or she needs. Meanwhile, students performing well in academic outcomes will be told that they have responsibility for helping their classmates who had failed in learning. In the class, the subject representatives (the best students in a certain subject such as Chinese, math, English), student leaders from CC, CCYL, YP, and SA are always valuable resources to help those at-risk students. Many activities they run as shown before are linked to improving troubled students' academic achievements. For example, they had conducted a program called "hand-in-hand—helping a student who is more difficult than me." Through this activity, students in the class donated money, food, and any other things to help their classmates who live in extreme poverty. They also organized learning groups to assist their peers who experienced academic failure.

The class director plays a central role in the network to assist students who need help. He or she is responsible for taking care for the whole class and supervising all the programs and activities conducted by students. If a student has any problem, he or she will be the first one who will be contacted. More detail will be discussed in the next chapter.

The school teachers are supposed to be the strong supporters in the chain of helping at-risk students. As long as students have any problems in academic learning, they are always there to offer their aid. In their daily teaching, they have to make sure if every student understood what they have taught in the classroom. If not, they will ask students to come to their offices to make up the part students missed in the class.

Students who have serous problems in learning and behavior, and have family difficulties will be assigned to the head of the grade while the most difficult students are directly referred to the teachers in the Department of Teaching and Supervision and the school leaders, even the Principal himself. At the beginning of a semester, the class director will report the number of students who needs special help from the school. For example, through interview and observation, I learned that every school leader on the old campus—two vice principals, the secretary of the school Party committee—was responsible for helping one at-risk student. They talked with the students once a week and took care of problems in those students' life (e.g., organizing students to donate money) and helped them in learning. Becoming a friend with the at-risk students, they tried to understand the students, and always encouraged them when they made any progress. It has been reported that this one-on-one help model has received very positive results. Many good examples have been documented.

In all, collaboratively, the school tried all attempts to help at-risk students. The network and well-organized methods shed many lights on approaches toward improving at-risk students' schooling.

In summary, with an obvious political purpose, moral education is a challenging subject to teach and to manage in China. Today, middle school students in modern China generally show a tendency of declining interests in this kind of activities. However, No. 8 School has carried out a moral education reform since it launched *success education* in 1987. By combining moral education with students' needs together, the school used moral education as a tool to rebuild students' self-esteem and self-confidence in learning. The evidence shows that the reform has achieved positive results. Especially, at the first stage, based on the data I have collected, the moral education group had taken a series of effective strategies to improve students' discipline, behavior, and academic learning. After establishing a new campus in 2001, moral education is characterized by helping students to develop their potentials through holding a variety of extracurricular activities. Criticism from some teachers I found in my investigation said that moral education has been ignored to some extent in the new school, compared with the early stage of the reform. These teachers worried that it will show a negative result in the future.

NOTE

1. Regularly, the Ministry of Education establishes national role models for students of the whole nation. The role models are usually students who sacrifice their life for saving others, or those who overcome tremendous adversaries to achieve academic and other types of success. Once the role models are officially established, schools are to organize activities to report on the role models' stories and students are urged to learn from them. These role models will be invited to schools to report their stories of struggle and triumph.

CHAPTER 10

THE ROLE OF THE CLASS DIRECTOR IN CLASSROOM MANAGEMENT

This chapter will examine a very special role—the class director in classroom management in No. 8 School. We will study the origin of the class director system in China, the primary function of the class director in improving at-risk students in the experiment, the strategies adopted by the class directors to create a loving, caring and positive learning environment for at-risk students, and the beneficial results at-risk students have received from the system in the reform. The professional development and training of the class directors in success education will also be explored.

THE ORIGIN, DEFINITION, FUNCTION, AND RESPONSIBILITY OF THE CLASS DIRECTOR IN CHINA

China is one of several countries (e.g., the former Soviet Union, and Japan) which have set up a system in which the class director is responsible for the classroom in the world. Originally, the system was created by the former Soviet Union after the victory of "the October Revolution" in 1917, aimed at reforming the old education from tsarist Russia and having a new educational system to serve all the working class people. Learning from

Success for All, pages 187–210
Copyright © 2008 by Information Age Publishing
All rights of reproduction in any form reserved.

the Soviet Union, the CCP introduced this system in the mid-1930s from K–12 to university level when the CCP was still exiled in the mountainous areas in Shanxi province. After the CCP took power in 1949, China officially stipulated in 1952 that the class director system was to be established in all schools (Li & Chen, 2003; Tan, 2003).

In China, the class is the basic unit of teaching and learning, normally with a body of 40–50 students under the leadership of a teacher called the "class director." Thus, the "class director" refers to the teacher who is in charge of the class management. More specifically, according to *the Temporary Regulation of the Work of Class Director in the Middle School* issued by the Ministry of Education in 1988, a class director is the organizer, educator, and supervisor of a class as well as the capable assistant to school leaders to implement school policy and the education plan. The functions of a class director are multiple: As an adviser of students in a class for their learning, life, and personal development; a coordinator of teaching and nurturing for the class; and a bridge to connect the school with students, teachers with students, students with students, and the school and the family.

The regulation describes that the fundamental task of the class director is to take full responsibility for educating, managing, and supervising students in a class under the principles of an all-rounded development—moral, intellectual and physical development—so that students can become the citizens with proper ideals, culture, discipline, and good health. Therefore, a class director must love students, respect students, and help students maintain right orientation in politics, accomplish all the learning tasks required by the school and run all kinds of activities inside and outside the school to develop their latent talents. The regulation states that a class director is designated by the principal, and enjoys certain allowance which varies from school to school.

Since a class director plays a crucial role in student management, school leaders in China always pay serious attention to the work of class directors. Especially, in at-risk schools like No. 8 School, class directors play an even more significant role in school improvements than that in regular schools, for at-risk students need more caring and training. The following section will examine the work performed by the class directors in No. 8 School during the implementation of *success education*.

A CLASS DIRECTOR AS PARENTS

As described in earlier chapters, many students in No. 8 School came from divorced families, living in extreme poverty. Also, the community around the school is an area with a high criminal rate in Shanghai even today. A street I visited near the school, called Dili Gang, was claimed as the street of drugs. Among 100 householders, more than 50% were suspected of trafficking in narcotics. Living in this poor and highly dangerous environment, students were greatly influenced by those negative factors. Lacking proper love and caring from home, children in the school had many mental and behavioral problems. Struggling for life, they did not have enough to eat and wear. They were lonely, unconcerned, dirty, ill-disciplined, impolite, reckless, and some even committed crimes.

To educate and manage these disadvantaged children, teachers in No. 8 School realized that just as the sun is vital for plants, love and caring in daily life are also vitally important to children's growth. Thus, many class directors acted as parents to take care of their students and tried their best to make up for students' deficiency in love from their families. Principal Liu also required teachers to give preferential treatment to at-risk students and rebuild them starting from forming basic behaviors. "Our class directors have to teach students everything," said Ms. Zhou, the former director of Moral Education Office. She said:

> For example, we had to teach them how to eat properly, how to dress neatly, how to clean the washroom, how to greet people, how to get to the class on time, and how to concentrate in the class (otherwise, they would still wander everywhere when the class began, and walk back and forth, in and out of the classroom during the class).

Many touching stories have been documented in the history of *success education*. In these stories, class directors help students in many ways. First, they took care of at-risk students starting from their daily life. Mr. Xu, an English teacher, described a story in his presentation for the experience exchange in the school teacher meeting. He told us that "S" was a very special student in his class. His father was in prison twice and his mother ran away from the family. He was raised by his grandparents without a stable income. Lacking care from the family, S developed into a hooligan at an early age. He often swore at and beat up people, turning himself into the overlord of the campus. He was a truant and did not do any homework.

On the first day when Xu became the class director in S's class, he saw all the students dressed up in school uniforms except for S, who was in a very dirty coat. After school, Xu brought S to a clothing store and purchased a set of school uniforms for him. Xu wished that S could go to school every day and S nodded his head. On the second day outside the class, Xu assisted S in doing homework. S said he did not have any exercise books. Xu purchased all the needed exercise books for him. He was surprised and started to do his homework. Every morning, Xu asked S to come to school earlier so he could help him do his homework, teach him English, and then, have breakfast together. When S was ill, Xu bought Chinese herbal medicine for him. Through Xu's persistent effort, S eventually passed all the exams, becoming a national star of the Youth Pioneer, a high honor for students.

Second, class directors created a supportive environment to assist at-risk students. Ms. Su (1993a,b), a senior class director in the school, wrote about her experience of helping a girl who lived in extreme poverty. Looking very depressed and pale, Xie was Su's new student. Through talking with her individually the first day of the new semester, Su learned that Xie lived in a very poor family: Her father had been suffering from a mental disorder and had not worked for a long time, and her mother worked in the community making a very low salary to raise Xie and her older brother. Su reported this special case to the school. Before long, Xie received financial support from the school.

One day, Xie was ill in the hospital. The doctor diagnosed her illness as long-term malnutrition. Su organized the whole class to donate food and money to Xie. Also, she sent all kinds of food to her family during the holidays. Furthermore, to help Xie out of poverty, Su went to Xie's father's work unit in the hot summer and begged the leaders of his father to provide financial support for his two children. The leaders of his father's work unit were touched by Su's love for her students and decided to give a certain amount of money to support Xie and her brother who was also a student in No. 8 School for their miscellaneous expenses in school. Furthermore, a letter signed by all the classmates to ask for support for Xie was sent to Mayer Zhu Rongji (later, he became the Prime Minister of China), asking for assistance for Xie's family. As a result, her father's monthly sick leave allowance was increased from 53 yuan to 92 yuan. By taking all of these actions, Su helped Xie and her family in resolving their financial problems. Xie and her family were deeply moved. Consequently, Xie improved her academic learning impressively.

Although not all the class directors acted the same way as Su, they always went a long way to support their at-risk students either by asking for community help or by organizing the student's classmates to make contributions. The support for the student is not limited to money but more important, it is through these efforts the class director guides all students to build up a loving and caring environment to help those students with special needs. For example, many students told me that their class directors always taught them to take good care of those classmates with learning difficulty. Any discrimination against the disadvantaged students was not allowed in the class.

Third, giving special care to those students who were at risk of dropping out. Before the experiment, student dropout was a big challenge in No. 8 School. When *success education* was launched, Liu required teachers to never give up on a single student. Therefore, prevention of dropouts was the priority for class directors to pay attention to. In the book, *One Hundred Case*

Studies of Success Education (Guo & Liu, 1993), Mr. Liu shared his experience on how to keep a girl in school by visiting her family and talking with her and her parents twenty times! Another class director, Mr. Wang, prevented his student Wei from being a truant through chatting with him from time to time during the school day and arranging his classmates to play with him. Feeling a lot of fun in school life, Wei eventually maintained a stable schedule in the school.

From my interview, I found that class directors in No. 8 School worked extremely hard to take care of their students. Ms. Qing described her daily routine as a class director in school: She arrived in school around 7:00 a.m.. Before going to her office, she went to her class first. Through the windows, she looked at her students to see if they were doing their morning reading. At 7:30 a.m., she brought her kids to join the flag-rising ceremony and do the morning exercises. Usually there are seven classes a day for students. For each class, she has to go to the class and see if her students get into the classroom on time. Also, there are two physical exercises during the break between classes and two eye-protection exercises during the day. Qing has to keep in touch with students and see whether they are doing their activities properly. Class was over at 5:00 p.m.. After class, she may find the students who need help with their homework or have problems during the day. If so, she has to talk with and help them. Qing said that she arrived home daily around 6:30pm or 7:00 p.m.. Even though she is at home in the evening, if students have any problems, she is ready to go and help them. Parents can phone her at any time and ask for help. For a class director, it is always a long day with heavy responsibilities. I interviewed several students who have graduated from the school and they commented on their class directors: "They are really great! They are just like our parents. To some extent, they even know us better than our parents since they spent more time with us than our parents did."

A CLASS DIRECTOR AS AN EDUCATOR

As an educator, helping students improve their academic achievement is always their major task. Particularly, the main purpose of success education is to see that no at-risk student is left behind in academic learning. Thus, class directors are regarded as the soul of a class, and were expected to be the catalytic agent to push students to go forward. Trying to help students improve one point of a score at a time, class director in No. 8 School put all their efforts to help students improve their learning.

One of the most effective methods used by class directors is that they raised students' achievements by identifying students' strengths and putting them into an important role in the class. In an exam-oriented system, low academic performing students have always been the insignificant figures, looked down upon by their peers and the society. Suffering from low self-esteem, these students tend to feel hopeless. To encourage at-risk students, class directors made every attempt to identify any of students' strengths, and promoted those students to a relevant leadership position in the classroom. In so doing, students felt that they were respected, trusted and useful, and experienced feelings of joy they had never experienced before. Consequently, they transformed themselves into new persons and their academic outcomes were improved as a result. These kinds of stories have been heard from most of class directors in No. 8 School.

Known as one of the most mischievous students in the school, Gu was Ms. Lou's student. His father died before he was born. Leaving him to his grandparents, his mother remarried right after she gave birth to Gu. He was brought up by his grandparents, both of whom were more than seventy years old. His grandpa was paralyzed while his grandma was almost blind. Living in such a disadvantaged family, Gu was not only a low academic achiever but also a troublemaker in the classroom. When teachers were teaching, he blew soap bubbles in the class, played with paper-folded aircraft, and even lit firecrackers in the classroom. To flee morning exercises, he lay prone on the water pipe on the second floor like a house lizard. Instead of walking the stairs, he climbed the water pipe in and out of the classroom.

To help this student, Ms. Lou paid close attention to Gu, trying to identify any strengths he might have. She found that Gu could do a good job cleaning the classroom. Many students might simply leave the dirty mop in the corner after cleaning, but Gu washed all the dirty mops and put them in order on the windowsill. Lou noticed this careful act by Gu and promoted him as a person in charge of labor for the class. Gu was very happy since he had never been a leader in the classroom in his whole life and never had been praised by the teachers. After being named the leader of labor in the class, Gu worked harder in all kinds of labor work. Lou told him if he could only do that kind of work well, it was not good enough. As a student he also needs to do well in his study and have a future for himself. We are living in an era of rapid development of science and technology, and learning knowledge is extremely important. Gradually, Gu began to understand the importance of learning and improved his academic achievement greatly. Successfully passing the graduating exams for middle school students, he went on to a technology school.

Besides being responsible for the classroom management, all class directors are teachers in a subject area. In their own fields, they tried very hard to help their students. There were three popular words in No. 8 School that described clearly how teachers help at-risk students, especially in the early stage of the reform: "fixing" (*ding*), "closing" (*guan*), "following up" (*gen*). That is to say, teachers, particularly class directors, have to fix their eyes on those at-risk students all the time, helping and taking care of them whenever needed. If at-risk students did not understand the courses taught on that day or were not able to do their homework, teachers have to keep student in school and help them make up for the knowledge they missed in class. Although some students have shown they can keep up with their learning for a period of time, teachers have to follow up on those students' academic progress in case they have a relapse. This strategy was very practical to help the slow learners.

By using the above approach, Ms. Kui, an English teacher, had successfully helped four students with extreme difficulty in learning the English language. Among these four students, two were stammers, the third was hyperactive and the fourth was a few-word person. Their basic knowledge of English was so poor that some of them could not recognize the 26 letters of the alphabet. Kui assisted them every day outside the class. Although she needed to repeat words and sentences again and again, she never gave up. She designed "the prize of learning progress" to motivate them. After three years' strenuous work, these four students easily passed the exams to graduate, with one student achieving a high score of 89 out of 100. They were very proud of themselves and their self-confidence had also been increased.

In addition, as a supervisor, class directors help with their students is not limited to their own fields, but included other subjects as well. Students from two classes I observed shared the same feelings with me that their class directors educated them in many ways. In particular, Mr. Xu's students on the new campus told me that Xu not only taught them English but also assisted them in Chinese, math, and history. "He is a genius," student Zhang said to me, "it seems to me our teacher Xu knows everything."

Xu explained that,

> As a class director, I not only pay attention to the course I teach but also care about my students' achievement in other subjects. For example, I asked a Chinese teacher to give me all the Chinese tests taken by my kids and found that they made many mistakes in spelling. That is because, instead of reading, students today are more interested in playing games and chatting on the computer. To deal with this problem, I decided to establish a class library and run all kinds of reading activities in the classroom. I required my students to take notes and write down whatever they learned every day. The activity stimulated students' enthusiasm with learning and they have made great progress. For example, so far the class discipline was improved. Spelling problems in Chinese had been reduced greatly and students' writing skills had been enhanced as well. The average math scores had reached 91.2 at the end of the semester in 2002, placing the class in the second position among all classes in the same grade. The number of failing students in English had been reduced from 13 students at the beginning to 3 at the end of the semester.

I did a group interview of other subject teachers (Chinese, math, history, and physics) in Xu's class. They informed me that Xu's class used to be an indolent class, and 50% of the students were not motivated to learn. Many students in this class did not want to do homework. They all agreed that the class had been changed dramatically because of Xu's persistent and creative efforts. The class library and reading activities initiated by Xu had played an important role.

Furthermore, as educators, class directors take great responsibility for nurturing students' personal development. All of the students I interviewed, whether they had graduated or were still in school, conveyed a strong message to me that their class directors were their mentors as well as their models of behaviors. They were influenced tremendously by their class directors during four years of junior high. Especially, students all agreed that their class directors always told them that to be morally good is the most important thing for them to learn and cultivate. They need to learn subject knowledge, but they always should first and foremost learn to be a good human being. Only if their behaviors are good can their study be improved. Therefore, class directors put a lot of energy into students' behavior training. They talked with students during the school day and after class whenever they found they were having any problems. They helped students set up a big goal for the future and urged them to make great contributions to the betterment of the society. They also made frequent visits to students' families to get strong support from the parents.

In my investigation, I noticed that class directors have used the weekly journal to cultivate their students. I collected some students' weekly journals from Mr. Xu's class in the Fall semester of 2003 and found that all the journals almost followed the same themes. Their topics focused on the existing problems in the classroom, or a moral code they should abide by. For example, a journal at the beginning of the semester talked about how they should prepare themselves for the new life and new learning task of their third year in junior high. In the major body of the log, they discussed study habits (e.g., being quiet in the classroom during the evening self-learning section, learning seriously), moral principles (e.g., honesty and trust), and the problems that existed among students (e.g., smoking, discipline, etc.). The journals reflected Xu emphasis of behavior training each week. It is also a way for Xu to communicate with his students. The most impressive thing that caught my attention is Xu's response to those at-risk students. He always wrote down sentences like "You are great!" "You made progress recently. I am happy for you," or "Keep going!" He also put a standard sentence in all the journals, which says: "If you have any difficulty in learning, please ask for the teacher's help." Many other class directors did the same things like Xu and students felt that they received much support from their class directors. My comment is that if the weekly journals can be written in more diverse approaches, meaning if students can choose their own topics, the students' real thoughts may be reflected in the journal better.

A CLASS DIRECTOR AS A MANAGER

Classroom management is the core of the class director's work in China. In other words, a class director is the leader of a class; she/he is responsible for the management of teaching, learning, and various related activities. The job of the class director in the period of junior high is particularly tough and challenging since adolescence is viewed as in a "disturbed state" caused by a rapid physical, sexual, psychological, cognitive, and social change (Mussen et al., 1979). Further, the class directors in No. 8 School face more problems: (1) They have many at-risk students; and (2) most students are an only child. China has been carrying out a one-child-per-family policy since the 1980s in order to control its population, meaning a couple is only allowed to have one child. Pampered and spoiled by the family, these children have been reported to have many negative traits, such as being selfish, dependent, lonely, impulsive, and irresponsible. To cope with all the problems, a class director has to put a lot of his/her energy into developing capable leadership skills.

In my research, I interviewed thirty class directors in both the old and new campus, and gathered 34 summary papers written by class directors. My observation, interviews, and the summarization articles I collected indicate that hard work, diversity, creativity, loving and caring attitude, stimulation, and dedication are the main characteristics of class directors' work in No. 8 School. A clear mandate for classroom administration in *success education* is to help all students, especially those at-risk students, achieve success, form good habits in learning, develop their moral attribute, and finally promote self-regulation. Although the experience of the class directors in student management is diverse, many strategies they have employed are in common. The following section attempts to explore the role of a class director as a manager and measures used by them for classroom improvement.

1. Setting up an Example

Many class directors have learned from their own experience that teaching by precept and example is very important in managing a class. Ms. Liang, a young class director with five years of experience, wrote that in school the class director is the person who influences students the most since he or she extensively conducts the activities of teaching and learning for students and interacts with students for the longest time. In front of students, the class director himself/herself is a mirror and a book. Hence, Liang tried to be a good example for her children. For example, she asked her students to be polite and have good manners, and in reality, she had respected and cared for every student, made good friends with them, and never mocked them. Since she told her students to love manual labor (many only-child students do not enjoy any physical labor), every early morning and afternoon she participated in the task of cleaning the campus and the classroom, together with her students. To train students to have a good and neat handwriting, she always wrote on the blackboard carefully and neatly when she gave a lecture. In doing so, she had built up a very good relationship with her students and influenced her kids through her own role model.

2. Build up a Capable and Self-regulated Committee of Class

In their summarization papers, every class director mentions that training student cadres and organizing a capable class committee are essential in leading a class. In China, the Committee of Class is the body of student organization, which, under the leadership of the class director, leads a class to implement policies from the school and assists teachers to operate all teaching and learning activities required by school. Thus, the Committee of Class is the heart of the class.

In No. 8 School, the Committee of Class in each class consists of eight students: monitor, vice monitor, and five other committee members in charge of learning, communication/ publication, life, hygiene/labor, and recreational and sports activities. Specifically, each member of the committee has his/her responsibility. For example, the monitor is the head of the class, who is fully responsible for chairing the work of the committee, proposing and implementing the work plan for his/her term, organizing the class meetings, and arranging routine work for each day. The vice monitor is the assistant to the monitor, taking full responsibility for the class when the monitor is absent. The learning coordinator usually is the academically highest achieving student in the class. Besides supervising the student representatives of various subjects (who are also chosen for their achievement in a specific subject learning) to collect and submit classmates' homework and organize learning activities in the regular school, the learning coordinator in No. 8 School was required to report their classmates' learning information to the class director from time to time, to assist the class director to know the students who have learning difficulty, and to arrange one-on-one help with at-risk students. The communication and publication coordinator is mainly responsible for publishing the blackboard newspaper in the back of the classroom and editing weekly news etc., while the life coordinator helps classmates with their lunch, dinner (if it is a boarding class), and financial aids in life. Meanwhile, the work of campus cleaning every morning and classroom cleaning every afternoon is organized by the hygiene/labor coordinator. PE classes, morning exercises, and other sports activities are very important for students' health. The duty of overseeing them is taken by the PE coordinator. In the meantime, the recreational coordinator serves the class by organizing all kinds of art performances and other entertainment activities.

There are two other important student sub-organizations in the class which a class director can rely on: the Communist Youth League branch and the branch of Communist Youth Pioneer (YP) These two student organizations are very active. Usually, many major activities such as a science and arts festival, sports games, and holiday celebrations (e.g., the National Day, New Year, etc.) will be co-organized by the three student organizations. Thus, the secretary of the League and the team leader of YP are often invited to participate in the meetings of the Committee of Class.

In regular schools, particularly in key schools, the Committee of Class is not difficult to form since there are many excellent students in the class. However, in No. 8 School, it was a challenge for the class director to organize a capable work team among at-risk students with low motivation in learning and in life. Ms. Lou and Mr. Xia, two experienced class directors in the first stage of the experiment, used many methods to train student leaders. For example, both of them asked their students to take turns being the leader for one day or one semester. In this way, everyone has an opportunity to develop his/her competence and achieve success. Lou shared her experience that when she practiced "Today I am the master" in her class, everyone was excited by this original idea. One student smiled heartily when he tied up the name tab with words "The small master" on his chest. Lou asked him why he was smiling. He told Lou that before, he had always been led by others since he was a student of failure, and he never thought he would become a leader in the class someday. In the traditional classroom, student leader positions are always reserved for those high achieving students. Therefore, he was very excited to be chosen as a leader that he could not keep himself from smiling.

Today in No. 8 School, they have two monitors in the class: one is a semester long monitor and another one as "the monitor on duty" just for one day. The latter are especially designed for every student to take turns in assuming leadership roles, aimed at developing children's potential. Through the turn-taking approach, class directors found that many at-risk students were very capable and responsible in managing the class. They worked seriously and very hard on duty. By adopting this measure, the class director identified many excellent talents and in the meantime, students' self-confidence had been enhanced. Currently, in China the system of "the monitor on duty" has been adopted throughout the country. However, as early as in the mid-1980s, No. 8 School had pioneered in creating this technique to train at-risk students.

Finding students' strengths to develop was found to be as another effective method for class directors to train student leaders. In her work, Ms. Lou noticed that when student leaders had meetings or reported their classmates' information, they were inclined to tell her about their counterparts' negative sides. As a result, many students did not like their student leaders and were not willing to be a leader since they regarded those student cadres as teachers' secret agents. Lou trained her student leaders to pay attention to the good deeds done by their classmates and then, praised them in the class. Gradually, the relationship between student leaders and their classmates was improved. The committee's leadership skills had been enhanced.

To develop the student leader's ability for self-regulation, the school required that all activities should be designed and organized by students, yet also be supervised by class directors. "The class topic meeting" is a main activity held by the Committee of Class. What is "the class topic meeting"? In China, this is an activity used in the classroom from K–12 with a specific title and topic, which may meet a political purpose or resolve an existing problem in the class. Supervised by the class director, "the class topic meeting" is a method of moral education and also a way to manage the class.

In No. 8 School, class directors have facilitated students to run many class topic meetings with a clear purpose of helping at-risk students overcome their mentality of inferiority. The topic of the meetings can be very broad such as one on "Our ideals, achievement and motivation," "Work hard for our beautiful dreams," and "the glory of the sixteen years old."The forms of meetings can also be very diverse, including public lectures, presentations, discussions, debates, impromptu meetings, games, visits, exhibitions, and so on. To hold a successful class topic meeting, the Committee of Class has to work hard. For example, they have to select the topic meticulously, design the program seriously, fix up a place for the meeting carefully, and choose the host cautiously. After the meeting, they also collect feedback in time to learn lessons from the meeting and improve the next one to come. This process is carried out by student leaders with the class director's supervision. Through the class topic meetings and other activities, class directors have gradually built up a competent class committee that can work independently.

3. Creating a Harmonious, Upgraded, and Well-Disciplined Class Climate

Every class director in No. 8 School has invested a lot of energy on the formation of a harmonious class climate since children will grow up together for their whole four years of junior high education. The class environment exerts a tremendous impact on students' personal development during their teenage period. Without exception, class directors in No. 8 School put great effort into building a homelike class environment for the children as soon as the student entered the school. They educate their students to love the school and love the class. Ms. Shi, a class director in grade 9, told her students when they met together the first time, that "the class is our new big family and we are the family members. We should love each other, help each other, and unite like one person." As part of a family, every student should make contributions to the class. Many other class directors have a similar experience. Through organizing the class to participate in all kinds of activities conducted by the school such as the "star class" competition, science and arts festival, and sports matches, class directors emphasize the importance of group honor. Gradually, a deep feeling about the class has been cultivated.

To advance their classes, class directors have helped classes set up their common goals, which are divided into three periods: short-term, midterm, and long-term under the principle of *success education*. For example, in her summarization paper in 2003, Ms. Jin wrote of her class' goals as: In the near future her class should foster students' good behavior and have good study habits; during the midterm period, the class should become a self-regulated one; and for their highest goal, the class in the future should be an excellent group with self-management, self-support, creativity, and have an ethic of hard-working.

In the process of fulfilling their common class goals, each class makes efforts to form its own class spirit. In No. 8 School, each classroom has a big slogan posted above the blackboard in front of the class, which can be regarded as an indicator of the class spirit in that specific period of time. The slogan will be changed according to the goal they want to reach in that academic year. Ms. Ren, a class director in the second stage of the reform, in her article presents three different slogans in her class to meet different reform goals in three years. Starting from 6th grade onward, the slogan was: "Be hopeful and be indomitable," "Rally our forces and uplift our youth's elegant demeanor," "Be dauntless and advance bravely." In some ways, these slogans function as a reminder to encourage students to conquer any difficulty in learning and life, while little by little internalizing the spirit to be part of their self-motivation.

A well-disciplined classroom is a very important part of the class environment as well as an essential prerequisite for any teaching and learning. As a leader of the class, the class director is regarded as the key person accountable for improving classroom discipline, a serious problem in the school before the reform. Even though different class directors may have different methods, an obvious common experience shared by these teachers is: To make rules and responsibilities clear and get students to help each other.

Besides all regulations issued by the school, to discipline their students, many class directors have stipulated their own class regulations through discussion with students, based on their class' situation. "The class pledge" contains rules which are more specific, more basic, and easier to achieve than the general regulations set by the school. To implement the regulations and rules, every day the class director supervises and inspects the work done by the Committee of Class and any other students on duty.

The following is a typical example to help one understand how a class director maintains the classroom management. Mainly, Ms. Jin used two measures to manage her class daily. The first is called as "the system of the monitor on duty," a school-wide practice mentioned above. The student who functions as a monitor will take responsibility for the whole day's work in the class. The daily duty includes checking the morning cleaning, inspecting students' compliance with appearance codes by checking if all students wear uniform, red scarf, and CYL badge with them, inspecting homework submission, maintaining classroom discipline, organizing exercises, and dealing with unforeseeable events. After class, the on-duty monitor will report his/her work to the committee. The second measure applied by Jin is "the system of daily class behavior regulation recording." That is to say, the monitor or other student leaders will keep a daily record and write down all the work done during the day, and other things such as students' learning needs, good deeds done by classmates, or incidents that happened during the day. In this way, students have a clear understanding of what they should do.

In fact, to keep everything in order, class directors even give a list of all the tasks to the student in charge of maintenance of order that day. The list covers works for windows, desks, chairs, doors, lights, TVs, computers, the class library, the blackboard, the drinking machine. If there is any problem, the class director will find the right person to do it. Through this approach, they enhance the students' sense of responsibility and keep the classroom in good order.

In addition, many class directors have established the system of rewards and punishments. As a part of moral education, students' behaviors will be evaluated. Ms. Wang wrote that in her class she had 100 score as basic line for each student weekly. If a student follows all school rules well and does good deeds, he or she will be given higher scores. Otherwise, his/her scores will be reduced. Every month, Wang will award her students who did a good job in learning and behavior. Students who were rewarded were happy.

4. Cultivating and Motivating Students to Learn

Students' learning is always the first priority for class directors. The main problem for at-risk students in No. 8 School was that, lacking good study habits, they failed again and again and were sick of learning. How did class directors inspire students to be interested in studying? First, they have paid a lot of attention to foster students' good learning habits. According to Principal Liu, the focus of school work for the first year students should be the cultivation of students' good behaviors and habits in learning since students in 6th grade are facing the transition from elementary education to secondary education. A good beginning would result in much less effort for them to succeed in the future. On the contrary, if one has acquired a bad habit during the teenage period, it is very difficult to change. Therefore, all the class directors are required to emphasize nurturing students' good habits.

For helping new students who will be entering No. 8 School, Ms. Zhou said:

> To train children's good habits, we will hold a one-week school-wide summer camp for new students in late August each year right before the new academic year starts. In the camp, students will be given some military training such as lining up and gathering. In fact, this is a discipline training. Then, our class directors will organize students to learn the Regulations of Shanghai Middle School Students, and explain rules issued by the school as well. After that, another important program should be study habit training. Our class directors will teach students how to do homework in different subjects, the format for homework, and how to write a journal etc. All these will go into great detail. We have a pamphlet to present all the programs we have. In the end of the training, we will have a test for evaluation of students. This really helps students to get used to school life that is going to come.

After this intensive training, class directors nurture students' good habit in learning through their daily work. Ms. Shi said that she has paid special attention to training her students on how to do their homework, how to prepare their class, and how to concentrate in class. Ms. Wang even trained her students on how to keep the desk clean so that nothing could distract them in class, and also how to answer a question distinctly and how to read aloud.

"How long does it take to teach students' learning habits?" I asked when I did the class director group interview. They told me that it will take them half a year to do it. After six months, most students will gradually get used to all the rules in school and greatly improve their learning skills.

To stimulate at-risk students' enthusiasm in learning, class directors have made tremendous efforts. One of the approaches that many class directors adopted is to build up a competitive mechanism in the classroom. Ms. Lou described that at the early stage of *success education,* facing a large number of disadvantaged children, she aroused her students' learning interests by collaborating with teachers of other subjects to hold a competition among the students in a class and between students of different classrooms. Especially, she designed a program called "the secret action of a golden apple" to improve students' learning. She asked every student to write a letter to her and tell her who is his/her competitor in the exams this time and then draw an apple on the envelop. The letter was confidential. She also told her students to keep their own goal a secret until the end of exams. The program was full of mystery and challenge. All students were so interested that they invested all their energy in the learning. As a result, they improved their academic outcomes greatly. In the end of the program, the award Lou gave to the children who won was an apple. Many children treasured that apple very much. Instead of eating it, they put the apple in their cupboards to continue savoring their prize.

Lou also introduced a master-disciple system into students' learning. She assigned high achieving students as masters to help the low academic achievers. If the disciple achieved success in learning, the master would be rewarded and wear a big red flower in front of his/her chest. This strategy inspired students very much. Through this one-on-one help, many students' academic achievement improved rapidly.

Moreover, many class directors encouraged their students to actively participate in extracurricular activities to explore new interests and learning after class. For instance, under Ms. Jin's encouragement, many of her students became young artists, dancers, photographers, journalists, judges, and scientists after school. As a result, being active in all kinds of learning, the average academic score of her class was ranked among the best of the successful classes in the school.

A CLASS DIRECTOR AS A COMMUNICATOR

As an administrator of a class, class directors manage students' daily teaching and leaning while they also take responsibility for collaborating with other school teachers and communicating with students' families. The work of classroom management is comprehensive, complex, and challenging, making it necessary to develop a network of resources. Since success education aims at helping at-risk students with their learning and life, data reveals that the class directors in No. 8 School have been trained to show special care for those children from disadvantaged families. Therefore, when a class director takes over a class, it is important for him/her to identify those learners with problems and difficulties. Then, he or she will find ways to help them. Acting as a communicator, the class director needs to call for help from any sources. Besides students assisting each other, helps from other teachers and from students' families coordinated by class directors have been proven to be effective approaches for helping at-risk students.

In practice, the school realized that since students who were failing academically had a shortage of too much basic knowledge, the only solution was to ask all subject teachers to collaborate so that they could speed up the process of improving learning for at-risk students. Thus, when class directors noticed that some students were struggling for their learning and with some other problems, they would report the information to the school and ask for help. During the school days, the class director would exchange information about the at-risk students with those subject teachers who were teaching the class and discuss a plan to help them. Working cooperatively together, they improved many students' learning results.

Liu had been a typical at-risk student with serious problems in both learning and behavior in Ms. Zhang's class. Liu's father died when he was only three years old. The family of four relied on his mother's meager salary to survive. Because of poverty, he did not have a desk and a lamp to study. Thus, he never read or did homework at home. He was not interested in learning at all and even tore up his textbooks and exercise books. He consequently failed in five subjects and his English score was only 8. As a disobedient student, Liu spent most of his spare time after class with other problem kids.

When Zhang learned about Liu's situation, she shared this information with all the teachers who were teaching him. The teachers sympathized with him and decided to help him. They deliberately expressed their high expectation of him and encouraged him whenever he made any progress. Some teachers offered him free remedial lessons in order to help him catch with up the class (Zhang, 1993). Ms. Zheng, an outstanding math teacher, wrote about how she helped Liu with his life and learning math (Zheng, 1993). Zheng told us that one day, she found Liu was dressed in rags, and she showed her deep sympathy for him. She went back home, got all the extra clothes she could find, and sent them to Liu's family. Liu was very moved. Moreover, Zheng bought lunch for Liu every day in order to provide enough nutrition for him. After lunch, Zheng offered him a make-up math course. Two years later, Liu became a successful student, passing all the examinations to get into higher level education. His English score had increased from 8 to 91. Similar stories could be heard from time to time during my interviews. Many teachers enjoyed their collaboration and felt it was meaningful for them to provide help to needy students.

In China, the class director is the most familiar person for parents in their children's school. Parents may not know who the school principal is, but they must know who is their children class director. To build connections with students' families, the class director contacts parents all the time regarding their children's education. In No. 8 School, the connection between the class director and parents even starts before children enter No. 8 School. Liu required his class directors to visit the families of all students before the new students enter the school. In the middle of August, class directors, who will take over a new class, usually spend one week visiting each student's family so that they become familiar with the new student and his/her family background. Class directors may need to go to some students' former primary schools to obtain information about students with serious problems in learning and behavior. Many class directors responded that, although intensively visiting 40–50 families in the hot weather of summer was a little bit tough, it is very helpful and worth doing as the investigation helps tremendously with their future classroom management. Students and their families are also very pleased to see the teacher coming to visit their home. They thought that the visit is an indication of the teacher's care for the student. Thus, through the visits, class directors build up a close relationship with students and their families. In doing so, it is much easier for teachers to get the parents support.

For returning students, Liu required class directors to visit one third of the students' families before each new semester starts. This is to say, they select two kinds of students and visit their families—those students who have made the biggest progress in learning and behavior, and those who still have problems. The purpose of visiting these two kinds of students' families is to thank parents for their support, to report to parents about their child's new development in school, and to encourage students who had made the biggest progress in that semester. Also, when visiting the families, they discussed their plans and strategies with parents to help the problem students.

In fact, the class director makes a connection with students' families every school day by asking parents to sign the student's agenda book. I collected one student's agenda book as a sample. Through the sample, I found that the small notebook is a daily means of communicating between the class director and parents, and between school and students' families. In this particular notebook, the message is brief and clear. The task of homework for each subject on that day is the primary item on the agenda book. The class director writes down anything that required parents' cooperation or special attention. For example, in the sample I collected, Ms. Sun, a class director in grade 7 on the old campus, put notes to tell parents about the exam days a week ahead of time. She made appointments with the parents to meet her in school if the student had any problem. She also informed parents about any special schedule adjustment in school. On the parent's side, I saw the father's signature on the agenda book every day. He replied to the teacher's requirements very politely and cooperatively. He also asked the teacher to do something since the student made some mistakes outside the school. If he could not come to school on the day assigned by the teacher, he would write a note to her and explain the reason. The daily communication for the class director is with more than forty students' families. It is a heavy workload.

Moreover, the class director's office, home, and cell phone numbers are available to every student's family. Parents or any family members can call the class director at any time if the student has any problem at home or they want to discuss anything with the teacher about helping the student. The class director usually receives many phone calls from students' families after school. Also, the class director will make a call to parents at any time if necessary. I heard that some teachers have to pay more than 50 yuan for their calls monthly.

Ms. Cui told me that one day she received a phone call from a student's mother around 11:00 p.m. when she was already asleep in bed. The mother asked Cui to help her because her son ran away from home. This was an at-risk student's family. His mother is a housewife and the father often beat the student and his mother. The reason for the students running away was that his father had hit him that day because he wrote something about his father in his journal. Cui tried any way she could to help the family find the child. She could not sleep for the whole night until 5am when the child was taken home by the police. Later, Cui visited the student's family and had a serious conversation with the father. She discussed the art of teaching a child with the family. From then on, the father did not hit his wife or son anymore. In all, the function of the class director as a communicator with students' families works in many ways. Some aspects will be examined in the next chapter.

THE PROFESSIONAL DEVELOPMENT OF THE CLASS DIRECTOR IN NO. 8 SCHOOL

As presented above, to be a qualified or an outstanding class director in an at-risk school not only needs enthusiasm for helping disadvantaged children, but also high proficiency in leadership skills. How has No. 8 School trained its class directors? Data shows that the school used three ways to train class directors.

First, the school used the philosophy of *success education* to educate class directors and believed that every class director has a desire and potential to be a successful leader of classroom management and can achieve success in his/her work. The school leaders helped class directors to have high expectations for at-risk students, to develop confidence in their ability to manage a class, and to motivate them to be "a star of success." To enhance class directors' leadership skills, the school holds "Class Director Workshops" at the beginning of each new academic year. Through the training, the school leaders made class directors aware of their important role in at-risk students' learning and nurturing. The essential part of the training is to coach class directors to love and respect at-risk students, and adjust their strategies to facilitate transformation of classroom management from a teacher-centered model to a student-centered (self-regulated) model.

In particular, after having achieved much success in the first stage of reform, the school leaders and teachers summarized their experience and lessons, and worked out "six elements of efficient classroom management" as the following: (1) Class directors need to deeply understand students by collecting and analyzing students' information in time; (2) class directors need to stress students' non-cognitive education, improve students' mindset, and cultivate students' success mentality; (3) class directors should actively conduct all kinds of activities, and train students' ability to educate themselves; (4) they are to continuously have high expectations and requirements, and help students internalize these expectations and requirements; (5) they should evaluate students with encouragement, and continuously create opportunities for students to achieve success; and (6) they should pay attention to school regulation education, and foster students' good habits of behavior and learning (Liu, 1997). Synthesized from conducting the first phase of the experiment, these six principles have become the guidelines and heart of *success education* in classroom management. Naturally, they have become the most important part of class directors' professional training.

Second, the school has developed a master-disciple system to train class directors. To help the first year young teachers with their professional development, the school assigned two experienced teachers as their masters: One is for teaching and the other for class director work. According to the school rules, the master takes the responsibility for teaching the disciple how to be a class director. They share experiences of being a class director with the disciples and help the young class directors with any work problems they may have. The young class director is required to attend as many activities, organized by his/her master, as possible and observe how his/her master deals with all kinds of student management problems. Similar with the master-disciple system in teaching, the masters' award is linked to the progress their disciples make.

Both one-on-one interviews and group interviews show that the master-disciple system is powerful and effective. All disciples agreed that their masters have helped them with class director skills tremendously. Ms. Tan recalled:

I felt very grateful having a master because when I have any troubles, my master is always there. My master is Ms. Qing. She is an excellent class director. I was influenced by her very much. She did not tell me what I should do or what I should not do. She used her actions to teach me. In the past, people usually said that if you want to be a teacher in No. 8 School, you have to be tough on students because they are too troublesome. However, I never found my master treated her students in that way. She is very nice to students, and loves and cares for them as her own children. She taught students by wisdom and heart. In return, her students loved her very much. That really impressed me. I have learned a lot from her and imitated her bit by bit.

Ms. Zhang, another new class director, also shared similar experience like Tang with me:

It is true that "example is better than precept." My master exactly showed this to me. When I started to work as a class director, I had no idea how I could do it. When I got into any troubles in my work, she always came to my classroom to help me. She taught me by her experience. When I met similar problems next time, I knew what I could do. She taught my students English for two years and helped me do a lot of things, including accompanying me to visit my students' families although she herself also managed a class and had to visit her own kids' families. Indeed, I have learned a great deal from her.

Through this mentoring arrangement, the school has trained many outstanding young class directors. In daily life, the relationship between the masters and disciples is very close. The disciples expressed their deep gratitude for their master's help.

Third, the school put class directors' training into its regular routine. Since student management is an ongoing task, it needs adjustment and summarization at appropriate time to meet students' changing situations. The school has a regular agenda for the class director training. At the beginning of the semester, class directors are required to submit their classroom management plans to the Department of Student Supervision while at the end of the semester they hand in their summaries to the school. The more than 30 papers I gathered are class directors' summarizations in the first semester for 2003–2004 academic year.

During work days, the school conducts a class director meeting every other Monday morning. All class directors participate in this meeting, report their work, and exchange their experiences in solving all kinds of students' problems. If the school leaders find a number of class directors who did an effective job in helping at-risk students, they will identify those teachers as good examples and ask them to describe their experience to all class directors in the meeting.

Sometimes, the school will have a highly effective class director do a presentation in the Friday school teacher meeting. In addition, at the end of every semester, in order to summarize the whole semester's work, the school will hold an "experience exchange meeting of teaching and cultivation" and ask all school teachers and staff to learn from the effective class directors. During my research period, I observed three class directors being promoted as good examples. Two young female teachers shared their experience in the class director meeting while the senior male class director had his presentation in the Friday school-wide teachers' meeting. This onsite training, to some extent, may facilitate class directors, particularly, for the new recruits, to get some fresh experience which might help them deal with similar problems in the future. At the same time, the training helps create a professional community that maintains a momentum of continuous growth.

SUMMARY

In summary, as a class leader, class directors have played a crucial role in the success education experiment in terms of transforming students' behaviors, nurturing students' self-esteem and self-confidence, and improving students' academic achievements. However, I also find that there are problems to be addressed. One of the problems is that the allowance for class directors is very low. Although the school has increased the subsidy for class directors from 150 yuan to 250 yuan monthly after the mid-1990s, it is still too low considering their heavy work load (more than 10 hours a day). Also, a class director manages a class and at the same time, teaches a class. It is too much for them. Every class director I interviewed felt very tired every day after working. Many class directors responded that if one takes the role as a class director, it means he or she will, to some extent, sacrifice much of their spare time and family life. Otherwise, they cannot do a good job taking care of so many teenage students. An improvement would be to assign another teacher as an assistant of the class director to manage the class together, which would be a more reasonable workload for the class director. In that way, they could have more time to develop themselves in their professional field. These problems are common issues in China. It needs strong support from the leadership from high levels as well as from the whole society to raise the position of class directors, recognize the importance of their work, and sustain them financially.

The Role of the Class Director in Classroom Management 209

Photo 10.1 The class director in the class meeting on the old campus, 2004.

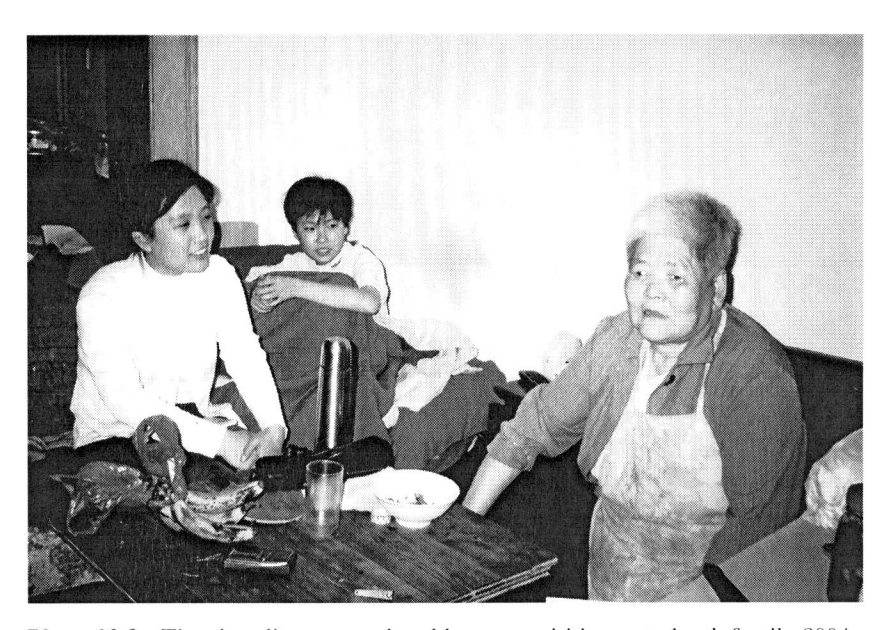

Photo 10.2 The class director on the old campus visiting a student's family, 2004.

Photo 10.3 The class director on the new campus in a moral education activity, 2004.

CHAPTER 11

PARENTAL AND COMMUNITY INVOLVEMENT

Effective Resources and Active Support for At-Risk Students

Effective parent and community involvement can be viewed as a strong support for school improvements, especially, for low-performing schools to meet their challenges (Ogden, & Germinario, 1994; Ward, 2004). This chapter examines how this special Chinese school interacted with parents and the community, how the school got support from parents and community, and how it helped at-risk students to succeed and in the meanwhile helped their parents establish confidence in their children's learning. Effective strategies for developing a close link between school and family, as well as establishing an open, dynamic education model for helping at-risk students, will also be discussed.

HELPING PARENTS DEVELOP CONFIDENCE IN THEIR CHILDREN

China has a long tradition in which parents hold very high value on education for their children. There is a famous Chinese saying: [all parents

Success for All, pages 211–228
Copyright © 2008 by Information Age Publishing
All rights of reproduction in any form reserved.

have the] "Longing to see their son become a dragon"—meaning, they all long to see their children succeed in life. Success in life, however, is to be achieved through a good education. Hence, most families have high expectations for their children's education. However, the parents in No. 8 School were the opposite. Poor family backgrounds contributed to student failure in school. And, because of the students' repeated academic failure, the parents had lost confidence and hope for their children, especially if their children were to enter No. 8 School. Parents thought it a waste of time and money to pay too much attention to their children's education. With a low level of education, they did not know how to educate their children at home either. As a result, they would be satisfied if their children made no trouble in school. When they received phone calls from teachers to report a problem their children had, or when their children brought home poor academic reports, they would simply beat their children. Many children were scared of their parents. This usually turned into a vicious cycle, and the poor relationship between parents and children further led to students' academic failure.

Facing problems in the students' families, Liu and the research group realized that the family is a place where children live and shape their views toward the world. Like teachers in school, parents are children's teachers at home. Therefore, to improve students' learning, the school decided to develop a new, multidimensional relationship with students' families and promote the idea of *success education* with parents.

To communicate with students' families efficiently, the school had adopted a series of innovative measures in the mid-1980s: For example, they had set up a monthly parent meeting system, established a parent's school, and organized parent committees at class, grade, and school levels. Further, they opened a direct line to the Principal and set up mail boxes to parents. Details will be given in the next section.

In order to help parents build up confidence in their children, the school had done three things. First, they put a great deal of effort into building mutual understanding between the parents and the school by showing their sincere care for each and every student. In the school-parent meetings, Principal Liu stated that the school valued and cared for every child and understood the deep love parents had for their children. An individual child might only account for one tenth of a hundred percent among the school's student population, but the child is a full one hundred percent to a family—especially since the only child carries the whole family's hope for the future. The school helped the parents realize that they shared a common goal with the families, that is, their effort to help a child succeed in learning would result in facilitating a family's getting out of poverty and having a better life. Parents felt that Liu's remarks were very practical and they were deeply touched by Liu's speeches. They were willing to cooperate with the school.

In practice, the school leaders made students' families feel that they were living in a big family who could share happiness as well as sorrow together. For example, the school would send teachers or staff to students' families to celebrate any big achievements made by students and the families, including students' progress in learning and behavior improvement, students' birthday, parents finding a new job, and the family moving into a new house. Also, when students' families were having difficulties in life such as illness, living in extreme poverty, or lose of a job, Principal Liu would organize donation campaigns within the school and send food, clothes, and other necessities to the family. In this way, the school would develop a friendly and close relationship with students' families.

Second, the school advocated *success education* literacy between parents and assisted them to believe that every child has special talents and has the potential to be successful. The school also treated every child as a genius and believed that they all would have a bright future. If the child has any difficulty in learning, teachers are always there to help. To do so, the school required teachers to always hold a positive attitude toward students and never criticize any children in the parents' meetings. Liu proposed that his teachers hold every parent's meeting as a celebration party, celebrating every tiny progress made by children. In the meetings, the school showed their sincere gratitude for parents' active support for the school's work. They also pointed out children's achievements to the parents and awarded students all kinds of names that were never considered before the reform. For example, they set up "the biggest learning progress award," "the behavior progress award," "the award of active participant in manual labor," "the award of active participant in extracurricular activities," etc. Through these activities, parents became keenly aware that their children had made progress and were moving forward in their life. Proud of their kids, they gradually regained hope and confidence in their children.

Third, the school involved student families as partners in *success education* reform. In the past, parents thought that their children were dull and slow-witted. Anxious for their children to improve, they resorted to swearing and hitting when their children got poor scores at school. Implementing the philosophy of *success education*, Liu told parents that through investigation, their children's intelligence was normal, but the children needed to raise their self-confidence and form good habits of learning. Liu set clear and practical responsibilities for school and families that while the school put their full efforts into students' academic improvement, the parents needed to cooperate with school to create a supportive learning environment for their children at home. Parents felt that the responsibility described by Liu was reasonable and doable for them. The school also invited parents to engage in the schools' major events as evaluators, such as the science and art festival and any other activities involving their children's class. By doing so, parents experienced their children's progress in person, in the process and gained a better understanding about their children and the school.

According to the parents, Liu's most efficient strategy was what is called the "four-one method." That is, Liu insisted on parents doing four things for their children at home: Setting one goal for their children, providing one lamp, having one desk (since Zhabei was the poorest area in Shanghai, some families could not even provide a lamp and a desk for their children to study), and spending one hour a day helping their children with homework until their children developed good study habits. Later, the school added another "one"—they suggested parents have a serious conversation with their children once a month.

The feedback on Liu's "four-one method" strategy was positive. Following Liu's method, parents felt that they found a specific and effective way to help their children. It was much better than simply blaming and hitting the children. The relationship between parents and children improved dramatically. Witnessing their children's improvement every day, the parents were very pleased and had hope for their children's future.

I interviewed several parents who participated in the early stage of reform. They all agreed that Liu's "four-one method was useful, practical, and had helped them a great deal. Mr. Chu stated that before the reform, he often beat his son, Qingsheng, who was one of the biggest troublemakers in the school. Like many parents, Chu wished to help his son, but he did not know how to do it except for scolding and beating. He said that he enjoyed attending the parent meetings held by the school and took note of the suggestions recommended by Principal Liu, the class director, and other teachers. In the end, he had learned much knowledge and many specific techniques on how to educate a child as a parent. Seriously following Liu's instruction of the "four-one method" at home, he found that his son gradually calmed down and was willing to study. By helping his son do his homework one hour every day, Chu noticed his son's many wonderful merits which he previously ignored. Without having to fear his father's anger, Qingsheng also felt relaxed and comfortable at home. As a result, Qingsheng had made dramatic improvement in his learning and transformed himself from an at-risk student to one enjoying high academic achievement.

Many similar stories had been documented and have been heard in my interviews. Parents were grateful for *success education* as it rebuilds their confidence in their children's education and changes their children's future.

OPENING EFFECTIVE CHANNELS TO COMMUNICATE WITH PARENTS AND SERVING THE FAMILIES

As discussed in previous section, to better interact with students' families, the school had initiated institutional innovations. This section will describe several major structured activities created by the school for getting the parents involved in their children's education.

The Parent Meetings

In the history of *success education*, parent meetings are regarded as one of the effective ways to promote the reform and communicate with students' families. In regular school, there may be one or two parent meetings per semester, and its chief function being to report students' performance to parents. In the initial stage of *success education*, Liu and the research group decided to hold a parent meeting once every month to set up a network with the families to change the serious situation of at-risk student education in the school. Also, rather than being obsessed with improving students' scores to pass the National Entrance Examination, as was the case in the parent meetings in most regular Chinese schools, the contents and formats of the meetings in No. 8 School were broader and more creative.

As in many other occasions, Principal Liu played an important role in promoting the philosophy of *success education* with parents. Interviewees recalled that, every time during the parent meetings, Liu was a keynote speaker to introduce the new education reform to the parents, to encourage them to have confidence in their children and in the school, and to call for support for their children's learning and the school's reform. Many parents felt that Liu's speeches were quite inspiring and acceptable.

I attended the parent meetings twice during my research period: One was in the old campus and another in the new campus. The procedure of the meeting I attended followed this format: First, the school leader started with an explanation of the reason for holding the meeting; then, the representative of class directors or school teachers made a speech to welcome parents and reviewed what they had done in school recently and what the school needed parents to help them with in students' learning. After these, the meeting got into its practical part: Parents met together in their children's classes to get more detailed information about their children. The class director hosted the meeting, introducing the class and the children's development at that period, answering questions and hearing parents' concerns. The meeting was usually held at night during the weekend so that it was more convenient for parents to attend, and the parents could speak with the class director for as long as they need.

In her presentations of sharing *success education* experience on different occasions, Ms. Lou, a class director in the earliest period of the reform, described what a parent meeting was like under the principle of *success education*. She wrote that the parent meetings were a very important way for the school to strengthen its connection with families. However, how a meeting was held was critical to attract the parents to come. Before the reform was implemented, the school also had regular parent meetings. However, only a few parents attended the meetings since the school teachers always criticized their children in the meetings. They felt ashamed to participate in the meetings because of their children's poor performance in school. Also, students did not want their parents to take part in the meetings, for they would be condemned or beaten by their parents after the meeting due to the bad report teachers would always have given their parents. Therefore, they usually hid the announcement of parent meetings issued by the school or simply tore it up.

Implementing *success education*, Lou changed her way to hold parent meetings. She shared her experiences with me that:

> I treated every parent meeting as a family celebration party, seriously preparing for it as I would have prepared for a class. In the past, I would simply ask a student to write a poster which said "Welcome, parents." However, in the experimental class, I carefully designed a theme with a clear purpose for each meeting. For example, I wrote down themes for my meetings: "Let's join hands for our children's future; "Let's collaborate to help our children's success"; or "Let's share our children's success together." Within this harmonious environment, parents felt joyful and pleasure in the meeting. To encourage parents and students, I highlighted the students' progresses and praised each student in front of their parents. They were all very happy. For those students who had made a big progress, I awarded a red flower to both the students and their parents to celebrate their success. This was usually the moment parents were so touched that they cried, as their children had never received any rewards but only blame.

In terms of the forms of the meeting, Lou also incorporated some changes. For example, instead of hosting the meeting all the time by herself as she did in the past, she asked students to host the meetings, demonstrating their achievements and reporting their work, or she let the students to put on an art performance for their parents. Sometimes, she asked parents to co-host the meeting with her or had a round table meeting with parents to discuss student issues. Stimulated by these interesting meetings, more and more parents attended her meetings. Students were also happy to see their parents in the meetings.

The example I gave above was an example of a parent meeting at the beginning of the experiment. At the time I did my field work, teachers told

Photo 11.1 Arriving at a parent meeting in the new campus, 2004.

me that they had the parent meeting twice a semester since the situation of their students was much improved than before. Also, they could use many other forms to communicate with parents, such as email and telephone.

The Parent School

The purposes of setting up the parent school are to help parents develop parental skills, to guide parents in understanding their children better, and to improve the relationship between the parents and students. Usually, the parent school ran seminars for the parents, lectured by experienced class directors. The seminar topics were based on parents' needs and problems that existed among parents in dealing their children education at home. For example, they held a number of seminars with the following titles: "How to deal with the problem of children addicted to computer games"; "What can parents do if the child makes friends with hooligans"; "If the child lies, what can parents do"; and "If a child always fails, what can we do as parents." The seminars were reported to be successful and very welcomed by the parents. The attendance of parents in the parent school reached 95% in the old campus in the early stage of the reform (Liang, & Lou, 1993).

In the parent school, special attention was paid to educating parents to change their traditional way in raising children. In China, there is a saying that "a child cannot become a useful person without parents [beating them with] sticks." Therefore, it is a common phenomenon in China for parents to scold and hit their children when they made mistakes or performed poorly in learning. Teachers in the parent school gave lectures to parents on how to use modern educational methods to nurture children at home. They taught parents to fully respect their children, communicate with their children equally, always encourage their children, and democratically discuss with their children when they make major decisions for their children.

After participating in these lessons or talking with teachers, parents felt they had benefitted greatly. Many of them changed their ways of treating their children. The book, *One Hundred Good Examples of Success Education*, documents some parents' stories. For example, students Zhu, Wei, and Guo's fathers used to beat them often and badly. Through the parent school, the father's parental skills were completely transformed. Zhu, Wei, and Guo improved greatly in their academic outcomes and behavior as a result (Guo & Liu, 1993).

In addition, the school invited parents with good parental skills to come to the school or find a place outside the schools to exchange experiences. I collected twelve parent experience-sharing papers from the parent school on the new campus in the Fall semester of 2001. The parents shared their experiences on how they educated their children at home. Some described their stories of nurturing children's learning habits, others explained how they set a role model by themselves to facilitate their children's personal growth. The contents are rich and diverse. Drawn from their own experiences, parents learned from each other through these papers. All in all, evidence shows that the parent school set up a new practice in the interaction between the school and parents in China as early as in the mid-1980s. Even today, many schools have not offered such a service.

The Parent Committee

The school set up a parent committee at class, grade, and school levels to obtain more resources for the reform from the community. The most active parent committee is the one at the class level as it has a close link with the children. To get more support from parents, the class director tried to create an environment conducive to involving parents in the classroom management. As discussed before, parents were welcome to participate in many activities held by the class. They were invited to join the process of student evaluation not only in extracurricular activities, but also in subject learning activities (as mentioned in chapter 9).

Some parents involved themselves by providing financial support for helping other poor families. For example, Mr. Xia, as a class director in the earliest experiment class in 1987, incorporated some important classroom reforms which were supported by parents. To encourage students, he initiated three levels of prizes to reward students' progress in learning. In most regular schools, the award is always given the top students. Xia thought this practice should be reformed in an at-risk school, otherwise, students would not be stimulated. Therefore, he donated 50 yuan (which was equivalent to a teacher's monthly salary in the mid-1980s) to the class as the fund to reward students. He discussed with the parent committee and asked if they could donate some money for this endeavor also. Being very cooperative and supportive, the parents all agreed with this idea and made their contributions to the award. By using the donation, Xia designed "the greatest progress award" to those at-risk students who had extreme difficulties in learning, but had made great progress. Although they might not pass the standard test, Xia rewarded their improvements to encourage them as well as other students. When Xia sent the award to the parents, they were so excited that some of them cried. With tears in his eyes, one parent said that "Before, when I attended the parent meeting, I lowered my head because of my son's poor academic achievements. This time I can raise my head. For the first time, I feel that my son has a future. Also, it is the first time I feel dignity as a parent." Evidence shows that this reform in award-giving has inspired a lot of at-risk students to make their advancement. As a result, this practice had been endorsed by the school and become part of the award system in the school today.

Ms. Lou also shared her experience that in her class, one student, who came from a disadvantaged family, had broken his leg. In a short time, other parents donated several thousand yuan to help cure him and were willing to give more if necessary. The above stories show that parents have become a reliable support for the school and for the reform.

The Regular Communication between Teachers and Parents

This refers to the basic connection between the school and families. The school required all teachers to treat parents equally and offer any help they can to the students and their families. The school also required its teachers to know each student's basic information, including their characteristics, learning situation, and their family background. To do so, teachers have to communicate with students and their families.

On this basic level of communication, the class directors and the other moral education teachers play a major role since they take the responsibility for managing the class and students. By using a network and the multiple communication methods such as phone, email, letter, note, and discussions in school (asking parents to come to school), and family visits, teachers have built up an effective and efficient interaction system with families.

In particular, drawn from the experience of educating at-risk students for decades, teachers in the school found that, among a variety of communication techniques, family visits are the most effective approach for transforming at-risk students, which is especially so for those extremely difficult students. Viewing the family visit as an important tool of moral education, the school specifies the visit time, and how often it should be for class directors. Teachers' performance in the family visit will be recorded and evaluated by school as part of the required task of moral education. As mentioned in chapter 11, at the beginning of each semester, a class director has to make visits to all the families of the new students, and visit 30% of the returning students' families. Meanwhile, if students are getting into trouble, the class directors and moral education teachers are required to visit the student's family at any time.

Why is the family visit treated as so important? Ms. Sun (1993), a formal head of CCYL and a psychology teacher in the old campus, described in detail what they did and how this technique worked. According to Sun, to help those problem students, teachers have to master all the information about the students, so that they would know what they can do to help the students. Therefore, when the teachers in the school visited at-risk students families, they did an investigation and researched the students and their families.

First, they asked the student for information about the circle of his/her friends, what kinds of friends he or she wishes to make, and how are his/her friends doing. Peer pressure is the main influence for children in this age. If teachers know the child's friends information, they will know what kind of problem the child has.

Second, they talked about the student's leisure life. Teachers usually asked parents what the student did outside the school, especially what the child did on weekends; what kinds of novels, magazines he or she liked; what kinds of music the kid preferred, and other information such as how the child did his/her homework, and what kinds of games the child played. In a relaxed and pleasant chat, teachers might recommend some helpful activities for parents to guide their children's energy in daily life.

Third, they observed the student's learning environment. Through the family visit, teachers noticed if the child had a quiet and good learning environment at home. For example, they would find out if the family could provide a lamp, a desk, and a tape-recorder for the child. If not, they would try their best to persuade parents to obtain all those necessary study tools for the child. If the family was not able to do it, teachers would try their best to help resolve the problem. For instance, in Ms. Gong's class, L often could not finish his homework. To know the reason, Gong visited his family. She found that L's father died and his mother lost her job. Deep in poverty, his mother was not willing to spend the little money they had to buy a lamp for L, as a result he could not do his homework in the evening at home. After failing to persuade his mother to get a lamp for L, Gong succeeded in getting the community head to agree for L to do homework in his home every day from 6:00–9:00 p.m.

Fourth, they tried to find out if the student had any extracurricular activities. If not, teachers would suggest that the family offer some in order to develop the child's diverse potentials. Overall, with multiple functions, teachers found that only through family visits could they deal with at-risk students' problems properly and efficiently.

Furthermore, interviews and documents indicated that, growing up in a disadvantaged environment, the school had to assume double responsibilities: They had to transform both the students and the parents. Sometimes, only after changing the parents first was it possible for the student to be changed. Mr. Du, a senior moral education teacher, shared his experience with me. He said that in an at-risk school, the toughest thing was not the students but the task of educating the parents. He gave me a story about Mr. Li, a PE teacher and a class director, who was on site when I interviewed Du.

Li had a painful experience: One day, he was beaten severely by a student and his criminal gang outside the school. He, however, still loved his career and enjoyed teaching at-risk students. Li had a student whose father was in prison for seven years. He might have some mental problems because of his life in prison. He would hit his son for the slightest offense. For example, one day on a cold day, his son had a little discipline problem in school. He came to school and started to beat his son until they arrived home. Then, he ordered his son to take off all his clothes, and with only his underwear on, to stand outside. His son was scared to death. In another occasion, because of a very small thing, he came to the school, smashed the classroom and dirtied the wall. To help his student, Li started to make friends with the father. He visited his student's family numerous times, and sometimes they went to restaurants and drank wine together. After years of hard work, gradually the father felt that Li respected him and that he was understood and accepted by society again. Finally, persuaded by Li, the father stopped beating his son. In gratitude, the student studied very hard and passed the exams to a vocational school. His father was also a changed person, feeling hope in his life again because of his son's progress. Similar stories were many. Some parents, however, were changed little although teachers worked very hard. Through these stories, I realized that the transformation of at-risk students was a difficult task that needs all society to work together.

A NEW EDUCATION MODEL LINKING SCHOOL, COMMUNITY, AND SOCIETY

In the implementation of success education, the school leaders realized that the school is not an isolated sector in today's rapidly developing era, rather it should build up a web, weaving parents, communities and the whole society together to help children grow in an open and fully supportive environment. Getting greater community involvement in the school's reform effort and attempting greater school involvement in the community are two key thrusts for the school to strive for. Service integration between community and school can be discussed as follows.

1. Practical Support from the Community

The school leaders stated that support from the community was crucial throughout the reform. The school leaders involved the local community in the reform from the very beginning. They invited the leaders of the community to the school and attended their meetings in order to share decision-making. In return, the local community provided the school with support in many ways.

In terms of school safety, for example, the school contacted the local police station often to create a secure environment for students. At the beginning of the reform, criminal gangs went to the school very often to recruit students to join in their criminal activities. To create a safe environment, the school asked the police station to place several policemen in the school so that students could go to school and back home safely. If students were sent to the police station for an offence, the police officers would collaborate with the school and give the students counseling. Thus, the local police station has been an important link in the success of the school reform.

Another practical way for the community to support the school was that they prioritized providing financial aid to students' families living in extreme poverty. The director of the Committee of Residents told me in the interview that even in 2004 there were still more than 30% of the families in their area living in poverty. The committee would try their best to send a living stipend from the government to those families whose children attend the No. 8 School. That was very important for a family which has only minimal money to survive.

In the implementation of the reform, the leaders of the community were invited to participate in many activities. For example, as mentioned before, the director of the Committee of Residents was invited to attend new teachers' meetings and become the counselor of the new teachers in the school in order to help them understand the community better. All these practical supports from the local community had become precious resources for the school to implement its reform.

2. Cultivating Children to Serve the Community and Society

Indirect support from the community could be examined in many ways. The school found that learning by serving always benefits both the students and the community. Therefore, the school initiated many activities for students to serve the community and learn how to care for others. For example, they held a program called "Giving love" in which students were organized to go to kindergartens, nursing homes, special education schools, etc. to provide services to small kids, elderly people, and specially challenged children. Another activity they organized was called "sending apples" to the elders who lived in nursing homes. Every child was required to send one apple, with a note that contains the student's name and a red heart drawn by him/herself, to an elderly person. The activity received a positive effect in that the elderly people were very excited and felt warm to have children's respect and caring. Every Thursday, they would look forward to the children who would come to see them on Friday.

In 1996, the school conducted an activity called "four-ones service" initiated by a key school in the Zhabei District and promoted by the city government. Concretely, the "four-ones service" means that it requires every student to help his/her family in one specific thing every day, to do one good deed for the neighborhood weekly, to participate in one activity held by the community monthly, and to attend one activity of social practice organized by the district and city each semester. During these activities, students cleaned the streets of the community, gave art performances, helped elderly people, and worked as journalists, photographers, and radio announcers. With the diversity, students were very active in participating in those activities which were provided outside academic learning. Meanwhile, they learned to take responsibilities for the family, community, and society.

3. Learning from the Society

In the reform, the school had tried many ways to ensure that the resources of the community were available to support the development of students' abilities. For example, they organized students to go to government offices, factories, and the community to do investigations for their social study. Mr. Chen, the former vice principal, recalled that some students conducted an investigation—"Zhongxing Street is developing rapidly." The investigated street is near the school. It used to be one of the poorest and the most backward areas in Shanghai before the undertaking of the economic reform in 1978. To help students get to know their neighborhood's social changes, the school obtained active support from the community so that students were able to visit many work units, families, and factories, and interview people from all walks in life. As a result, they collected a wealth of data, composed many vivid stories, and had a good experience learning about the society they live in.

Collaborating with the community, the school also ran a number of activities to stimulate at-risk students' learning. For instance, they invited alumni to come back to school and shared their experience of how they overcame the difficulties in learning to be successful, and how knowledge is important in one's professional field today. Sometimes, they invited students' parents, who lost jobs or regained jobs, to give a talk to students. Using their living experiences, the parents told the children that learning is the first priority for them in today's highly competitive world. Without knowledge, one would not be able to capture opportunities in the job market. Generally, this kind of activity exerted powerful impacts on students since the speakers came from their real life.

4. Transforming Students through Efforts of the Parents and the Community

Moral education in China is so deeply ingrained in Chinese education that schools would take every opportunity help transform students morally. In this section, I will describe an activity called "the fourteenth birthday party" held by the school to demonstrate how parents, community, and school cooperated together to educate children in No. 8 School.

In Shanghai, teachers told me that when children reach a certain age such as 14 or 18, the school would hold some solemn ceremonies for the students to celebrate their new roles in life. The age of 14 means a person has moved from being a child to becoming an adolescent, while 18 means a person has moved from being an adolescent to becoming an adult. Therefore, the school will have a group birthday party for students who reached these two important landmarks (in China, children go to school at 7. Therefore, students in the same grade should be at the same age).

During my fieldwork, on April 15, 2004, "the fourteenth birthday party" was held by the Moral Education Office for grade 8 students. The school selected a base for adolescent education (something like summer camp) run by a local company, as the place for the party, located in a beautiful small town near a lake in the suburb of Shanghai. It took us more than two hours by bus to get there. Lasting for two days, the event was both a moral education activity as well as a spring camp for children. Under the leadership of class directors, students started their activity in the evening and continued the second day. The party was full of fun and stimulating. They had assorted fruit dishes' competition, art performances, tug-of-war matches, canoeing, etc.

There were three things which impressed me the most. The first was, when the party began, two students ran into the room from the back, each holding a torch while passionate music was being played. The torches were passed from one hand to another, symbolizing that the students have passed from childhood to youth, thereby entering a new stage of life. The children were very excited about this moment. The second inspiring thing was "the 14 oaths," a poem with 16 sentences. The pledge expressed students' passion, responsibility, hope, dream, and ambition to serve the country and the society. The main idea in the pledge is for students to study hard and become a useful person to society. Led by the host, a gentleman who was an expert in conducting this kind of party from the local community, students raised their right hand, repeatedly reading sentence by sentence the pledge. The students looked solemn and excited. The third thing was parents' letters. After the oath, students were told by the host to read their parents' letters. This was a product of collaboration between the school and the families. Many children were surprised that they received this letter. Maybe this was the most touching moment of the party. Many children

Photo 11.2 The fourteenth birthday party: Participating in assorted fruit competition, provided by No. 8 School, 2004.

226 *Success for All*

Photo 11.3 The fourteenth birthday party: The torch ceremony, 2004.

Photo 11.4 The fourteenth birthday party: A girl crying touched by her Parents' letter, 2004.

cried when they read their parents' letter. I collected some parents' letters and found that they were all written in a very moving way. In their letters, parents expressed their deep love and high expectation for their children, hoping their children would study hard and have a bright future. After the activity, I interviewed some students about the activity. Many students reflected that they enjoyed it very much. Feeling a sense of being a grown-up, they said that they should work hard and not let their parents worry about them anymore. Clearly, this is the point when the family, the community, and the school arrived at the common goal to educate children. In such a special occasion with passion and enthusiasm, it was not surprising that children had an unforgettable experience.

5. A Broader World

The school's interaction with the community was not limited to the local community where No. 8 School was located, rather the school's interaction with the outside world become national and international after 1990, when the school fulfilled its reform goals successfully. Many principals around the country have come to the school to learn from the reform. Many scholars from Europe, North America and Asia have visited the school. Therefore, the school teachers and students have had more opportunities to learn from a broader world. For example, because of the *success education* program, students in No. 8 School come from all over the country. That has brought a diverse culture to the campus, in which students can learn from

Photo 11.5 The delegation from Macao University, 2004.

each other. To receive foreign guests, the students were trained to practice their English more fluently. Also, they had participated in shooting several TV special programs and had some exchange programs with students from Hong Kong. During my investigation, I met a delegation from Macao University visiting the school. They were undergraduate students, majoring in mathematics. Liu introduced success education to the delegation and arranged the school's experienced math teachers to demonstrate how No. 8 School conducted its math teaching reform. These activities enriched students' lives and opened their minds up to other people and possibilities. All these factors might make contributions to the school curriculum reform with a clear emphasis on the combination of the Eastern and Western education systems.

6. Sharing Resources with the Community

In the new campus with modern equipment, the school started to share their resources with the community. They opened their sports ground, library, reading rooms, dancing rooms, computer labs to the community. On the weekends, while teachers were free, they taught computer courses to residents in the community. Students participated in art performance programs held by the community. Also, students were organized by the school to publish blackboard newspapers for the community. All these activities were welcomed by the community and benefitted the community. In all, to improve at-risk students, the school has put tremendous efforts into collaborating with the community. Through multidimensional approaches, the school attempts to develop a new education model that can integrate the school and society and Western and Eastern systems together.

SUMMARY

In sum, No. 8 School has valued parental and community participation in the school's reform and encourages their involvement in many ways. The school first helped parents to increase their confidence in their children and collaborate with the school in their children's learning. A variety of creative approaches were initiated by the school to improve communication with families and community. With persistent efforts for more than a decade, the school has developed an effective system of interaction with parents and the community at large, which have contributed greatly to the successful implementation of success education.

CHAPTER 12

SUMMARIES, REFLECTIONS, AND CONCLUSIONS

In this concluding chapter, I will first outline how success education sheds light on strategies and innovations for helping at-risk students. Further, as any reform will encounter problems and challenges, I also analyze the problems and dilemmas in the school's implementation of the experiment, and describe the main challenges the school is facing today. Second, I will reflect on the use of CSR, the model of Comprehensive School Reform, as the theoretical framework for this research. How has China's experience enriched and extended this model? In what way the international education community will be illuminated on helping disadvantaged students will be discussed.

THE MAJOR CONTRIBUTIONS OF SUCCESS EDUCATION AS A COMPREHENSIVE SCHOOL REFORM MODEL

Based on literature review in chapter two, the CSR model is described as a school-wide and comprehensive approach that focuses on the reconstruction of the whole process of schooling—management, teaching, learning, and parents and community involvement. Meanwhile, the other two features of the CSR model: Research-based practice and helping disadvantaged students in high-poverty schools—the two original ideas of developing the reform model, are also accounted as the important components of CSR programs. Using these criteria of the CSR models, I will summarize the major contributions of success education reform carried out by No. 8 School as follows.

1. The Success Education Model Is a Research-Based Educational Reform in China

China is a country with highly restrictive political control. Educational reforms before 1978 were almost always the results of political policy, with their directions changing constantly with the up and down of political tides at the time. Since 1978, with the restoration of the higher education system and the training of a new generation of researchers, Shanghai, as the dragon head of economic reform and educational restructuring in China, have trained and encouraged educators and researchers to conduct educational research and seek ways to improve educational efficiency and equality. Under such a circumstance, many new educational experiments emerged in 1980s. The *success education* program is one of them and has become the most successful one. As a pioneer in research-based reform, *success education* has set up a unique reform model in China, that is, to use scientific approach for making educational policies and carrying out an educational reform.

Specifically, throughout the reform, the school has grounded its policymaking and instructional innovations through deliberate efforts in research data collection, experimental design and theory building from experience. For example, Principal Liu initiated the experiment based on his own research and the research done by the research group he led. As described in chapter 6, from 1983 to 1985 when he studied in the Department of Education Administration of Shanghai Normal University to get his second bachelor's degree, Liu had spent those two years doing literature review on at-risk students' education, collected data on this issue, and tried to find solutions to help disadvantaged students. In 1987, Liu submitted his research proposal to the Shanghai Municipal Committee for Education (SMCE) and started this educational experiment as a three-year experimental research program.

Also, through research, Liu and the research group identified the problems hampering the learning of at-risk students and determined their main strategies for the implementation of *success education*. Shown in chapter 6, in the early stage of the experiment, Liu and the research group began the implementation of the reform through careful research design. Using five months from May to September 1987, the school organized the research group and teachers to study and edit literature review on school success and improvement of at-risk students in both Chinese and English. At the same time, they did an investigation on the average IQ and the psychological characteristics of at-risk students among schools in the district to compare the differences between high academic achievers and low academic achievers. Through analyzing all the data they collected, the school found that the main reason causing at-risk students' academic failure was their low self-esteem and low self-confidence. Therefore, Liu and the research group focused their strategies on enhancing students' self-confidence by providing all kinds of opportunities for children to achieve success in their daily learning. It is after doing research and practicing various innovative measures for two years, that in 1989 the research group named the education reform they were conducting as *success education*.

In chapter 7, we highlighted how the school tried to find effective teaching methods through making videotapes of teachers' lessons and facilitating teachers to write research papers. This is a significant endeavor. Over the years, the school had recorded more than one thousand videotapes of teachers' classes, especially, of those outstanding teachers' classes. Through organizing teachers to analyze outstanding teachers classes, the school identified the patterns of outstanding teaching and promoted them for all teachers to follow. In this way, the school improved its quality of teaching rapidly. Also, by creating all kinds of opportunities and fostering a favorable research environment, teachers in the school had published numerous papers in professional journals and a number of books on *success education*. Evidence indicated that the research-based reform resulted in improved effectiveness and this may be one of the main reasons why *success education* has been lasting for nearly two decades.

2. The School Has Made Significant Contributions to the Development of At-Risk Student Education in China

As indicated in literature review, Chinese education is an exams-driven system that labels most students as school failures. Focusing on helping high achieving, top students to pass the National Entrance Examination for higher education, Chinese schools and society have neglected and even looked down upon at-risk students. Meanwhile, the field of at-risk student education had also been ignored by the mainstream researchers for a long time. As a result, the exam-oriented system led to a large number of low performing students who experience painful failure and suffer great damages in their self-esteem. Although there were strategies proposed for and research done on improving at-risk students before the mid-1980s, all of them were mainly description of individual teachers' experiences, not a reform that is systematically designed and that requires collective actions taken by the government, school, and society as it is the case in *success education*. As a school-wide reform, *success education* has become a pioneer in the field of at-risk students' schooling. Based on much research done by the school and many living experience drawn from teachers for more than a decade, it is obvious *success education* has made a ground-breaking contribution to the Chinese society, maybe the international community as well, in terms of creating a comprehensive philosophy and designing rich and multiple practical measures for improving at-risk students. This research-based practice has been promoted to many schools within the country and attracted attention from the international community as well.

3. Success Education Proves Multiple Levels of Leadership Support is Essential for Conducting a CSR Program

In chapter 6, by examining the supports from all levels of governments in Shanghai and even in China, I found that leadership is the key to run a whole school reform. Since a CSR model is a complicated and systematical project, it needs strong support from multiple layers of leadership, legislatively, financially, and morally. Especially, in China's case in which politics still plays a dominant role in people life, leadership from higher levels has the power to determine whether a reform is to be promoted or not, and what directions a reform should take. The case of No. 8 School is the positive result of the cooperation of Shanghai governments at all levels. Using a Chinese saying to express it, this special reform has occurred at "the right time, the right place, and with right people's support" (*tiansh dili renhe*). In other words, *success education* met the demands by many sectors of the society for changes. At the state level, it met the need of universalizing the nine-year compulsory education in the mid-1980s and implementing quality education around the country after the 1990s. At the municipal level, *success education* was regarded as a very important tool to implementing the Compulsory Education Law issued by the central government and enhancing the quality of education in the poorest area in Shanghai. For the leadership at the district level, the reform was a result of their bold plan and determination in changing the serious problems of poor education. All these factors indicated that this was the reason why the alternative approach in No. 8 School could attract much attention from many forces in society. The case of *success education* may tell us that, to wisely and successfully implement a CSR model, reform sets its goal as meeting the needs from multiple levels of the society is essential. Only in that way can a reform be fully supported by all forces from a society.

4. Teacher Training Needs to be Given Top Priority

Teachers are the center of a school, which, to a great extent, determines the quality of education in school. Therefore, professional development is regarded as a key to implement a school-wide reform. To improve the quality of the teaching force, No. 8 School placed its first priority to training its teachers. In chapter 7, I described a variety of alternative teacher training programs that were initiated by the school. Through analyzing the experience of No. 8 School, one can find that highly effective teacher professional development is possible when a school undertakes well planned and coordinated efforts to motivate teachers and provide continuously learning opportunities for them.

Among seven strategies adopted by No. 8 School for improving teachers' quality, as discussed in Chapter 8, the first and the second measures—"making developmental plans" and "*success education* theory and methodology training"—work on teachers' motivation and give teachers the skills to actualize the concepts of *success education*. These measures are crucial to make a CSR model a success since only after teachers understand the importance of the reform can they actively involve themselves in the successful implementation of the reform. The rest of the five specific strategies provide original in-service training for teachers in the fields. They build up a network of effective teacher training, engaging teachers within the school and drawing from sources and expertise from outside the school. For example, they study outstanding teachers' teaching and spread their teaching approaches to other teachers. This practice has been proven as a speedy way to enhance teachers' teaching quality. In the meantime, team teaching training has created a professional learning community in which teachers learn from each other and collaborate to achieve a common goal. Young teachers, who have little teaching experience, have benefitted the most from the master-disciple teaching training arrangement. The master teachers not only passed their teaching experience to young teachers, but also gave their loving care to their young colleagues and established a harmonious relationship between each other, which could facilitate young teachers to be able to teach effectively as soon as possible. Through having the going-out and inviting-in teaching training method, the school effectively builds a network with the broader society so that teachers could refresh their knowledge and learn educational theories and practice from other schools and experts. It is a very important way for teachers to continuously grow in a rapidly changing era. Although the research-based teaching training is a challenge for any schools, No. 8 School has made great efforts and achieved great success. In a research-based teaching format, teachers can be upgraded to a higher level of teaching in both theory and practice. Overall, the campus-based teacher training became an essential factor for the successful implementation of *success education*.

5. Designing a Flexible Curriculum and Evaluation System that Fits the Situation of At-Risk Students and Encourages Students to Learn

As we have known, the Chinese educational system is a uniform, exam-oriented system. To achieve the goal of helping students pass the National Entrance Examination, a national curriculum and unified teaching outlines have been compiled by the State Education Commission and local education departments. The curriculum and guidelines tend to emphasize difficult contents, which benefits mostly only the top students who are expected to successfully pass the national entrance examination. The unified teaching curriculum itself made most students a failure and did not fit the situation of at-risk students who lacked much basic knowledge. Liu and the research group initiated a bold innovation in their curriculum and evaluation system, as described in chapter 8.

Data shows that the strategies of altering the curriculum and the criteria of evaluation were fundamental, powerful and practical approaches in No. 8 School to transition at-risk students from experiencing failure to savoring success. Many students experienced educational failure because the unusually difficult curriculum and a stiff evaluation system cannot stimulate students to learn. Many strategies of teaching innovation created by No. 8 School such as "low," "small," "more," and "fast," were designed to help the at-risk students, and they have been proven to have improved at-risk students' academic achievement because these measures cater to the level of students' knowledge and the students specific needs. The alternative evaluation system provided many opportunities for students to experience success and improved their confidence in learning. The most significant contribution made by *success education* to at-risk students' education was that the school directly worked on students' motivation system to facilitate students to establish a positive mentality and a high self-esteem. In that way, the alternative approach eventually transformed students from a person of low self-esteem to a person full of confidence in their learning and future.

6. Effective Class Management through the Class Directors and the Power of Love and Care to Stimulate Students Motivation to Learn

At-risk students usually display problems in behavior, discipline, and learning due to their disadvantaged family background and poverty in the community. To change this situation, No. 8 School reformed its moral education from serving solely a political purpose, as is practiced in most regular schools in China, to combine it with multiple approaches to meet students' needs. They initiated many creative, interesting, and practical programs and activities to rebuild students' self-esteem and self-confidence with promising results as indicated in chapter 9.

Especially, the school emphasized the crucial role of the class director in classroom management. This special Chinese practice had been shown as an effective method to manage at-risk students with multiple problems in learning, behaviors, and discipline. By giving their love and care to students, the class directors had built up a close relationship with their students which made it possible to influence students to make changes. Assuming roles as students' parents, and as an educator, manager, and communicator, the class directors in No. 8 School made special and significant contributions to the at-risk student education.

7. Building an Effective Relationship between School and Families, and School and Community

Under the traditional educational model, the communication between parents and school focuses on a narrow goal, namely having students achieve high scores in the National Entrance Examination. Teachers usually pay more attention to high achieving students' families while low achieving students' families feel ashamed in their interaction with the school. To rebuild parents' confidence in their children's learning, No. 8 School established a dramatically new relationship with at-risk students' families in many ways. They helped students' families financially, held parent meetings to promote the ideas of *success education*, set up a parent school to improve their parental skills, and visited families to discuss with parents on how to deal with students' problems. Through providing all kinds of services, the school established a common goal with the families and community, and they worked together as a team to improve the at-risk students' learning and personal growth.

PROBLEMS AND CHALLENGES IN THE IMPLEMENTATION OF SUCCESS EDUCATION

Like any CSR model, the success education reform has faced many problems and challenges during its implementation. In this section, I will discuss these difficulties confronted by the school.

Financial Problems

One of the biggest challenges faced by Principal Liu are financial problems. Unlike CSR programs in the United State, which is funded by the government largely, the financial support from the Chinese government for the *success education* model was far from enough. With only a 30,000-yuan grant from the Shanghai municipal government, Liu started the reform. Although the Zhabei District government also gave 30,000 yuan for the purchasing of lab equipment, the school still lacked money to pay its large expenditures such as teachers' allowance, stipend, teaching facilities (e.g., computers, desks, chairs) and so on. After 1990, due to decentralization of educational funding, the governments at all levels reduced their investment in education. Schools had to find the extra funding by themselves. To continuously run the program and maintain the school, Liu had to try very hard to find resources for the school. As described in chapter 6, Liu used to run factories, stores, restaurants and so on, to generate income for the school. During our interview, Liu told me that during the ten years from 1994 to 2004 while he worked as the principal of the school, for nine years he had to borrow money from outside the school to pay the premium of his teachers and staff at the end of every year.

Another example could reflect the situation of the school's financial problems. From my interviews, I learned that from January to April 2004, the district government provided 280,000 yuan monthly to the school. However, the total expenses of the school were 580,000 yuan per month for teachers' and staff's salary and other cost. It means that the school had to find the other 300,000 yuan by itself. Liu told me that this is the reason why he expanded his school as a "complete school" which was no longer just a middle school, but it also included both junior high and senior high in the new campus. Since compulsory education in China is only for nine years, the school can charge the senior high school student 2,400 yuan per semester in tuition. Through this means, the school could resolve part of its financial problems. Also, in the new campus, Liu could recruit students nationally and charge them 10,000 yuan per year for tuition. Through these measures the school was able to partially resolve the shortage of funding.

The most negative impact of lacking money is that it is difficult for the school to hire high quality teachers from the local area. Also, it is difficult for the school to keep its outstanding teachers. Although the Zhabei District has developed very rapidly since 1978, it is still one of the most underdeveloped areas in Shanghai due to historical reasons. The school leaders told me there was a gap in teachers' salaries between the Zhabei District and the other advanced areas in Shanghai. For example, teachers' average salary in No. 8 School was around 30,000 yuan per year, yet in the Xuhui district, an area where the rich people in Shanghai reside, it was around 50,000 yuan per year. As a result, many of the school's teachers were hired from outside Shanghai. Also, Liu shared with me that the major challenge he was facing was that every year he lost a number of outstanding teachers because of a lack of funding. "We put in a lot of efforts to train our teachers. However, after years of efforts, some of them jumped to other schools which can offer more money to them. I have no choice for that. It is the reality because everyone needs money in life," Liu said.

The Challenges of Transforming Teachers, Staff, Students, and Parents to Embrace the Idea of Success Education

My investigation shows that transforming people's mindset was a tough process for the school. At the beginning of reform, Liu and the research group invested a lot of time and energy in transforming the school culture from focusing on students failure to emphasizing their strengths. The teachers, having worked in a desperate environment for a long time, at the beginning of the reform did not know what the reform was about, what they could do, and what would be the result. Generally, they did not have confidence in students. So, informing teachers and helping them to embrace success education has been a difficult path. For the first stage, since there were only two classes, it might be easier to change a small number of teachers' minds. However, in the second stage the reform was enlarged to the whole school. Liu said that they had to instill the new educational philosophy in the minds of every teacher and staff member in the school. It was the most difficult task for the reform. The biggest challenges for school leaders to face were: How to explain the significance of *success education* reform to teachers and staff? How to encourage teachers to be persistent when they were having difficulties in helping at-risk students? And what should be done to build up a close relationship with the students and parents?

Through years of hard work, the teachers gradually accepted the new education philosophy. However, the old campus would be closed due to the city government's plan to demolish the whole area of Zhabei. The school hence built up a new campus in 2001. In the new campus, Liu organized a new team of school leaders and recruited many new hands who did not know *success education* well in terms of its philosophy and practice. Making a comparison of the two campuses, I felt teachers in the old campus obviously had a better understanding of the idea of *success education* than the teachers in the new campuses. The dedication of teachers to the reform was a challenge as well in the new campus, since the new leaders were more concerned about their economic rewards than their fellow teachers are in the old campus. Many teachers and staff, who transferred to the new campus from the old one, told me that they missed the time when they were working in the old campus. Although the school conditions of the old campus were not as good as the new campus, teachers enjoyed their work very much since they shared a lofty goal and a spirit of helping needy students. They collaborated together all the time without thinking about monetary reward. In the new campus, even though they earned more money than while they were in the old campus, they felt the collaboration among teachers was much more difficult than in the past. Thus, it was a big challenge for Principal Liu to promote *success education* to his new colleagues under a changing social and cultural context.

Transforming at-risk students is a complex and hard call which demands time, energy, and cooperation among teachers, and which requires support from parents and the community. In the first and second phases, the reform had achieved great success in improving at-risk students' academic outcomes and enhancing their personal development. However, not all the students have followed the same pace in making progress. Also, students' progress might be up and down with a relapse. Teachers might take years to work on a student for his/her change. Some works done by the teacher might not be effective at all. Thus, improving at-risk students requires teachers to be patient and persistent. In addition, teachers found the most difficult thing to change at-risk students was to identify the right way to understand the students and the right method to bring transformation in the individual student. It needs time but more important, it requires teachers to be loving and caring and know the art of communication and management.

In the year I visited the school, students' academic achievements at the old campus were not as high as before. The reason causing this backslide was that, bothered by the uncertainty of the school's approaching closure, teachers and students worried about their future. In this sense, to ensure the continuous success of the reform, the school has to keep its energy and support to ensure teachers have a stable environment to work together for students' learning and growth.

I found that it was impossible to change a high at-risk school unless it also transformed the parents. Many teachers, especially class directors, stated that the most difficult thing for them to do during the reform was to help parents transform their way of educating their children at home. Since parents came from a variety of backgrounds, it was a difficult task for the class teacher who has to communicate with all parents after taking a heavy work load in and after school. Many class directors and teachers told me that they had some unhappy experiences with the parents, who did not understand the reform and in one occasion kept the visiting teachers waiting outside of their house for a long time before admitting them in. Parent school is a good way to educate parents to improve parental skills. However, it is hard for it to last long since it consumes too much of teachers' time preparing and giving all the lectures for parents.

Many other problems also existed in the school. For example, the school needs to continuously enhance teachers' teaching quality; especially, it needs to develop senior teachers' capabilities of using computers and other technology. Moreover, teachers have worked very hard but they were paid too low. In terms of students' management, although the school has reduced students' behavioral problems and discipline problems due to its adoption of a tight management system, students should have been given more free rooms to develop. All these problems may take a long time to address and find solutions.

Where Will Success Education Go?

In fact, a very serious problem faced by Liu and the school is where *success education* will go after Liu retires in 2010? In the first and second stages, the reform had been reported to have great positive effects under collaborative leaderships from governments at all levels. The model had been expanded to many schools in the Zhabei District after the mid-1990s. However, the score-up movement did not reach an ideal result. By 2004, only Liu's three schools still carried out the reform while other schools have stopped. During the height of the development of *success education*, there were 10 scholars working in the Shanghai Institute of Success Education, established in 1997; the number, however, was reduced to two in 2004. With the closure of the old campus in 2006, *success education* is facing a critical time. Moving into a new area, most students in the new campus came from peasant families in the suburb of Shanghai with a stable and decent income. They were not disadvantaged students anymore. Liu's other school was a private school, serving children from well-to-do families. Under such a situation, many teachers in the school were worried about the future of *success education*. Where will it go?

Success education calls for more support from a higher level of leadership. In the past, the very important reason for the reform to achieve a great success was the strong support and collaboration from the governments at all levels. However, after the late 1990s, the support from the governments has become more on paper than action, and the government and the school seldom work as partners in the reform anymore. Especially, after the leaders at the district and city level, who fully supported the reform in the first and second stages, retired from their positions, the new leaders might not feel an urgent need to put energy into the reform since the average level of education in the district has been raised. Therefore, they might shift their attention to other educational reforms in other schools since leaders in China always attempted to achieve his/her own success in a certain field during his/her term. As a result, they gave their support in lip service rather than participating in and providing supports of all kinds, as leaders did in the first and second stages. This challenge arises from the problems of the Chinese political system, not from the personal defects of any individual leader, as everyone has to show his/her own political achievement (*zhengji*) during his/her term.

Another shortcoming from the system is that after one became successful in a certain field, the system will use the tool of propaganda to set up him/her as a good model for everyone to learn from and give the person a great deal of honors, ignoring the achievement and support from other members of the work team. As a result, it might hurt the feelings and enthusiasm of those fellow workers who also participated in the reform and made great efforts and contributions. Indeed, Principal Liu gained tremendous honors from the governments at all levels after his success in leading the reform. He was given titles such as the "special grade principal" at municipal and at national level, "special grade teacher" at municipal and at national level, named one of "ten outstanding young primary and secondary school teachers," and so on, all highest honors for the teaching profession. He was received by the central governmental leaders, even the former president of CCP Jiang Zhemin, as a model citizen.

Liu said during our interview that he never imagined he could receive so many honors from his work, and in fact he did not want to have so many honors; he would rather have more active and practical support from the government. For example, he had a very strong wish that the government could grant more money to the school, such as 5,000 yuan in operating budget for every student in his school, so that he could run a boarding school for at-risk students who come from disadvantaged families as well as those from wealthy families. In that way, he could do a comparative research on disadvantaged students from different family backgrounds. He is still full of enthusiasm for helping at-risk students and needs more support for the research and practice.

A shortcoming of the Chinese culture also contributed the decline of the reform. That is to say, the Chinese people cared for their face a lot. Since the school became famous, many educators, scholars, and guests from the domestic and international fields visited the school. The government leaders might think the old campus was too backward with old buildings and poor equipment. They believed the school should be presented as a modern one with modern equipment and better conditions. According to my interviewees, this might be a part of the reason why they shut down the old campus. In fact, it hurt the feelings of the school leaders and teachers who worked in the old campus. They loved the school and loved *success education* program very much. A number of teachers cried when they knew the school would be closed. Most leaders and teachers were very anxious about the result. When I visited the families around the school, some parents cried and they did not know what they were going to do for their children's future. The leader of the Committee of Community I interviewed also said the school should remain open until all the old houses are gone (it might take many, many years for the government to do it), since the students living nearby needed the school. Otherwise, the schools near this area would be too crowded. Also, No. 8 School was full of experience to deal with at-risk students in this area and children might get more benefits from *success education* than attending other schools. It is clear a strong leadership is very much needed to energize the school.

Contradiction with the Existing Exam-Oriented Chinese Educational System

Although China has called for quality education for more than a decade, the exam-driven system still plays a central role. The main purpose of all the schools in China is still to help students pass the National Entrance Examination. Therefore, No. 8 School is facing a big challenge from the whole system. Especially on the new campus, it has senior high school students now. Liu told me that he could not extend to the senior high students *success education* because of the National Entrance Examination. Even for the junior high students, the school has to pay much more attention to the scores of the students. Teachers in the school said that they had on choice because parents and the whole society expected students to pass all kinds of exams, especially the National Entrance Examination. Otherwise, the school could not survive.

I observed that after a unified standardized examination was administered in all schools at the district level, the school had to organize the teachers to analyze each student's test carefully and find the way to help him/her. They also ranked the scores of the students, a practice which puts great pressure on students. I interviewed some students about this issue. They told me that they did feel pressure from the exams and their future as well.

Because of the national exams, the school is challenged by the parents' choices as well. Many parents tried all possibilities to send their children to go to key schools or to better private schools in order to pass the National Entrance Examination. That might influence the school in terms of recruitment and student composition.

All of the problems presented above may require much more attention from the whole society to support the *success education* reform. It is a comprehensive process and no single factor can accomplish the work.

THE IMPLICATIONS OF THE REFORM

Although success education occurred in China, we may learn some lessons from this unique Chinese reform and shed light on the CSR model. Having been carried out for more than two decades, the success education reform bears a number of implications for at-risk education from an international perspective.

1. Leadership

As shown in the literature review, the leadership is essential in implementation of CSR. The case of No. 8 School indicates that the important roles of leadership from district, city, and state are the prerequisites to make the reform successful. At the district level, leaders have functioned as collaborators to organize a research team, provided financial support, and gave autonomy to the school for policymaking. At the municipal level, leaders have provided an open environment and given strong support. At the state level, the school reform was endorsed by the central government as a model and promoted for wide adoption within the country. Among multiple leadership, the school principal plays a significant role in school reform. In No. 8 School, it is Principal Liu who initiated, developed, and persisted in the school-wide reform. Without a principal's ambition for change, big vision for education, perseverance in reform, and behavior as a good example, a CSR cannot be implemented and succeed.

2. Unification

Once a CSR model is selected, setting up a common goal and a shared ownership with teachers, staff, students, and parents is essential for school leaders. In other words, the principal should clarify the missions of the new education reform and the goal to reach, makes clear the expectations for everyone on the campus, followed by all attempts to transform the attitudes and beliefs of all the members in the school community. The evidences indicate that Liu and the research group promoted the major principles of *success education* to administrators, staff, teachers, students, and parents. They need to convince all stakeholders that they can achieve success in their efforts. For example, to administrators, the school helped them believe that every teacher has desire and potential to succeed and is able to achieve many aspects of success. The school also helped teachers and parents establish their confidence in students. Functioning in a coherent way, "the beliefs" of *success education* had been deeply built into the school culture and instilled into people's minds. The transformation resulted in a powerful synergy of efforts to make the reform a success.

3. Construction of a Loving and Caring Environment

Disadvantaged children, like the plants needing soil, sun, water, and good weather to grow, need love and care from teachers and parents to heal the wound in their damaged hearts. No. 8 School made a clear requirement at the very beginning of the reform that all the teachers and staff must pay special attention to students from the disadvantaged families and show their love to these at-risk students. They established a network to help the disadvantaged students both in their life and learning. The school tried its best to help at-risk students financially and academically. At the class level, the class directors made great contributions to create a family-like learning environment in which students can access teachers' help at any time and in any occasions. At home, the school helped parents restore their confidence in their children and cultivate better parental skills in educating their children. With the school's effort going way beyond technical and academic help, at-risk children improve their learning and life nurtured by good will and a lofty spirit of love and care.

4. Collaboration

Collaboration was an inherent part of the efforts throughout the process of the *success education* reform. Firstly, collaboration emerged among leadership at all levels. As mentioned above, without support from district, city, and state governments, the school could not make *success* education so successful. In particular, at the school level, Principal Liu and his assistant principals, heads of different departments, and teachers and staff, all shared decision-making in drafting the plans and crafting strategies for the successful implementing of the reform.

Teachers' collaboration played a central role in professional development and students' learning. The cooperation among teachers in the *success education* model could be seen in the whole process of schooling, including team working, mentoring in teacher training, the preparation for lessons, and the voluntary collaboration among teachers to help at-risk students.

The cooperation between school and family in No. 8 School was dynamic and creative. The school gave families in extreme poverty financial support, and helped parents maintain their hope for their children, invited parents to participate in school activities, and so on. The class director is the key to make the cooperation happen. In all, it is the collaboration from multiple levels and in multiple forms that allows the school to function efficiently so that the reform could be implemented smoothly and successfully.

5. Accountability

Accountability is an important concept in CSR models. Only when a school assures accountability in its policies and strategies can the school reform be effective. The *success education* model firstly made sure there was leadership accountability at all levels. It proved to be an essential support for the reform. Secondly, the accountability can be seen to come from teachers' training. The school initiated all kinds of original and effective training programs based on the campus. It created a sustained community for teachers' professional growth. Thirdly, accountability is ensured by the school changing its curriculum to guarantee students to achieve success easily in the classroom and enjoy the process of learning. A flexible curriculum, which meets at-risk students' needs, is the foundation for students to improve their academic achievement. Fourthly, accountability also emerged during the communication with family and community. All the measures adopted by the school ensure that students' families provided active support for the reform. Accountability at every aspect in teaching and learning facilitated the long term achievement of *success education*.

6. Motivation

Throughout the process of reform, instead of adopting reform measures through coercive means, the school leaders worked on the motivation system of teachers and students to push the reform forward. Using the idea of *success education*, the school encouraged teachers to succeed in their teaching. Specifically, the school helped teachers make their developmental plan so that teachers were actively involved in the reform with a big goal and high expectations.

Students in *success education* were highly motivated in learning. The school discarded external approaches employed in the past such as forcing students to learn or scolding students for their failure, and replaced them with creative measures to build up students' self-esteem and confidence in learning. Though an elaborate curriculum, students experienced as much success as they could in the classroom. By conducting all kinds of extracurricular activities, teachers identified students' strengths and encouraged their development to boost up the students' self-confidence. In all, the school believed that only by providing more opportunities for students to achieve success can students be motivated to learn by themselves.

7. Diversity

In the traditional education system, the school applied uniform textbooks, curriculum, and evaluation criteria to every student, ignoring his/her personal characteristics, learning style, and pace. In the *success education* model, the school designed a flexible curriculum to fit students' pace, edited textbooks and study materials to meet at-risk students' needs, and reformed the evaluation system to encourage students to learn. In sum, the process of teaching and leaning in *success education* was full of variety that made possible for at-risk students, who missed learning much basic knowledge since their elementary education, to catch up with other students in academic learning.

All the above experiences were drawn from the *success education* program. They were also strategies and rules that have been proven to be effective in improving at-risk students' academic learning through the school's practice for more than two decades. I hope that these principles and strategies summarized from the Chinese case can be applied to the international educational field that can make its due contributions to at-risk student education.

CONCLUDING REMARKS

As shown in the literature review sections of the research, both the issues of success for all and at-risk students are burning issues of the day for all countries in its process of modernization and globalization. With rapid strides in both science and technologies, education is being more and more seen as a panacea for nations in the world to survive and to win in the global economic competition. Education is generally believed to be the key to ensure equality of opportunity for all children, a goal for all to achieve in the 21st century. Although many countries have focused their attention, energy, and efforts on improving at-risk students, today more than ever before, the results of these measures are not obvious. On the contrary, because capitalism is being adopted globally, more and more people are becoming poor while fewer people are becoming richer. Increased inequality in educational opportunity and treatment are becoming serious problems that cause many students to suffer school failure. Therefore, success for all and the existence of a large number of at-risk students are dilemmas and challenges faced by almost every country around the world in the 21st century.

The *success education* model in China which I investigated attempted to provide some answers to the challenge of improving at-risk students' learning, a worldwide challenge faced by educators. I used CSR models as a guideline to analyze the case. At the same time, I employed ethnographic methods such as interviews, participant-observation, and critical reviews of documents, to evaluate the experiment of *success education* and study how it improves students' academic performance and personal growth as a whole. The research found that through carrying out the *success education* program for more than twenty years, this at-risk school, located in a run-down area in Shanghai, China, has been transformed into a successful school. The innovations introduced by the school, which were related to the whole process of teaching and learning, have worked in a coherent way to make school-wide change possible. The core of *success education* is to establish a loving and caring environment, to design a flexible curriculum which can meet at-risk students' needs, and to involve parents as partner to help students succeed in learning. I propose that the above three aspects may provide a solution to achieving educational equality so that no at-risk student are left behind. The research I conducted as a case study may have some limitations. However, I hope that the principles that the case advocates and have proven to be effective can be applied to the international educational field.

APPENDIX A

MISSION STATEMENT

Our school is founded upon the principle of "success education," and upholds these as the school's motto: That we aim to help students "understand themselves, transcend themselves, and contribute themselves to the wellbeing of society." We place stress on all the students' development, and give priority to training students with the spirit of liberal arts. We aim to cultivate students' scientific qualities and cultural understanding. We strive to foster the harmonious development of students' knowledge, abilities and character. The goals of our school are: We will build our special niche in "success education," serve the local district mainly while we also serve Shanghai city and the whole country. We aspire to build our school into a nationally and internationally well-known school with high efficiency and effectiveness.

248 *Success for All*

APPENDIX B

Class Schedule for Grade 7, No. 8 School, Shanghai, China (Fall, 2006)

	Class order	Time	Monday	Tuesday	Wednesday	Thursday	Friday
Morning	1	7:50–8:35	Chinese	Math	Chinese	Math	English
	2	8:45–9:30	Arts	English	Chinese	Math	Math
		9:30–9:45	Physical exercises during break			
	3	9:45–10:30	English	Computer	English	Chinese	Civic Education
		10:40–10:45	Eye-protection exercises			
	4	10:45–11:30	Math	Labor	Geography	Biology	PE
		12:40–13:00	Lunch Break			
Afternoon	5	13:00–13:45	Geography	Chinese	PE	English	Biology
		13:45–14:00	Physical exercises during break			
	6	14:00–14:45	PE	PE	History	English	Chinese
		14:55–15:00	Eye-protection exercises			
	7	15:00–15:45	History	Biology	Math	Music	Class meeting
		16:00–17:00	Extracurricular activities			

APPENDIX C

Timetable of Teacher and Administrator Activities, No. 8 School, Shanghai, China

	Class	Time	Monday	Tuesday	Wednesday	Thursday	Friday
Morning	1	7:50–8:35	Moral Edu. meeting	Group meeting of preparation for Geography and Arts	Group meeting of preparation for Chemistry and labor	Group meeting of preparation for Music and PE	
	2	8:45–9:30	Group meeting of preparation for History				School Administrative Meeting
	3	9:45–10:30	Class Director meeting (biweekly) Grade Director meeting (weekly)				
	4	10:45–11:30					
Lunch break							
Afternoon	5	13:00–13:45	Group meeting of preparation for Foreign Language (English) and Civic Education	Group meeting of preparation for Math	Group meeting of preparation for Biology and Physics	Group meeting of preparation for Chinese	Meeting of the head of teaching and Research group
	6	14:00–14:45					Class meeting with theme at school level
	7	15:00–15:45					
			Interest group activities				School staff meeting

APPENDIX D

Middle School Students' Regulations in Shanghai, China (6–9 grades)

1. Love our motherland, love the people, support the Chinese Communist Party, study hard, and prepare ourselves for making contributions to the modernization of socialism.
2. Arrive at school on time, do not be late, do not leave school early, and do not skip classes.
3. Pay attention during class, think and reflect diligently, finish homework seriously.
4. Do physical exercises persistently, and actively participate in extracurricular activities.
5. Take part in labor activity, and treasure the fruits of labor.
6. Live thriftily, pay attention to hygiene, no smoking, no drinking, no spitting.
7. Observe school regulations, comply with public order, and abide by the laws of the country.
8. Respect teachers, unite with classmates, be polite to people, no swearing, and no fighting.
9. Love the collective, take care of public property, and do not do anything that harms other people.
10. Be honest and modest, and every wrong will be righted.

APPENDIX E

The Objectives of Cultivating Basic Qualities for Compulsory Education from Grade Six to Nine in Shanghai, China

I. Quality of Ideology and Moral Character
   1. Love our motherland, love people, support the Chinese Communist Party and be concerned about current political affairs; develop self-respect and self-confidence, and make unremitting efforts to improve oneself; begin to acquire a certain level of consciousness for diligence, cooperation, and social responsibility.
   2. Love the collective, observe school regulations and abide by the law of the country; respect teachers and elders, honor one's parents, be honest and dependable, be polite, be ready to help others; participate actively in all kinds of activities organized by the school and community, and develop certain abilities of communication and organization.
II. Quality of Culture and Science
   1. Study earnestly, and diligently, have good study habits, be highly motivated in learning, and develop an ability of self-learning.
   2. Master the basic knowledge in various subjects and command the basic learning skills; broadly learn knowledge through studying popular science; grasp some scientific learning methods and mode of thinking, and preliminarily develop abilities of collecting data and handling information.
   3. Have healthy interests and habits and certain aesthetic judgment.
III. Physical and Psychological Quality
   1. Have a healthy physique and stamina, develop a good habit of doing exercises; actively take part in all kinds of activities in sports, and master certain basic skills in athletics; grasp some knowledge and skills of hygiene, develop good habits in hygiene, and have a balance time schedule for study and rest.
   2. Be broad-minded; have a bright and cheerful disposition; get along with others well and cooperate with others well; cultivate the strong willpower and the ability of self-control.

IV. Quality of Labor Skills
   1. Love labor, have a good habit in labor; cultivate the feelings of loving working people and the spirit of arduous struggle; preliminarily master some basic housework and labor skills in public welfare; actively participate in all kinds of social activities, and have certain abilities that he/she can live independently.
   2. Understand social division of labor; preliminarily master basic knowledge of occupations and employment, and have a good grasp of some basic skills in professional work.

APPENDIX F

Newspaper Report (Translation from Chinese) (1):

Liu Jinghao Arrived in Hong Kong from Shanghai and Shared his Experience on How to Educate At-Risk Students: Carrying out Evaluation of Encouragement to Eliminate Students' Feelings of Frustration

"In the symposium on how to educate at-risk students, which was held yesterday, a number of speakers emphasized the importance of rebuilding students' confidence. They also showed some positive results of educational reforms during the years.

Co-sponsored by the Department of Curriculum Development of Educational Bureau of Hong Kong, the Department of Education in Hong Kong University, and the College of Education of Hong Kong, the symposium invited Liu Jinghao, Principal of No. 8 School in Shanghai, to share his experience on carrying out *success education*.

Liu Jinghai revealed that "at-risk" students were defined as those with normal cognitive ability but low academic achievement. The main problems of those students are that with a mind set of failure, they lacked self-confidence in themselves and had low motivation to do school work. Although the reasons why students became at risk are various, there was a similar phenomenon that those students have all experienced repeated failures in school. It is these negative experiences that made students have low self-esteem and lose their enthusiasm for schooling. The solution for dealing with this problem is quite simple; we just need to help students achieve success constantly so that their confidence in learning will be restored. S*uccess education* was initiated for this purpose.

Liu said that the core of *success education* is to transform the ideology and method of traditional education. At the beginning, at-risk students achieved success with teachers' help; then, after making progress, students were motivated to learn independently; finally, through the *success education* approach, students were totally transformed from being at-risk to succeeding in academic learning. In the traditional education model, labeling all students by only using the uniform testing standard, the school itself became the important factor that made learning more difficult for at-risk students. Under this system, students, in particular those at-risk students, could not be evaluated properly. To deal with this problem, we designed the test based on students' starting point of learning, namely their real knowledge level. We also helped students set up their academic goals according to their own learning pace. Whatever progress students made, the school would encourage them. Called "evaluation with encouragement", the new evaluation system used multiple ways and dimensions to measure students. Those measures included teacher evaluation, student group evaluation, and student self-evaluation etc.. (The alternative assessment system has been proven to achieve positive results in terms of helping at-risk students achieve success in their academic learning)."

—Selected from *Ta Kung Pao* in Hong Kong, March 20, 1996.

APPENDIX G

Newspaper Report (Translation from Chinese) (2):

Success Education in Zhabei No. 8 School Has Achieved Remarkable Success: Helping At-Risk Students to Develop their Confidence in Learning

"The Community of Zhongxing in the Zhabei District first held a symposium on how to promote *success education*, a well-known educational reform around the country, from a broad scale. The conference also awarded an outstanding prize in *success education* to Liu Jinghao who was appointed Principal of No. 8 School last year.

Liu Jinghai was the Director of Department of Teaching and Research of Education Bureau of Zhabei District. Under his leadership, *success education*, a research-based educational reform, helped many at-risk students with normal cognitive ability but low academic achievement restore their confidence in learning, and experience academic success, showing continuous progress in their study. There were 12 at-risk schools in the District, characterized by "a large number of at-risk students, poor quality of the teacher force, and low family income." After carrying out *success education*, the percentage of qualified students who passed the standard graduation examination for middle schools, was raised to 80% or higher from 30% in 1987. The students' performance in No. 8 School was raised from the bottom level when they entered into the school to above-average level in the Zhabei District last year upon graduation. The rate of students meeting the requirement for compulsory education had reached 100%, while the rate of excellence had reached 85% . The level of students' motivation in learning was near that in the key middle school in the District. With a zero percent of criminal record for eight years, the school has been rewarded as "an excellent school" three times by the Shanghai city government. *Success Education* became famous in both the domestic and international educational fields. *Success education* was awarded the first prize in achievements in scientific research of basic education in Shanghai, and the third prize of achievements in excellent works in philosophy and social science in Shanghai for eight years. Li Lanqing, the Vice Premier of the State Council in China, fully recognized the remarkable achievements made by *success education*, and intended to promote its experience to the entire country."

—*The Wen Hui News*, Shanghai, China, February 25, 1995.

BIBLIOGRAPHY

Ai, L. (1993). The cultivation of students' ability of self-regulation in moral education. In M. Huang (Ed.), *Collectanea of expanding research on success education*, vol. 1. *Proceeding for the Second National Conference on Success Education* (pp. 371–376). Shanghai, China: The Education Bureau of Zhabei District, Shanghai and Shanghai Institute of Success Education.

Aimaiti, M. (2001). Low achievers: A group who we cannot ignore. *Journal of Xinjiang Education Institute*, 17(2), 32.

American Institutes for Research. (1999). *An educators' guide to schoolwide reform*. Arlington, VA: American Association of School Administrators.

Ames, N. (2004). Lessons learned from Comprehensive School Reform Models. In S.C. Thompson (Ed.), *Reforming middle level education: Considerations for policymakers* (pp.131–154). Connecticut: Information Age Publishing.

Baker, J. A., Terry, T., Bridger, R., & Winsor, A. (1997). Schools as caring communities: A relational approach to school reform. *School Psychology Review*, 26, 576–588.

Balfanz, R., & Mac Iver, D. (2000). Transforming high-poverty urban middle school into strong learning institutions: Lessons from the first five years of the Talent Development Middle School. *Journal of Education for Students Placed at Risk*. 5 (1/2), 1082–4669.

Bandeira de Mello, V. & Young, B. A. (2000). *State profiles of public elementary and secondary education, 1996–97. Statistical analysis report.* Washing D.C: U.S. Department of Education. Retrieved on July 21, 2008, from http://www.eric.ed.gov/ERICDocs/data/ericdocs2sql/content_storage_01/0000019b/80/16/04/93.pdf

Bao, P., & Huang, Y. (1995). Learning how to survive, how to care, and how to create: Reflection on elementary education into the 21st century. Retrieved on July 21, 2008, from http://www.cnki.com.cn/Journal/H-H2-SHJZ-1995-02.htm

Barr, R. D., & Parrett, W. H. (2001). *Hope fulfilled for at-risk and violent youth: K–12 programs that works*. Boston: Allyn and Bacon.

Success for All, pages 257–278
Copyright © 2008 by Information Age Publishing
All rights of reproduction in any form reserved.

Barr, R. D., & Ross, B. (1989). *Teenage parent programs: The problems and possibilities.* Corvallis, OR: Oregon State University.

Bateman, S., & Karr-Kidwell, P. J. (1995). At-risk programs for middle school and high school: Essential components and recommendations for administrators and teachers. Retrieved on July 21, 2008, from http://www.eric.ed.gov/ERICDocs/data/ericdocs2sql/content_storage_01/0000019b/80/14/14/1b.pdf

Bennett, N. G., Li, J., Song, Y., & Yang, K. (1999). *Young children in poverty: A statistical update.* New York: NCCP/Publications.

Berends, M., Bodilly, S., & Kirby, S. N. (2002). Looking back over a decade of whole-school reform: The experience of New American Schools. *Phi Delta Kappan,* 84(2), 168–175.

Berends, M., Chun, J., Schuyler, G., Stockly, S., & Briggs, R. J. (2002). *Challenges of conflicting school reforms: Effects of New American Schools in a high-poverty district.* Santa Monica, CA: RAND.

Berends, M., Kirby, S. N, Naftel, S., & McKelvey, C.(2001). *Implementation and performance in New American Schools: Three years into scale-up.* Santa Monica CA: RAND.

Berger, P. L., & Huntington, S. P. (Eds.). (2002). *Many globalizations: Cultural diversity in the contemporary world.* New York: Oxford University Press.

Bhalla, A. S. (1995). Recent economic reforms in China and India. *Asian Survey,* 35(6), 555–572.

Bodilly, S. J., Purnell, S. W., Ramsey, K., & Keith, S. J. (1996). *Lessons from New American Schools development corporation's demonstration phase.* Santa Monica, CA: RAND.

Borman, G. D., Hewes, G. M., Overman, L. T., & Brown, S. (2004). Comprehensive School Reform and achievement: A meta-analysis. In C.T. Cross (Ed.), *Putting the pieces together: Lessons from Comprehensive School Reform research* (pp. 53–108). Washington DC: The National Clearinghouse for Comprehensive School Reform.

Borman, G. D., Hewes, G. M., Oveman, L. T., & Brown, S. (2002). *Comprehensive School Reform and student achievement: A meta-analysis* (Report 59). Baltimore, MD: Johns Hopkins University, Center for Research on the Education of Students Placed at Risk.

Borman, G. D., & Hewes, G. M. (2001). The long-term effects and const-effectiveness of success for all. Center for Research on the Education of Students Placed at Risk. Retrieved on July 21, 2008, from http://www.eric.ed.gov/ERICDocs/data/ericdocs2sql/content_storage_01/0000019b/80/19/a0/b8.pdf

Bourque, M.I., & Byrd, S. (Eds.). (2000). *Student performance standards on the national assessment of educational progress: Affirmations and improvements.* Washington, DC: National Assessment Governing Board.

Bowles, S., & Gintis, H. (1976). *Sociology of education.* Homewood, IL: The Dorsey Press.

Boyd, W. L., & Shouse, R. C. (1997). *The problems and promise of urban schools.* (LSS publication series no. 97-12). Philadelphia: Temple University Laboratory for Student Success.

Bradley, D. F., Pauley, & J. A., Pauley, J. F. (2005). *Effective classroom management: Six keys to success,* Lanham, MD: Rowman & Littlefield Publishing Group.

Bronfenbrenner, U. (1986). Ecology of the family as a context for human development: Research perspectives. *Developmental Psychology*, 22, 723–742.

Brookover, W., Beady, C., Flood, P., Schweitzer, J., & Wisenbaker, J. (1979). *School social systems and student achievement: Schools can make a difference*. New York: Praeger.

Bush, G. W. (2001). No child left behind. Arlington: Educational Research Service.

Bush, T., Coleman, M., Si, X. (June, 1998). Managing secondary schools in China. *Compare: A Journal of Comparative Education*, 28(2), pp. 183–195.

Cale, J. (1992). Motivating at-risk students through flexible summer school opportunities. *NASSP Bulletin*, 76 (545), 106–109.

Cai, L. (Ed.). (1995). *Shanghai: Building a new international economic center*. Shanghai, China: Shanghai People's Press.

Campbell, J. R., Hombo, C. M., & Mazzeo, J. (2000). *NAEP 1999 trends in academic progress: Three decades of student performance* (NCES 2000-469). Washington, D.C.: U.S. Department of Education.

Cao, J. (1991). Pay attention to ten warning signs on educating at-risk students and do a good job in transforming at-risk students. In J. Liu, & Q. Ge (Eds.). *Studies on at-risk students* (pp. 223–225). Shanghai, China: The Education Bureau of Zhabei District in Shanghai.

Carnegie Council on Adolescent Development. (1989). *Turning points: Preparing American youth for the 21st century: Report of the task force on education of young adolescents*. Washington, DC: Carnegie Council on Adolescent Development.

Carnoy, M. (2000). Globalization and educational reform. In P.N. Stromquist, & K. Monkman (Eds.), *Globalization and education: Integration and contestation across cultures* (pp. 43–63). New York: Rowman & Littlefield Publishers, Inc.

Catterall, J. S. (1985). *On the social costs of dropping out of school*. Stanford, CA: Center for Education Research, cited in Alliance for excellent education. (2004, December). *Measuring graduation to measure success*. Washington, DC: Author.

Central Research Institute on Educational Science (2003). *The development and problems of universalizing nine-year compulsory education: A report on the development of basic education in China (2002/2003)*. Beijing, China: Educational Science Publisher.

Chan, D., Mok, K., & Tang, A. (2004). Education. In L. Wong, L. White, & S. Gui (Eds.), *Social policy reform in Hong Kong & Shanghai: A tale of two cities* (pp. 85–126). New York: M.E. Sharpe.

Chang, C. (1996). Vision on Chinese education in the 21st century. *Education*. 5, 91–95.

Chen, C. (1991). The influence of family's cultural background on students' academic learning. In J. Liu, & Q. Ge (Eds.). *Studies on at-risk students* (pp. 170–171). Shanghai, China: The Education Bureau of Zhabei District in Shanghai.

Chen, C. (1993). Nurturing students' mentality of success and ability of self-education: The second round of moral education through success education. In M. Huang (Ed.), *Collectanea of expanding research on success education*, vol. 1. *Proceeding for the Second National Conference on Success Education* (pp. 282–291). Shanghai, China: The Education Bureau of Zhabei District, Shanghai, and Shanghai Institute of Success Education.

Chen, C. and the Other. (1993). A study on carrying out "success education" in low performance middle schools: A research report on strengthening the cultivation of non-cognitive dimensions in education. In T. Guo (Ed.), *The exploration of success education: The experience of success education in Zhabei District of Shanghai* (pp. 76–93). Tianjin, China: Tianjin Education Press.

Chen, D. (2005, March 3). The elevation of people's consumption level in order to stimulate economic growth. *The Newspaper of International Finance.* Retrieved from http://news.xinhuanet.com/fortune/2005-03/03/content_2641737.htm

Chen, D. (2003). *Liu Jinghai & success education.* Beijing, China: International Culture Publisher Inc.

Chen, D. (2002). *The theory and practice of success education.* Shanghai, China: Shanghai Education Press.

Chen, J. (1991). Creating a good psychological environment and strengthening at-risk students' positive self-concept. In J. Liu, & Q. Ge (eds.). *Studies on at-risk students* (pp. 198–200). Shanghai, China: The Education Bureau of Zhabei District in Shangha

Chen, K., & Oster, S. (2006, March 14) Politics & economics: China's Premier continues to push market changes. *Wall Street Journal* (Eastern edition), A.8.

Chen, N. (2004). Strategies on transforming at-risk students. *Tianfu New Forum,* 12, 318–319.

Chen, X., & Yang, Y. (2005, November 8). Dramatic changes through instituting competition at different levels. *Economic Information Daily.* Retrieved from http://202.84.17.25/www/Article/2005111883845-1.shtml

Chen, Y. (1991). A dialectic perspective on the concept of at-ris students. In J. Liu, & Q. Ge (Eds.). *Studies on at-risk students* (pp. 223–226). Shanghai, China: The Education Bureau of Zhabei District in Shanghai.

Chen, Y. (1993). On designing new teaching tools. In T. Guo, & J. Liu (Eds.). *One hundred case studies of success education* (pp. 47–49). Tianjin, China: Tianjin Education Press.

Cheng, A. (1991). An analysis on the correlation between difficulty in teaching and students' low academic achievement. In J. Liu, & Q. Ge (Eds.). *Studies on at-risk students* (pp. 152–156). Shanghai, China: The Education Bureau of Zhabei District in Shanghai.

Cheng, K. M. (1995). Education—Decentralization and the market. In L. Wong & S. MacPherson (Eds.), *Social change and social policy in contemporary China* (pp. 70–78). Aldershot, England & Brookfield USA: Avebury.

Chubb, E. J., & Loveless, T. (Eds.). (2002). *Bridging the achievement gap.* Washington D.C.: Brookings Institution Press.

Church, M. B. (2000). Comprehensive School Reform demonstration program: The third wave and its preliminary effects. *Prel Briefing Paper.* Honolulu: Pacific Resources for Education and Learning.

Collins, K. M. T., & Onwuegbuzie, A. J. (2001). Effect of an after-school tutorial program on academic performance of middle school students at-risk. Paper presented at the Annual Meeting of the Mid-South Educational Research Association. 30th, Little Rock, AR, November 14–17.

Commentator of China Education Daily. (1997, November/December). Broadly promoting quality education. *Chinese Education & Society,* 30(6), 86–87.

Corbett, D. (2002). *Effort and excellence in urban classrooms: Expecting and getting success with all students.* New York: Teachers College Press.

Cornford, F. M. (1975). *The republic of Plato* (Trans.). London: Oxford University Press.

Cotton, K. (1996). *School size, school climate, and student performance* (School improvement research series). Portland, OR: Northwest Regional Educational Laboratory.

Cox, T. (Ed.). (2000). *Combating educational disadvantage: Meeting the needs of vulnerable children.* Landon and New York: Falmer Press.

Cross, C. T. (Ed.) (2004). *Putting the pieces together.* Washington DC: The National Clearinghouse for Comprehensive School Reform.

Datnow, A. & Castellano, M. E. (2001, April). Managing and guiding school reform: leadership in success for all schools. *Educational Administration Quarterly.* 37(2), 219–249.

Datnow, A., & Stringfield, S. (2000). Working together for reliable school reform. *Journal of Education for Students Placed at Risk,* 5(½), 1082–4669.

Day, C., Van Veen, D., and Walraven, G. (Eds.) (1997). *Children and youth at risk and urban education,* research, policy and practice. Leuven/Apeldoorn: Garant Publishers.

Delany, D., & Paine, L. W. (1991). Shifting patters of authority in Chinese schools. *Comparative Education Review,* 2, 23–43.

Deng, D. (2006). A brief note on transforming at-risk students: We should rely mainly on love and appreciation instead of punishment. *The People's Teachers of China,* 2, 100.

Deng, X. (1984). Respect knowledge, respect talented people (May 24, 1977). *Selected works of Deng Xiaoping: 1975–1982.* Beijing: Foreign Languages Press.

Desimone, L. (2000). Making Comprehensive School Reform work. *Urban Diversity Series,* No. 112. Retrieved on July 21, 2008, from http://www.eric.ed.gov/ERICDocs/data/ericdocs2sql/content_storage_01/0000019b/80/16/3e/c7.pdf

Dewey, J. (1956). *Democracy and education: An introduction to the philosophy of education.* New York: The Free Press.

Donahua, P. L., Voelkl, K. E., Campbell, J. R., & Mazzeo, J. (1999). *The NAEP 1998 reading report card for the nation* (NCES 1999-500). Washington, DC: U.S. Department of Education.

Dorn, J. A. (Ed.). (1998). *China in the new millennium: Market reforms and social development.* Washington D.C: Cato Institute.

Duan, Z. (1989). The psychological conflicts of at-risk students and the art of transforming at-risk students. *Jiangsu Education,* 9, cited in J. Liu, & Q. Ge (Eds.). (1991). *Studies on at-risk students* (pp. 227–230). Shanghai, China: The Education Bureau of Zhabei District in Shanghai.

Edmondson, A. H., & White, J. (1998). Tutorial and counseling program: Helping students at risk of dropping out of school. *Professional School Counseling,* 1(4), 43–47.

Education Commission on the State. (1999). Comprehensive School Reform: Five lessons from the field. Retrieved July 21, 2008, from www.ecs.org.

Education Week (2001, February 27). Violence and safety. *Education Week.* Retrieved on July 21, 2008, from http://www.edweek.org/context/topics/issuespage.cfm?id=39

Edwards, V. A. (Ed.) (1998, January 8). Quality counts' 98: The urban challenge: Public education in the 50 states [Special Issue]. *Education Week* XVII (17). Retrieved on July 21, 2008 from http://www.edweek.org/media/ew/qc/archives/QC98full.pdf

Epstein, J. (2001). *School, family and community partnerships: Preparing educators and improving schools.* Boulder, CO: Westview Press.

Fan, M., & Li, B. (1991). On effectively transforming low-performance students. In J. Liu, & Q. Ge (Eds.) (1991). *Studies on at-risk students* (pp. 186–189). Shanghai, China: The Education Bureau of Zhabei District in Shanghai.

Fashola, O. S. (1998). *Review of extended-day and after-school programs and their effectiveness.* Report No. 24. Center for Research on the Education of Student Placed at Risk, Baltimore, MD. Retrieved on July 21, 2008, from http://www.eric.ed.gov/ERICDocs/data/ericdocs2sql/content_storage_01/0000019b/80/16/fb/7d.pdf

Fashola, O. S., & Slavin, R. E. (1997). Promising programs for elementary and middle schools: Evidence of effectiveness and replicability. *Journal of Education for Students Placed At Risk,* 2(3), 251–307.

Feinberg, W., & Soltis, J. (1998). *School and society.* New York: Teachers Colleges Press.

Feng, L. (2005, September, 25). The Zhabei government investigated the low income families which received 'minimum-living-standard guarantee' and proposed to help those families by giving them job training in order to be reemployed. *Evening News Report.* Retrieved from http://news.sina.com.cn/s/2005-09-25/12487030651s.shtml

Feng, W. (2004). An educational philosophical inquiry on several problems in current basic education reforms. *The Journal of Western Normal University,* 3, 87–91.

Feng, Z., Zhu, Z., & Cao N. (Eds.) (2002). *Zhabei's yesterday, today, and tomorrow.* Shanghai, China: Shanghai Social Science Academy Publisher.

Finn, C. (1987, Spring). The high school dropout puzzle. *Public Interest,* 87, 3–22.

Finn, J. D. (1989). Withdrawing from school. *Review of Educational Research,* 59, 117–142.

Flaxman, E. (1992). *Mentoring in action: The efforts of programs in New York City.* New York: Institute for Urban and Minority Education.

Foster, P. (1992). Teacher attitudes and Afro/Caribbean educational attainment. *Oxford Review of Education,* 18(3), 269–281.

Fraser, B. J., & Walberg, H. J. (Eds). (1991). *Educational environments: Evaluation, antecedents, and consequences.* Oxford: Pergamon.

Freire, P. (1970). *Pedagogy of the oppressed.* New York: Seabury Press.

Friedland, S. (1992). Building student self-esteem for school improvement. *NASSP Bulletin,* 76(540), 96–120.

Frieman, B. (2001). *What teaches need to know about: Children at-risk.* Boston: Mcraw-Hill.

Fu, A., & Shi, L. (2001). *The psychological characteristics of children from divorced families.* Hangzhou, China: Zhejinag Education Publisher.

Fullan, M. G. (1992). Successful school improvement: The implementation perspective and beyond. Philadelphia: Open University Press.
Gan, M. (2008). A brief analysis on the main traits of, factors shaping, and psychological rehabilitation of at-risk students. Retrieved on July 21, 2008, from http://www.148com.com/html/lunwen/03/08/20080324/370484.html
Gao, A. (1991). Discussion on the factors causing primary and middle school students to lose interest in study and strategies of dealing with this problem. In J. Liu, & Q. Ge (Eds.) *Studies on at-risk students* (pp. 161–162). Shanghai, China: The Education Bureau of Zhabei District in Shanghai.
Garfinkel, I., & McLanahan, S. S. (1986). *Single mothers and their children.* Washington, DC: Urban Institute Press.
Garnaut, R., Song, L., Tenev, S., & Yao, Y. (2005). China's ownership transformation: Process, outcomes, prospects. Washington D.C.: International Finance Corporation, Australian National University, China Center for Economic Research, Peking University.
Geng, G. (2005). A reflection on how to reduce the gap between the poor and the rich in our country. *Journal of Yanan College of Education,* 19(3), 15–18.
Gewertz, C. (2001, May 2). The Breakup: Suburbs try smaller high schools. *Education Week,* Retrieved on April 20, 2006, from http://www.edweek.org/
Gibbs, J. T., & Huang, L. N.(1990). A conceptual framework for assessing and treating minority youth. In. J. T. Gibbs, and L. N. Huang (Eds.). *Children of Color: Psychological interventions with minority youth* (pp. 1–29). San Francisco: Jossey-Bass.
Goldenberg, C. (2003, March). Settings for school improvement. *International Journal of Disability, Development and Education,* 50(1), 7–16.
Gong, J., & Xu, S. (1995). A report on applying success education in high schools. *Elementary and Secondary Education,* 9, 24–28.
Gong, L. (1991). "Five avoidances" in at-risk students education. In J. Liu, & Q. Ge (eds.), *Studies on at-risk students* (pp. 221–223). Shanghai, China: The Education Bureau of Zhabei District in Shanghai.
Gong, Y. (2005, November 28). An investigative report: One-quarter of a family's total income has been spent on children's education in Shanghai. *Chinese Youth Newspaper.* Retrieved from http://edu.cyol.com/gb/edu/2005-11/28/content_1108512.htm
Gordon, R., Piana, L. D., & Keleher, T. (2000). *Facing the consequences: An examination of racial discrimination in U.S. public schools.* Oakland, CA: Applied Research Center.
Greer, C. (1972). *The great school legend.* New York: Basic Books.
Greene, M. (1988). *The dialectic of freedom.* New York: Teachers College Press.
Gu, X. (1991). An analysis of at-risk students from a psychological perspective. In J. Liu, & Q. Ge (Eds.), *Studies on at-risk students* (pp.127–128). Shanghai, China: The Education Bureau of Zhabei District in Shanghai
Guo, T., & Liu, J. (Ed.) (1993). *One hundred case studies of success education.* Tianjin, China: Tianjin Education Press.
Halpern, R. (1991). *The role of after-school programs in the lives of inner-city children: A study of the urban youth network after-school programs.* Chicago: University of Chicago, Chapin hall Center for Children.

Hawkins, J. N. (2000). Centralization, decentralization, recentralization: educational reform in China. *Journal of Educational Administration*, 38, 442–454.

Hayhoe, R. (1984). *Contemporary Chinese education.* New York: M.E. Sharpe, Inc.

He, G.. (1992a). Chapter 5: Shanghai's roles as an economic centre. In G. Totten, & S. Zhou (Eds.). *China's economic reform: Administering the introduction the market mechanism* (pp. 67–73). Stockholm, SF: Westview Press, Boulder, Oxford and Center for Pacific Asian Studies, Stockholm University.

He, G. (1992b). Chapter 16: Economic reform in Shanghai. In G. Totten, & S. Zhou (Eds.). *China's economic reform: Administering the introduction the market mechanism* (pp. 225–235). Stockholm, SF: Westview Press, Boulder, Oxford and Center for Pacific Asian Studies, Stockholm University.

He, J. (1991a). A preliminary exploration of the polarization of achievements among middle school students. In J. Liu, & Q. Ge (Eds.), *Studies on at-risk students* (pp. 128–129). Shanghai, China: The Education Bureau of Zhabei District in Shanghai.

He, J. (1991b). An analysis on at-risk students' problems in elementary and middle schools and an exploration of solutions. In J. Liu, & Q. Ge (Eds.), *Studies on at-risk students* (pp. 176–179). Shanghai, China: The Education Bureau of Zhabei District in Shanghai.

He, J. (1991c). On the criteria of defining, the types of, the factors creating, and the strategies of transforming, at-risk students. In J. Liu, & Q. Ge (Eds.), *Studies on at-risk students* (pp. 105–108). Shanghai, China: The Education Bureau of Zhabei District in Shanghai.

Hertling, E.(2000, April). Evaluating the results of whole-school reform. *Educational Leadership*, 57(7), 10–15.

Hess, F. (1999). *Spinning wheels: The politics of urban school reform.* Washington, DC: Brookings Institution Press.

Heyns, B. (1985). The influence of parental work on children's school achievement. In S.B. Kamerman, & C. D. Hayes (Eds.). *Families that work: Children in a changing work* (pp.229–267). Washington DC: National Academy Press.

Holdzkom, D.(2002). *Effects of Comprehensive School Reform in 12 schools: Results of a three-year study.* Charleston, WV: AEL, Inc.

Holliday, D. C. (2002). Using cooperative learning to improve the academic achievements of inner-city middle school students. Paper to presented at American Educational Research Association national conference, New Orleans, La. Retrieved on July 22, 2008, from http://www.eric.ed.gov/ERICDocs/data/ericdocs2sql/content_storage_01/0000019b/80/19/fe/40.pdf

Hollister, R. G. (2003). The growth in after-school programs and their impact. Brooking Institution, Washington, DC. Retrieved on July 22, 2008, from http://www.eric.ed.gov/ERICDocs/data/ericdocs2sql/content_storage_01/0000019b/80/1a/ea/fd.pdf

Hong, X. (2006). The father of "success education". In Y. Zhang, & Y. Zhu, (Eds.), *The archives of wisdom from sixteen well-known educators* (pp. 206–210). Shanghai, China: The Eastern Chinese Normal University Press.

Hook, B. (Ed.). (1998). *Shanghai and the Yangtze Delta: A city reborn.* New York: Oxford University Press.

Hu, L., & Yang, L. (2004, April). The disparity between the poor and the rich in China and the strategies to deal with this problem. *Academic Exchange,* 121(4), 108–112.

Huang, C. (2005). Let unemployment become beneficial: A study on improving the system of minimum living standard guarantee in Shanghai. *The Analysis on Population and Market,* 3. Retrieved on July 22, 2008, from http://www.usc.cuhk.edu.hk/wk_wzdetails.asp?id=3850

Huang, J. (2004, November). A brief talk on how to transform at-risk students. *Character Education of China,* 11, 91.

Huang, J., & Xu, M. (1991). The investigation on low performance students in elementary and middle schools in Shanghai. In J. Liu, & Q. Ge (Eds.), *Studies on at-risk students* (pp. 225–227). Shanghai, China: The Education Bureau of Zhabei District in Shanghai.

Hunter, A., & Sexton, J. (1999). *Contemporary China.* New York: St. Martin's Press.

Huston, C. A. (Ed.) (1991). *Children in poverty: Child development and public policy.* New York: Cambridge University Press.

Jencks, C., & Mayer, S.E. (1990). Social consequences of growing up in a poor neighborhood. In L. E. Jr. Lynn, & M. H. G. McGeary (Eds.). *Inner city poverty in the US* (pp. 111–186). Washington, D.C.: National Academy Press.

Ji, Y. (1989). *The impacts of family factors on children's intelligence and academic achievements.* Shanghai, China: Eastern China Teachers University Publisher.

Jimerson, S. R. (1999, Fall). On the failure of failure: Examining the association between early grade retention and education and employment outcomes during late adolescence. *Journal of School Psychology,* 37(3), 243–272.

Jin, X., & Guo, D. (1991). The exploration of the factors placing new students at-risk in elementary school. *Psychological Development and Education,* 1, cited in J. Liu, & Q. Ge (Eds.). (1991). *Studies on at-risk students* (pp. 119–124). Shanghai, China: The Education Bureau of Zhabei District in Shanghai.

Jordan, G., Snow, C., & Porche, M. (2000). Project EASE: The effect of a family literacy project on kindergarten student's early literacy skills. *Reading Research Quarterly,* 35(4), 524–546.

Kagan, D. M. (1990). How schools alienate student at risk: A model for examining proximal classroom variables. *Educational Psychology,* 25, 105–125.

Kang, Y. (2001). *Interpreting Shanghai: 1990–2000.* Shanghai: Shanghai People Press.

Kaufman, P., Kwon, J. Y., Klein, S., & Chapman, C. D. (2000). *Dropout rates in United States:1999* (NCES 2001-022). Washington D.C: U.S. Department of Education.

Kaufman, P., McMillen, M., & Sweet, D. (1996). *A comparison of high school dropout rates in 1982 and 1992* (NCES 96-893). Washington D.C: U.S. Department of Education.

Kingery, P. M., Coggeshall, M. B., & Alford, A. A.(1998). Violence at school: Recent evidence from four national surveys. *Psychology in the Schools,* 35, 247–258.

Land, D., and Legters, N. (2002). The extent and consequences of risk in U.S. education. In S. Stringfield, & D. Land (Eds.), *Educating at-risk students: One hundred-first yearbook of the national society for the study of education* (pp. 1–29). Chicago: the University of Chicago Press.

Law, W. W. (2000). Schooling and social change: The People's Republic of China. In K. Mazurek, M. A. Winzer, & C. Majorek (Eds.), *Education in a global society: A comparative perspective* (pp. 355–370). Needham, Heights: Allyn & Bacon.

Leading Group of the Project on Shanghai into the 21st Century. (Ed.). (1995). *Shanghai into the twenty-first century: Strategic research on Shanghai's economy and social progress from 1996 to 2010.* Shanghai: Shanghai People's Press.

Lee, G., Wang, D., & Li, S. (2004). Chapter 5: Labor. In L. Wong, .L. T. White, and S. Gui (Eds.), *Social policy reform in Hong Kong and Shanghai: A tale of two cities* (pp. 127–157). New York: M. E. Sharpe Inc..

Lee, G. O. M., & Warner, M. (2005). The management of human resources in Shanghai: A case study of policy responses to employment and unemployment in the People's Republic of China. In R. Smyth, M. Warner, & C. J. Zhu (Eds.), *China's business reforms: International challenges in a globalized economy* (pp. 124–138). New York: Routledge Curzon.

Lei, S. (1995a). Educational experiment and reform in elementary and secondary schools for the past fifteen years. *Elementary and Secondary Education*, 5, 11–14.

Lei, S. (1995b). Educational trends and educational experiments in contemporary China. *Educational Research*, 2, 29–62.

Leithwood, K. & Jantezi, D. (1990). Transforming leadership: How principal can help reform school culture. Paper presented at the annual meeting of the American Educational Research Association.

Levin, H. M. (1989). Financing the education of at-risk students. *Education evaluation and policy analysis,* 11, 47–60.

Li, B. (2004). A survey on Shanghai migrant children's compulsory education. Retrieved on September 08, 2005, from http://www.ngocn.org/?action-viewnews-itemid-654

Li, B. (2002). The exploration and analysis on factors causing students to be at risk and the strategies for their transformation. *Journal of Henan Teachers' College*, 21(3), 53–55.

Li, H. (2005). Transforming at-risk students relies mainly on affection. *Education and Management in Primary and Middle Schools,* 144(5), 26.

Li, J. (2004). Educating low performance students through applying the theory of multiple intelligences. *Journal of the Chinese Society of Education,* 3, 15–18.

Li, J. (2004). An analysis on social factors leading to disparity between the poor and the rich in our country: A social transformation perspective. *Ganshu Social Science,* 3, 106–110.

Li, N. (2006, March)). Enlightening "late shining star" by using your heart. *China Education Research and Innovate,* 3(3), 113.

Li. S. (2001, Steptember). A discussion on how to educate at-risk students. *Journal of Heilongjiang College of Education,* 20(5), 117.

Li, X., & Chen, X. (Eds.) (2003). *Class directors in middle schools.* Nanjing Normal University Press.

Li, Y. (1989). Discussing the issues and the problems on at-risk student education in the middle school. Shanghai *Scientific Research on Education,* 3, 192–193.

Liang, Y. (1993). Enhance the effectiveness of moral education by carrying out success education. In M. Huang (Ed.), *Collectanea of expanding research on success education*, vol. 1. *Proceeding for the Second National Conference on Success Education* (pp. 356–362). Shanghai, China: The Education Bureau of Zhabei District, Shanghai and Shanghai Institute of Success Education.

Liang, Y. & Lou, R. (1993). Strengthening the supervision of parents' home education ability and enhancing the level of education at home. In M. Huang. (Ed.), *Collectanea of expanding research on success education*, vol. 1. *Proceeding for the Second National Conference on Success Education* (pp. 407–411). Shanghai, China: The Education Bureau of Zhabei District, Shanghai and Shanghai Institute of Success Education.

Lin, J. (2006). Educational stratification and the new middle class. In G. Postiglione (Ed.), *Education, Stratification and Social Change in China: Inequality in a market economy* (pp. 179–198). Armonk, NY: M. E. Sharp.

Lin, J. (2000). Reform in primary and secondary school administration in China. In C. Dimmock, & A. Walker (Eds.) (2000*), Future school administration: Western and Asian perspectives (*pp. 291–309). Hong Kong: The Chinese University Press.

Lin, J. (1999). *Social transformation and private education in China.* New York: Praeger.

Lin, J., & Chen, Q. (1995, Spring). Academic pressure and impact on student's development in China. *McGill Journal of Education*, 30 (2), 149–168.

Lin, J. (1994). *The opening of the Chinese mind: Democratic changes in China since 1978.* New York: Praeger.

Lin, J. (1993). *Education in post-Mao China.* New York: Praeger.

Lin, J., & Ross, H. (1998). Potential and problem of diversity in China's educational system. *McGill Journal of Education*, 33(1), 31–49.

Jin, X., & Guo, D. (1991). An exploration of factors leading to elementary students' low academic performance. In J. Liu, & Q. Ge (Eds.), *Studies on at-risk students* (pp. 119–124). Shanghai, China: The Education Bureau of Zhabei District in Shanghai.

Lippman, L., Burns, S., & McArthur, E. (1996). *Urban schools: The challenge of location and poverty.* (NCES 96-184). Washington DC: U.S. Department of Education.

Liu, A. P. L. (1991). Communication and development in post-Mao mainland China. *Issues and studies,* 27 (2), 73–99.

Liu, B. (1998) Liu Bin on quality education. Beijing, China: Beijing Normal University Press.

Liu, J. (2001). Strengthening the function of school-based training, and carrying forward the s*uccess education* training. In Huang, M. (Ed.), *Collectanea of expanding research on success education*, vol. 1. *Proceeding for the Second National Conference on Success Education.* (pp. 130–137). Shanghai, China: The Education Bureau of Zhabei District, Shanghai and Shanghai Institute of Success Education.

Liu, J. (2001). Encouragement-based evaluation in success education. In M. Huang (Ed.), *Collectanea of expanding research on success education*, vol. 1. *Proceeding for the Second National Conference on Success Education* (pp. 118–125). Shanghai, China: The Education Bureau of Zhabei District, Shanghai and Shanghai Institute of Success Education

Liu, J.. (1997). (Ed.). *Success education.* Fuzhou, China: Fujian Education Press.

Liu, J., & Ge, Q. (Eds.) (1991). *Studies on at-risk students.* Shanghai, China: the Education Bureau of Zhabei District, Shanghai.

Liu, J., & the Other. (1993). A preliminary summary of success education conducted by low-performance schools. In T. Guo (Ed.), *The exploration of success education: The experience of success education in Zhabei District of Shanghai* (pp. 51–75). Tianjin, China: Tianjin Education Publisher.

Liu, K.. (2004). *Globalization and cultural trends in China.* Honolulu: University of Hawaii Press.

Liu, L. (1998). Retrospection and future perspective on methods of educational experiments in the past several decades. *Educational Research,* 6, 64–69.

Liu, X. (1993). Modern educational experiments have moved forward and transcended the traditional Chinese culture. *Educational Research,* 5, 55–58.

Lou, R. (1991). Cultivating a mentality of success in our students. In J. Liu, & Q. Ge (Eds.), *Studies on at-risk students* (pp. 193–195). Shanghai, China: The Education Bureau of Zhabei District in Shanghai.

Lu, M. (2004). Introduction: The changing geographies of China. In C. Hsieh, & M. Lu, (Eds.), *Changing China: A geographic appraisal* (pp. 1–16). Westview Press, A Member of the Perseus Books Group.

Lun, N. K. & Chan, D. K. K. (2003). Chapter 5: Towards centralization and de-centralization in educational development in China: The case of Shanghai. In M. Ka-Ho (Ed.), *Centralization and decentralization: Educational reforms and changing governance in Chinese societies* (pp. 81–98). Hong Kong, Norwell, Massachusetts: Comparative Education Research Centre, The University of Hong Kong, Kluwer Academic Publishers.

Jia, J. (1997). Strengthening the government's role: Pushing quality education forward. *Chinese Education & Society,* 30(6), 61–63.

Maccoby, E. E., & Martin, J. A. M. (1983). Socialization in the context of the family: Parent-child interaction. In E. M. Heatherington (Ed.), P. H. Mussen (Serirs Ed.), *Handbook of child psychology (vol. 4): Socialization, personality and social development (4th ed.)* (pp. 1–101). New York: Wiley.

Maciver, D. J, Maciver, M. A., Balfanz, R., Plank, S. B., & Ruby, A. (2000). Talent Development Middle Schools: Blueprints and results for a Comprehensive Whole-School Reform Model. In M. G. Sanders (Ed.), *Schooling students placed at risk: Research, policy, and practice in the education of poor and minority adolescents* (pp. 261–288). Mahwah, NJ: Lawrence Erlbaum Associates, Inc..

Mackerras, C., Taneja, P., & Young, G. (1993). *China since 1978: Reform, modernization and 'socialism with Chinese characteristics'.* New York: Longman Cheshire, St. Martin's Press.

Mason, J. T., Mason, B. J. & Martin K.(2001). *Problems and Solutions in Urban Schools.* Lewiston, New York: Melburn Press.

Massachusetts Advocacy Center, (1988). *Before it's too late: Dropout prevention for the middle schools.* Carrboro, NC: Author.

Masten, A. S., & Garmezy, N. (1991). Risk, vulnerability and protective factors in developmental psychopathology. In D. B. Lahey, & A. E. Kazdin (Eds.), *Advances in Clinical Child Psychopathology,* 8(1–51) New York: Plenum.

McAndrews, T., & Anderson, W. (2002, January). School within schools. *ERIC Digest 154*, Eugene: University of Oregon, Clearinghouse on Educational Management.
McLanahan, S., & Sandefur, G. (1994). *Growing up with a single parent: What hurts, what help.* Cambridge, MA: Harvard University Press.
McLaren, P. (1994). *Life in schools: Introduction to critical pedagogy in the foundations of education.* New York: Longman.
McPartland, J. M., & Jordan, W. J. (2001). Restructuring for reform: The Talent Development Model. Principal Leadership, 1(8), 28–31.
Mead, G. H. (1934). *Mind, self, and society.* Chicago, IL: University of Chicago Press.
Miao, R. (2002, April). On the choices of developmental alternatives for China's education after her entry into the WTO. *Journal of the Chinese Society of Education,* 2, 2–5.
Mid-Continent Research for Education and Learning. (1999). *Guiding Comprehensive School Reform. Leadership Folio Series.* Washington DC: Office of Educational Research and Improvement.
Mok, K. H. (2004). Introduction: Centralization and decentralization: Changing governance in education. In K.H. Mok (Ed.), *Centralization and decentralization: educational reforms and changing Governance in Chinese societies* (pp. 3–17). Hong Kong, China: Comparative Education Research Centre, The University of Hong Kong, Kluwer Academic Publishers.
Montgomery F. A., & Rossi, J. R. (1994). Becoming at risk of failure in America's schools. In J. R. Rossi (Ed.), *Schools and students at risk: Context and framework for positive change* (pp. 3–23). New York: Teachers College, Columbia University.
Murphy, J., & Datnow, A. (Ed.) (2003). *Leadership lessons from Comprehensive School Reforms.* Thousand Oaks: Corwin Press.
Mussen, P., Conger, J., & Kagan, J. (1979). *Child Development and personality* (Fifth edition). New York: Happer & Row, Publishers.
National Assessment of Educational Progress. (1976). *Functional literacy and basic reading performance.* Washington, DC: Department of Health, Education and Welfare, U.S. Office of Education.
National Commission on Excellence in Education. (1983). *A nation at risk: The imperative for educational reform. An open letter to the American people. A report to the nation and the secretary of education.* Washington, DC: Author.
National Basic Education Bureau. (1997). Reflection on and future perspective for the development of basic education reforms. Retrieved on August 31, 2008, from http://www.hzjy.net.wenxian/cedu20/china4.htm.
National Development and Reform Commission. (2005, 07, 27). New China's achievements in education, culture, health, and sports in the past fifty-five years. Retrieved on September 1, 2008, from http://www.sdpc.gov.cn/gzdt/t20050727_38063.htm.
Nathan, J. (Ed.). (1989). *Public schools of choice.* St. Paul, MN: The Institute for Learning and Teaching.
Natriello, G., McDill, E. L., and Pallas, A. M. (1990). *Schooling disadvantaged children: Rating against catastrophe.* New York: Teachers College Press.
Nelson, B. S., & Hammerman, J. K (1996). Reconceptualizing teaching: Moving toward the creation of intellectual communities of students, teachers, and

teacher education. In M. W. McLaughlin, & I. Oberman. (Eds.). *Teacher learning: New policies, new practices* (pp. 6–7). New York: Teachers College Press.
New American Schools. (1998). *Blueprints for school success: A guide to new American schools designs.* Arlington, VA: Educational Research Service.
Ngan, R., Yip, N., & Wu, D. (2004). Chapter 6: Poverty and social security. In L. Wong, L. White, & S. Gui (Eds.), *Social policy reform in Hong Kong and Shanghai: A tale of two cities* (pp. 159–182). New York: M.E. Sharpe Inc..
Ngok, K. (2007, April). Chinese education policy in the context of decentralization and marketization: Evolution and implications. *Asia Pacific Education Review,*8(1),142–157.
Nord, C. W., Brimhall, D., & West, J. (1997). *Father's Involvement in their Children's Schools* (NCES 98-091). Washington DC: U.S. Department of Education.
Nye, B., Hedges, L. V., & Konstantopoulos, S. (1999). The long-term effects of small classes: A five-year follow-up of the Tennessee class size experiment. *Educational Evaluation and Policy Analysis.* 21(2), 127–142.
Office of Elementary and Secondary Education. (2000). Comprehensive School Reform demonstration program: Raising student achievement through research-based reform that strengthen the entire school. Washington DC. Reports.
Ogden, E. H. & Germinario, V. (1994). *The nation's best schools blueprints for excellences, volume 2, middle and secondary schools.* Lancaster, PA: Technomic Publishing Company, Inc.
Oxley, D. (2001, May). Organizing schools into small learning communities. *NASSP Bulletin, 85(* 625), 5–16.
Patrikakou, E. N. (1997). A model of parental attitudes and academic achievement of adolescents. *Journal of Research and Development in Education,* 31, 7–26.
Pearson, S. S. (2002). Finding common ground: Service-learning and education reform: A survey of 28 leading school reform models. Washington DC: American Youth Policy Forum. Retrieved on June 24, 2006, from http://www.aypf.org.
Pellicano, R. R. (1987). At risk: A view of social advantage. *Educational Leadership,* 44(6), 47–49.
Piania, R. C., & Walsh, D. J. (1996). *High-risk children in schools constructing sustaining relationship.* New York: Routledge.
Pittman, R. B., & Haughwout, P. (1987). Influence of high school size on dropout rate. *Educational Evaluation and Policy Analysis,* 9, 337–343.
Posner, J. K., and Vandell, D. V. (1994). Low-income children's after-school care: Are there beneficial effects of after-school programs? *Child Development,* 65, 440–456.
Protheroe, N. J. (1998). *Comprehensive models for school improvement: Finding the right match and making it work.* Educational Research Service.
Purkey, S. C., & Smith, M. S. (1983). Effective schools: A review. *Elementary School Journal,* 83(4), 427–452.
Qi, W., & Tang, H. (2004, December). The social and cultural background of contemporary moral education in China. *Journal of Moral Education,* 33(4), 465–480.
Reese, C. M., Miller, K. E., Mazzeo, J., & Dossey, J. A. (1997). *NAEP 1996 mathematics report card for the nation and the states* (NCES 97-488). Washington D.C: U.S. Department of Education.

Reglin, G. L. (1990). A model program for educating at-risk students. *T.H.E. Journal: Technological Horizons in Education,* 17(6), 65–67.
Reglin, G. (1998). *Mentoring students at risk: An underutilized alternative education strategy for K–12 teachers.* Springfield: Charles C Thomas Publisher, LTD.
Ren, J. (1998). Quality education and examination. *Educational Research,* 7, 64–68.
Ress, D. L., Argys, L. M., & Brwer, D. J. (1996). Tracking in the United States: Descriptive statistics from NELS. *Economics of Education Review,* 15, 83–89.
Rimmington, D. (1998). History and culture. In B. Hook (Ed.), *Regional development in China volume 3: Shanghai & the Yangtze Delta: A city reborn* (pp. 1–29). New York: Oxford University Press.
Roderick, M. (1994, Winter). Grade retention and school dropout: Investigating the association. *American Educational Research Journal,* 31 (4), 729–759.
Rogus, J. F., & Wildenhaus, C. (1991). Programming for at-risk learners: A preventive Approach. *NASSP Bulletin,* 75 (538), 1–7.
Rosen, S. (2000). Chapter nineteen: Education & economic reform. In C. Hudson, (Ed.), *Regional handbooks of economic development: The China handbook: Prospects onto the 21st century* (pp. 250–261). Chicago: Glenlake Publishing.
Rosenthal, R., & Jacobson, L. (1968). *Pygmalion in the classroom.* New York: Holt, Rinehart and Winston.
Ross, S. M. (2000). How to evaluate Comprehensive School Reform models. *Getting Better by Design,* Vol. 8. Arlington VA: New American Schools Department Corp.
Ross, H., & Lin, J. (2004, Spring). Schools of good will in China: Helping poor students succeed. *Journal of Thought,* 39(1), 131–147
Rossi, J. R. (Ed.) (1994). *Schools and students at risk: Context and framework for positive Change.* New York: Teachers College Press, Columbia University.
Rousseau, J. (1911). *Emile.* Translated [from the French] by Barbara Foxley. New York: Dutton.
Rowan, B., Camburn, E., and Barnes, C. (2004). Benefiting from Comprehensive School Reform: A review of research on CSR implementation. In C.T. Cross (Ed.), *Putting the pieces together: Lessons from Comprehensive School Reform research* (pp. 1–52). Washington DC: The National Clearinghouse for Comprehensive School Reform.
Sanders, M. G. (Ed.). (2000). *Schooling students placed at risk: Research, policy, and practice in the education of poor and minority adolescents.* Mahwah, NJ: Lawrence Erlbaum Associates, Inc., Publishers.
Sanders, M. G., & Jordan, W. J. (2000). Student-teacher relations and academic achievement in high school. In M.G. Sanders (Ed.), *Schooling students placed at risk* (pp. 65–82). Mahwah, NJ: Lawrence Erlbaum Associates, Inc..
Schorr, L. B. (1988). *Within our reach. Breaking the cycle of disadvantage,* London, Doubleday.
Shanghai Institute of Human Resource Development. (2005). A research report on Shanghai education and human resource development. Retrieved on August 18, 2006, from http://blog.hr.com.cn/index.php/viewnews-366.html
Shanghai Management Bureau of Housing & Land Resources (2005). The housing protection system for middle-and-low income families. Retrieved on July, 14, 2005, from http://www.shfdz.gov.cn/dsjy/detail.jsp?200505

Shanghai Municipal Commission for Education. (2006). Basic education. Retrieved on June 20, 2006, from http://www.shmec.gov.cn/web/concept/shedu_article.php?area_id=80&id=363

Shanghai Municipal Commission for Education. (2000a). *Shanghai's Yesterday, today, and tomorrow.* Shanghai, China: Shanghai People's Publisher.

Shanghai Municipal Commission for Education. (2000b). *Collection of documents of 1999 Shanghai Municipal Working Meeting on Education.* Shanghai: Century Publishing Group and Education Press.

Shanghai Municipal Statistic Bureau. (2005) The unemployment rate and the number of unemployed people registered in cities and towns. Retrieved on June 6, 2006, from *http://www.stats-sh.gov.cn/2003shtj/tjnj/nj05.htm?d1=2005tjnj/C0322.htm*

Shanghai Statistical Bureau (2005). The education expenses of Shanghai residents have an average annual increase of 23.2 percent during the past eight years. Retrieved on August 7, 2007, from http://web.xwwb.com/wbnews.php?db=1&thisid=330

Shanghai Statistical Bureau (1999). *Shanghai Statistical Yearbook.* Shanghai: Shanghai Statistical Bureau.

Shen, G. (2000, October). On educational changes of backward students. *Journal of Lingling Teachers College,* 21 (4), 18–79, 82.

Shouse, R. C. (1996). Academic press and sense of community: Conflict, congruence, and implications for student achievement. *Social Psychology of Education,* 1, 47–68.

Sjursen, K. (Ed). (2000). *Globalization.* The H.W. Wilson Company: The Reference Shelf.

Skiba, R., & Peterson, R. (1999). The dark side of zero tolerance: Can punishment lead to safe schools? *Phi Delta Kappan, 80,* 372–376, 381–382.

Slavin, R. E. (1989). Students at risk of school failure: The problem and its dimensions. In R. E. Slavin, N. L. Karweit, & N. A. Madden (Eds.). *Effective programs for students at risk.* (pp. 3–19). Boston: Allyn & Bacon.

Slavin, R. E., Madden, N.A., Dolan, L. J., Wasik, B. A., Ross, S., Smith, L., et al. (1996). Success for all: A summary of research. *Journal of Education for Students Placed at Risk,* 1 (1): 41–76.

Smith, A. E., Jussim, L., Eccles, J., VanNoy, M., Madon, S., & Palumbo, P. (1998). Self-fulfilling prophecies, perceptual biases, and accuracy at the individual and group level. *Journal of Experimental Social Psychology,* 34, 530–561.

Smith, C. J. (2000). *China in the post-utopian age.* Westview Press, A Member of the Perseus Books Group.

Snowden, P. E. (2001). An agenda for education reform in China. *Education,* 109(1), 23–26.

Song, J. (2001). Facilitating the transformation of at-risk students with love and patience. *Aihui Educational Forum,* 3, 83–85.

Spring, J. (2001). *The American School: 1642–2000.* New York: McGraw-Hill.

State Education Commission. (1997, April 14). Statistical report on educational achievements and development in China in 1996. *China Education Daily,* p. 2.

Stockman, N. (2000). *Understanding Chinese society.* Cambridge, UK: Policy Press.

Stringfield, S., & Land, D. (Eds.) (2002). *Educating at-risk students: One hundred-first yearbook of the national society for the study of education.* Chicago: the University of Chicago Press.
Stromquist, P. N. (2002). *Education in a globalization world: The connectivity of economic power, technology, and knowledge.* New York: Rowman and Littlefield.
Stross, R. (1990). The return of advertising in China: A survey of the ideological reversal. *The China Quarterly,* 123, 485–502.
Study group on at-risk students in Chaoyang district in Beijing (1990). An investigation on factors leading to students losing interest in learning in Chaoyang district middle school in Beijing. *Research on Juvenile Delinquency.* 2, 14–17.
Su, B. (1991). Educational problems of children from self-employed families. In J. Liu, & Q. Ge (Eds.), *Studies on at-risk students* (p. 174). Shanghai, China: The Education Bureau of Zhabei District in Shanghai.
Su, J. (2003). Shanghai stipulated the standard of fee for primary and secondary school. Retrieved on June 24, 2007, from http://www.edu.cn/20030825/3089785.shtml
Su, S., & Chen, J. (1994). *Fifteen years of education reform in Shanghai.* Shanghai: Shanghai Academy of Social Sciences Press.
Su, Y. (1993a). On warmth. In T. Guo, & J. Liu. (Eds.), *One hundred case studies of success education* (pp. 155–157). Tianjin, China: Tianjin Education Press.
Su, Y. (1993b). On transformation. In T. Guo, & J. Liu. (Eds.). *One hundred case studies of success education* (pp. 322–324). Tianjin, China: Tianjin Education Press.
Sui, Y. (1996). Education for all: Challenges and strategies in 2000. *Education,* 4, 77–83.
Sun, S. (2000, October). Shanghai between state and market in urban transformation. *Urban Studies,* 37(11), 67.
Sun, X. (1993). How to use family visits to supervise parents to educate their children at home. In M. Huang (Ed.), *Collectanea of expanding research on success education,* vol. 1. *Proceeding for the Second National Conference on Success Education* (pp. 412–417). Shanghai, China: The Education Bureau of Zhabei District, Shanghai and Shanghai Institute of Success Education.
Swedner, B., & Lubeck, S. (1995). *Children and families at-promise: Deconstructing the discourse of risk.* Albany, NY. State University of New York Press.
Tan, B. (Ed.) (2003). *A theory on class directors.* Changsha, China: Hunan Normal University Press.
Tan, S. (2000). Theoretical and policy issues in education reform and development in China. *Educational Research,* 3, 3–9.
Tang, J. (2002). The formation and situation of urban poverty in modern China. *The Forum of Cadres of Communist Party and Government of China.* Retrieved on July 21, 2007, from http://www.popinfo.gov.cn/popinfo/pop_docrkxx.nsf/v_rkbl/FAF3D9C7826DFB6848256E7C00235BE0
Tang, J. (2004). Let love warm the heart of at-risk students. *Character Education of China,* 5, 134–135.
Tang, Y. (2002). An investigation and analysis of factors causing students to be at risk and strategies for their transformation. *Journal of Sichuan College of Education,* 18 (12), 79–80.

Tao, W. (1999). An outlook on Chinese basic educational reform. *The Research of Education Science*, 9, 27–32.

Tong, Z. (2006, February). The development of China and world trade. *Journal of World Trade*, 40(1), 129–136.

Toppo, G. (2001, March 2). Report says blacks three times as likely to be special-ed students. *The Associated Press*. Retrieved from: http://www.wire.ap.org.

Trimble, S. B., & Peterson, G. W. (2000). Multiple team structures and student learning in a high risk middle school. Paper presented at the Annual Meeting of the American Educational Research Association. New Orleans, LA, April 24–28.

Tsang, M.C. (1991). The structural reform of secondary education in China. *Journal of Educational Administration*, 29(4), 65–83.

United Nations Development Program (UNDP). (1998). *Human development report 1998*, Oxford, Oxford University Press.

U.S. Bureau of the Census. (1999a). *Living arrangements of children under 18 years old: 1960 to present*. Retrieved on December 12, 2005, from http://www.census.gov/population/scodemo/ms-la/tabch-1.txt

U.S. Bureau of the Census. (1999b). *School enrollment – Social and economic characteristics of students (Update)*. Washington, DC: U.S. Department of Commerce.

U.S. Bureau of the Census. (1989). Marital status and living arrangements, March 1987. In *Current Population Report* (pp. 20–423). Washington DC: U.S. Government Printing Office.

U.S. Bureau of the Census. (1961). Household and family characteristics, March 1960. In *Current Population Report* (pp. 20–106). Washington DC: U.S. Government Printing Office.

U.S. Bureau of the Census. (1960). Marital Status and Family Status, March 1960. In *Current Population Report* (pp. 20–105). Washington DC: U.S. Government Printing Office.

U.S. Department of Education, (1995). *Mission and principles of professional development*. Washington DC: Author.

Vogel, E.F. (1969). *Canton under communism: Programs and politics in a provincial capital 1949–68*. Cambridge, Mass: Harvard University Press.

Wang, B. (1995). Let comprehensive educational experiments healthily develop in its own way. *Elementary and Secondary Education*, 6, 20–23.

Wang, G., & He, L. (1995). A report on applying success education in elementary schools. *Elementary and Secondary Education*, 11, 21–24.

Wang, J. (2006). Understanding, love, and integrated efforts: The transformation of at-risk students. *Education and Management in Primary and Middle Schools*, 159 (8), 28.

Wang, J. (1993). Comprehensive education reforms and the optimization of educational procedures. *Educational Research*, 1, 19–25.

Wang, J. (2005, June). On narrowing the gap between the poor and the rich and constructing a harmonious society. *Journal of Shandong University of Science & Technology (Social Sciences)*, 7(2), 42–46.

Wang, L. (1997). Devoting major efforts to carrying forward quality education and making a breakthrough in basic education—Summarization of an experience-sharing meeting of quality education in elementary and middle schools in the nation. *Educational Research*, 11, 25–28.

Wang, N. (2004). *Globalization and cultural translation* materialising Chinese series. Time Centre, Singapore: Marshall Cavendish Academic.

Wang, X. (2005). Three critical elements for transforming at-risk students. *Jilin Education,* 9, 43–44.

Wang, X. (2003). *Education in China since 1976.* Jefferson, N.C.: McFarland & Co.

Wang, X. (1993). A study on carrying out "success education" in low performance middle schools: A research report on an experimental reform in Chinese language teaching. In T. Guo, (Ed.), *The exploration of success education: The experience of success education in Zhabei No. 8 Middle School in Shanghai* (pp. 94–107), Tianjin, China: Tianjin Education Publisher.

Ward, R. E. (2004). *Improving achievement in low-performing school: Key results for school leaders.* Thousand Oaks, California: Corwin Press, A Sage Publications Company.

Waterman, J., & Walker, E. (2001). *Helping at-risk students: A group counseling approach for grades 6–9.* New York: The Guilford Press.

Waxman, C. H (1992). Introduction: Reversing the cycle of educational failure for students in at-risk school environments. In C. H. Waxman, H. Felix, J. W. D. Anderson, J.E, & H. P, Jr. Baptiste (Eds.) . *Students at risk in at-risk schools: Improving environments for learning (pp. 1–9).* California: Corwin Press, Inc., A Sage Publication.

Waxman, H., Felix, J. W. D., Anderson, J. E, & H. P, Jr. Baptiste (Eds) (1992). *Students at risk in at-risk schools: Improving environments for learning* . California: Corwin Press, Inc., A Sage Publication.

Wei, Q. (2006). How to transform at-risk students through teaching. *Comprehensive World,* 9, 117.

Weir, Jr., & Robert, M. (1996, September/October). Lessons from a middle level at-risk program. *Clearing House,* 70 (1), 48–51.

Wen, J. (2006). The governmental work report (Presented to the 4th Session of the 10th National People's Congress that opened in Beijing March 3, 2006). Retrieved on March 12, 2007, from http://www.gov.cn/ztzl/2006-03/15/content_227782.htm

White III., L. T. & Li, C. (1998). Politics and government and. In B. Hook (Ed.), *Regional development in China volume 3: Shanghai & the Yangtze Delta: A city reborn* (pp. 1–29). New York: Oxford University Press.

Wiles, J., and Bondi, J. (2001). *The new American middle school: Educating preadolesents in an era of change.* New Jersey: Prentice-Hall, Inc..

Wilson, W. J. (1986). *The truly disadvantaged.* Chicago: University of Chicago Press.

Winfield, L. F. (1991). Resilience, schooling and development in African-American youth: A conceptual framework. *Education and Urban Society.* 24, 5–14.

Wong, K. K., & Wang, C. M. (Eds.) (2002). *Efficiency, accountability, and equity issues in Title I schoolwide program implementation.* Connecticut: Information Age Publishing.

Wong, L., & MacPherson, S. (Eds.). (1995). *Social change and social policy in contemporary China.* Brookfield, Vermont: Ashgate Publishing Company.

Wong, L., & Mok, K (1995). The reform and the changing social context. In L. Wong, & S. MacPherson (Eds.), *Social change and social policy in contemporary China* (pp. 1–26). Brookfield, Vermont: Ashgate Publishing Company.

Wu, D. (1992). *Compulsory Education in China*. China: Shanxi People Publisher.

Wu, J. (2002, Fall). China's socioeconomically disadvantaged: Breaking the surface of a challenging problem. *Harvard Asia Pacific Review*, 6(2), 62–63.

Wu, J (1991). An investigative report on parents' expectation. In J. Liu, & Q. Ge (Eds.), *Studies on at-risk students* (p. 163). Shanghai, China: The Education Bureau of Zhabei District in Shanghai.

Wu, J. (1990). The Features, Causes, and Location of At-risk Students. *Education Commentary*, 2, 12–17.

Wu, K. (1995). Thoughts on several questions about comprehensive educational reform. *Educational Research*, 1, 37–42.

Wu, L., & Ginsberg, R. (1986). *Fundamentals of Chinese philosophy*. New York: University Press of America.

Wu, W. (1991). An investigation of pupils' interaction within class. In J. Liu, & Q. Ge (Eds.), *Studies on at-risk students* (p. 139). Shanghai, China: The Education Bureau of Zhabei District in Shanghai.

Xia, C. (1993). An experiment on encouragement-based evaluation in Chinese language teaching. In T. Guo (Ed.), *The exploration of success education: The experience of success education in Zhabei No. 8 Middle School in Shanghai* (pp. 37–40). Tianjin, China: Tianjin Education Publisher.

Xia, C. (1993). A brief discussion on how to help students form good habits in doing homework. In M. Huang (Ed.), *Collectanea of expanding research on success education*, vol. 1. *Proceeding for the Second National Conference on Success Education* (pp. 363–370). Shanghai, China: The Education Bureau of Zhabei District, Shanghai and Shanghai Institute of Success Education.

Xie, X., Li, Y., & Li, Q. (2006). A preliminary exploration on how to help at-risk students establish a sense of confidence. *Scientific Consult*, 6, 16–17.

Xinhua News Report (2006, May 5). The central government paid keen attention to the views of China's over 111 million internet users. Retrieved from http://latelinenews.com/news/ll/chinese/1415200.shtml?cc=

Xong, B., & Liu, G. (2004). A system and policy analysis on the formation of a poor class in urban China. *Jiangxi Social Science*, 2, 167–169.

Xu, H. (2006). A comparative analysis on learning differences between oustanding students and at-risk students. Chongqing, China: *Journal of Hetian Academy School*, 126 (5), 56–57.

Xu, L. (2004). An analysis on the current state of social stratification, problems and strategies during our country's transition. *Journal of Jingyang*, 6, 25–29.

Xue, D. (1993). From a score of seven points to seventy-four points. In T. Guo, & J. Liu (Eds.), *One Hundred of Examples of Success Education* (pp. 182–184), Tianjing, Ching : Tianjin Education Press.

Xue, M. (1981). *China's socialist economy*. Beijing, China: Foreign Languages Press.

Yan, G., & Liu, Z. 1997). *On quality education*. Jiangsu, China: Jiangsu Education Press.

Yan, X. (1991). An investigation and analysis on elementary school students' poor academic performance. In J. Liu, & Q. Ge (Eds.), *Studies on at-risk students* (p. 159). Shanghai, China: The Education Bureau of Zhabei District in Shanghai.

Yang, D., & Su, F. (2000). Taming the market: China and the forces of globalization. In A. Prakash, & J. A. Hart (Eds.), *Responding to Globalization* (p. 35). London & New York: Routledge.

Yang, F., & Campbell, C. (2006, January). China's Peaceful Rise. *Global Agenda,* 4(1), 162–163.

Yang, G. (2005, August). A system analysis of the current situation of social polarization between the poor and the rich in our country. *Journal of Anyang Institute of Technology,* 16(4), 59–64.

Yang, J. (2006). Shanghai: Several "key words" derived from the practice of helping the poor. Retrieved on January 18, 2006, from http://politics.people.com.cn/GB/14562/4038635.html

Yang, X. (Ed). (2001). *Chinese education: What are you waiting?* Beijing, China: Economic Daily Publisher.

Yao, S., & Liu, X. (Eds.) (2003). *Sustaining China's economic growth in the twenty-first century.* London & New York: Routledge Curzon, Taylor & Francis Group.

Ye, H., & Zhu, L. (2004). A policy study on the disparity between the rich and the poor in our country and the strategies of dealing with this problem. *Studies on Mao Zedong and Deng Xiaoping Theories,* 12, 67–71, 58.

Yep, R., Ngok, K., & Zhu, B. (2004). Chapter 8: Migration and competitiveness. In L. Wong, L. White, & S. Gui (Eds.), *Social policy reform in Hong Kong and Shanghai: A tale of two cities* (pp. 217–238). New York: M.E. Sharpe Inc..

Zeng, T. (2001). A macro analysis of basic educational reform and development. Jinan, China: *Songdong Educational Research,* 9, 5–7.

Zha, J.Y. (1995). *China pop: How soap operas, tabloids, and bestsellers are transforming a culture.* New York: The New Press.

Zhang, D. (2005, August, 22). Chongming: "Spring rain" nurtures education in rural areas of Zhabei: The whole society is helping students in poverty. *Liberation Daily,* Retrieved from http://news.sina.com.cn/o/2005-08-22/09126749740s.shtml

Zhang, D. (1995). Several questions about how to scientifically conduct educational experiments. *Educational Research,* 2, 50–58.

Zhang, G. (1993). On expectation. In T. Guo, & J. Liu. (Eds.). *One hundred case studies of success education* (pp. 95–97). Tianjin, China: Tianjin Education Press.

Zhang, H., & Liu, H. (2000). A brief analysis on the psychological impediment of at-risk students and the strategies teachers should adopt to help them. *Journal of Anya College of Education,* 2, 31–32.

Zhang, K. (2003). Chapter 8: Closing the productivity gap: The role of globalization in Shanghai's economic transformation. In D. Lu, G. J. Wen, & H. Zhou (Eds.), *China's economic globalization through the WTO* (pp. 87–100). Burlington, VT: Ashgate Publishing Company.

Zhang, J. & Li, X. (1998). *Social transition in China.* New York: University Press of American, Inc.

Zhang, L. and the Other (1993). A study on carrying out "success education" in low performance middle schools: A research report on experimental reform in mathematics education. In T. Guo. (Ed.), *The exploration of success education: The experience of success education in Zhabei District of Shanghai* (pp. 108–119). Tianjin, China: Tianjin Education Publisher.

Zhang, L. (2006). Talking about the psychological factors of causing at-risk students and the strategies of improvement. *Education and Management in Primary and Middle Schools,* 159 (8), 26–27.

Zhang, Y. (2006). A brief discussion about how to transform at-risk students. *Chinese Education Research and Innovation,* 3 (1), 51.

Zhao, Z. (2005). Zhabei No. 8 Middle School in Shanghai carried out the experiment on success education. In M. Xiong, & B. Yu (Eds.), *A history of educational experiments in contemporary China* (pp. 749–764). Jinan, China: Sandong Education Press.

Zheng, S. (1993). She is a teacher, but also a mother. In T. Guo, & J. Liu (Eds.), *One hundred case studies of success education* (pp. 157–159). Tianjin, China: Tianjin Education Press.

Zhou, G. (1993). An attempt to apply the model of success education to moral education. In M. Huang (Ed.), *Collectanea of expanding research on success education,* vol. 1. *Proceeding for the Second National Conference on Success Education* (pp. 367–370). Shanghai, China: The Education Bureau of Zhabei District, Shanghai and Shanghai Institute of Success Education.

Zhou, H. & Xiao, L. (2006). A research on the binary economic structure between cities and countryside and the labor market in Shanghai (II). Retrieved on June 6, 2007, from http://www.sass.org.cn/rlzy/articleshow.jsp?dinji=264&artid=10050&sortid=1835

Zhou, H. & Yang, X (2001). Research on the problems of educating children from migrant families. Retrieved on July 12, 2007, from http://www.popinfo.gov.cn/popinfo/pop_docrkxx.nsf/v_rkbl/D05FD6EF8F62979748256B2D002456D4

Zhou, X., Moen, P., & Tuma, N. B. (1998, July). Educational stratification in urban China: 1949–94. *Sociology of Education,* 71: 199–222.

Zhu, C. J., Nyland, C., & Cooper B. (2005). Employee perceptions of social protection reform in Shanghai: Diversity across ownership forms and occupations. In R. Smyth, O. K. Tam, M. Warner, & C. J. Zhu (Eds.), *China's business reforms: Institutional challenges in a globalized economy* (pp. 139–156). London & New York: Routledge Curzon, Taylor & Francis Group.

Zhu, H. (2003). How to develop at-risk students' potentials. *Hygiene Vocational Education,* 21 (10), 52.

Zhu, M. (2001, September/October). The education problems of migrant children in Shanghai. *Child Welfare,* 80(5), 563–569.

Zuo, X., Zhou, H., & Yang, X. (2003). A study on the relationship of population, employment, and the reconstruction of production structure in Shanghai. Shanghai New Intelligent Human Resources. Retrieved on May 17, 2006, from *http://www.sass.org.cn/rlzy/articleshow.jsp?dinji=264&artid=10073&sortid=1831*

CPSIA information can be obtained at www.ICGtesting.com
Printed in the USA
BVOW060854281111

276833BV00004B/2/P